Pei-Yi Liu
Care Logic in Diabetes Care and Nursing

Nursing Science | Volume 1

Pei-Yi Liu
Care Logic in Diabetes Care and Nursing

[transcript]

This thesis was accepted by the Faculty of Nursing Science of the Philosophical and Theological University of Vallendar (since 12/2021 Vinzenz Pallotti University) as a dissertation for the doctorate in nursing science (Dr. rer. cur.) and successfully defended on January 19, 2023.

Bibliographic information published by the Deutsche Nationalbibliothek
The Deutsche Nationalbibliothek lists this publication in the Deutsche Nationalbibliografie; detailed bibliographic data are available in the Internet at https://dnb.dnb.de/

© 2025 transcript Verlag, Bielefeld
Hermannstraße 26 | D-33602 Bielefeld | live@transcript-verlag.de

All rights reserved. No part of this book may be reprinted or reproduced or utilized in any form or by any electronic, mechanical, or other means, now known or hereafter invented, including photocopying and recording, or in any information storage or retrieval system, without permission in writing from the publisher.

Cover layout: Maria Arndt, Bielefeld
Printed by: Elanders Waiblingen GmbH, Waiblingen
https://doi.org/10.14361/9783839476284
Print-ISBN: 978-3-8376-7628-0 | PDF-ISBN: 978-3-8394-7628-4
ISSN of series: 2944-4055 | eISSN of series: 2944-4063

Printed on permanent acid-free text paper.

Contents

Abstract 7

Acknowledgments 9

Chapter 1: Introduction 11
Motivation and Background 11
Research Purposes and Questions 16

Chapter 2: Methodological Approach 19
State of the Art in Social and Nursing Science Research ... 19
Research Method 24

Chapter 3: Literature Review and Theoretical Framework ... 33
The Field 33
The Theoretical Nursing Care Approaches to the Subject ... 42
The Logic of Care 49
The Ethics of Care 55

Chapter 4: Practical Arena Analysis 67
Understanding the Disease 67
The Empirical Study of the Logic of Care 88
Other Care Logics in Practice 109

Chapter 5: Care Tensions and Ethical Dilemmas 125
Autonomy in a Vulnerable Body 125
Care Responsibility Without Authority 136
Professionalism Around Care Boundaries 147

Chapter 6: Conclusion 161
Brief Comment 161
A Logical Care Pattern for Diabetes Care and Nursing 163

References 167

Abstract

Within the German diabetes care practice, healthcare workers face various challenges associated with working in a commercial and economic healthcare society while simultaneously attempting to provide holistic care and preserving a relationship of trust with patients. Healthcare workers are required to act from a moral position within the hierarchy and to maintain professionalism in the face of uncertain responsibilities which can result in care conflicts and ethical tension. Based on the care theory of the Logic of Care introduced by Annemarie Mol in 2008, this study aimed to establish a logical care pattern to open a dialogue between the theoretical needs and practical obstacles encountered in diabetes care and nursing. This research was performed as a qualitative case study. The empirical data highlights the importance of the concepts described by Mol as components of the Logic of Care during diabetes care. However, three other types of care logic were identified in German care practice in congruence with the Logic of Care: the logic of choice, the logic of efficiency, and the logic of power. These parallel guiding factors can introduce care conflicts and ethical dilemmas for healthcare workers who must constantly respect the autonomy of a vulnerable body, take responsibility without authority, and fulfill their professional roles concerning care boundaries. To support healthcare workers who encounter ethical dilemmas during daily practice, tinkering approaches are encouraged over attempts to tame disease, shared responsibility should be encouraged over blame allocation, and nourished courage should be promoted to replace hidden bravery.

Acknowledgments

'If I'm not allowed to eat my favorite foods I'd rather die'. Thus spoke my first patient with diabetes when I was a student nurse. It made a lasting impression on me. Caring for patients with diabetes needs to consider not just their medical condition but also the impact this condition has on their daily life. I would like to thank the patients and the care workers in the Department of Diabetology, and the Home-Care Center 'Pflegenetz' at the University Hospital, Freiburg. Their hospitality, openness, and generosity allowed me to enter their lives with warmth and trust. Without sharing their valuable experience with me, this research and publication could not have been made.

This dissertation contains contributions from a great many people who gave me support, confidence, and courage at every step of my path. I wish to express my deep appreciation to my primary supervisor Helen Kohlen who has given so much time, patience, wisdom, and unwavering encouragement to bring me through to the end of this journey. I also wish to extend my gratitude to Carlo Leget to be the second supervisor of my dissertation. I am thankful to Professor Annemarie Mol for offering careful guidance and very helpful criticism over the dissertation.

I would like to acknowledge the help provided by my graduate colleagues and friends in the Department of Nursing at University Vallendar and at the 'Caring about Care' summer school in Freiburg. I have benefited a lot from their insightful comments, enlightening discussions, and frank assessments of my work. The assistance offered by my graduate colleagues Maria Peters and Christiane Gödecke, who read my revision and helped make some sense of the confusion, was greatly appreciated. My thanks go out to the Nursing faculty and staff for their friendly assistance throughout my graduate training.

A journey, such as this Ph.D. has been, can push one's spirit to a vulnerable and lonely place. I want to give special thanks to my husband Otto Schnekenburger, my family, and my friends for being there for me and providing enthusiastic assistance in the spiritual, linguistic, and financial spheres from beginning to end. I dedicate this dissertation to them for their never-failing support and encouragement. Without them, I would not have been able to undertake a Ph.D.

Chapter 1: Introduction

Motivation and Background

Care has diverse faces, and caring can be presented in a variety of ways. Joan Tronto (1993) viewed caring as "a species activity that includes everything that we do to maintain, continue, and repair our 'world' so that we can live in it as well as possible" (p. 103). Caring, from this perspective, is concerned about more than sick bodies, instead referring to all aspects of daily life and involving a range of people, including the patient, their family, healthcare professionals, and the social world in which we live (Gittell, 2009; Mol, 2008; Watson, 1985). Good care is, therefore, not a matter of making individual well-argued choices but represents the collaborative and continuous attempts to align existing knowledge and technologies with diseased bodies and complex lives (Gittell, 2009; Kodner & Spreeuwenberg, 2002; Mol, 2008).

The human body is complex, healthcare is full of unpredictable variables, and care practices have boundaries. As a practicing nurse, I often face various challenges associated with working in a commercial and economic healthcare society while simultaneously attempting to provide holistic care and preserving a trust-based relationship with patients. How healthcare workers act from a moral position within the hierarchy and maintain professionalism in the face of restrictions on the abilities to perform certain actions while being uncertain of their responsibilities, remain open questions. As a nursing scholar, I have begun to rethink the nature of care in nursing practice and question which phenomena guide whether the actual delivery of care aligns with the perception of care within the current care environment. In particular, I am interested in caring for patients with chronic diseases, especially diabetes.

By focusing on patients with diabetes care as my research target group, I was able to obtain a better understanding of what good care should be for two reasons. First, the debate regarding improvements in diabetes care is ongoing because diabetes represents one of the most pressing global health emergencies of the 21st century. The International Diabetes Federation (IDF) estimated that the total number of people with diabetes worldwide will increase from 463 million in 2019 to 700 million in 2045. In Germany, at least 8.0 million people were diagnosed with diabetes in 2019

(IDF, 2020). Based on AOK[1] data, the medical treatment of diabetes was estimated to cost EUR 21 billion in 2016 which corresponds to 11% of total health insurance expenditures (Deutsche Diabetes Gesellschaft [DDG], 2017). Healthcare organizations are under considerable pressure to identify cost-effective interventions to care for this population (Busse & Blümel, 2014; Schlette et al., 2009).

Second, diabetes is a chronic disease associated with life-changing complications. Patients with diabetes tend to have multiple comorbidities and symptoms that affect their daily lives. These patients must cope with symptoms, disability, emotional impacts, complex medication regimens, difficult lifestyle adjustments, and the process of obtaining medical care (DeBusk et al., 1999; E. H. Wagner, Austin, et al., 2001). Patients with diabetes are required and empowered to make multiple daily self-management decisions and perform complex care activities that must be successfully integrated into their daily lives (E. H. Wagner, Austin et al., 2001). However, the concept of self-management can vary according to individual personal values and be associated with multiple aspects of their lives (Callaghan & Williams, 1994; Mol & Law, 2014). What is the meaning of having diabetes? What are the needs for diabetes care that promote a holistic view of the patient while providing quality care? These questions require clarification when designing effective diabetes care in practice.

Based on the complexity of this chronic disease, a shift in medical practice has become essential, moving away from attempting to dictate behavior authoritatively to forming collaborative alliances that include healthcare professionals, patients, their families, care organizations, and society (Clark, 2005; Martin-Rodriguez et al., 2005; Mol, 2008). The integration of the health delivery system and collaborative practices among interprofessional teams has been described in the literature as an efficient, effective, and satisfying method for assisting individuals who are unable to obtain necessary assistance within the confines of traditional clinical practice, resulting in the structuring of interdependent professionals' actions towards patients' care needs (Kodner & Spreeuwenberg, 2002; Martin-Rodriguez et al., 2005; Maynard, 2006). A reciprocal practice that transpires within the framework of a relationship between the caregiver and the care receiver without abuse of power is recommended (Gastmans, 2006; Lachman, 2012). The questions that emerge in care practice include what types of care relationships are constructed and how the power between individuals and the environment affects these relationships and, in turn, influences care.

Today, the ideas that patients' preferences should be honored and that patients have rights and power in care are increasingly prioritized. Patients' views of satis-

---

1　AOK (Allgemeine Ortskrankenkasse) is one of the largest providers of statutory health insurance (Gesetzliche Krankenversicherung) in Germany. More than 24.7 million people, approximately one-third of the German population, are currently insured by AOK (DDG, 2017).

factory encounters are based upon respect for their autonomy and equality and depend upon the application of healthcare characterized by a genuine interest in the patient's self-management and emancipation rather than a focus on the authority and control of the healthcare provider (Fox & Chesla, 2008; Hörnsten et al., 2005). The global focus of healthcare has shifted toward patient empowerment[2] and the involvement of patients in self-care, and patients' satisfaction is often used to measure the quality of care when patient-centered care is supplied (Robin et al., 2008; D. Wagner & Bear, 2009).

The impacts of patient centralization on care practice and which facets of patient-centered care are best applied to diabetes care remain under debate. Based on the literature, the diversity of treatment strategies available for this illness and the various demands for care driven by both healthcare professionals and patients can result in conflicting expectations regarding treatment approaches, priorities, and outcomes; patients tend to focus more on how treatments will influence their daily lives, whereas healthcare workers are more focused on medical outcomes and economic efficiency (Clark, 2005; Hörnsten et al., 2004; Jasmine, 2009). Healthcare workers must view their patients subjectively, as people with feelings, and respect their patients' autonomy during decision-making processes while simultaneously taking an objective approach to the patient as an individual with a disease in need of care. Balancing these two views can be challenging for healthcare workers during daily practice.

Although team collaborations can improve the diversity of approaches, the current healthcare environment is often task-oriented, focusing on the disease and medical treatment instead of taking the time to address a patient holistically. This approach can limit the nurses' abilities to perform care by constraining the flexibility to negotiate with patients regarding care and instead requiring adherence to guidelines established by administrators, particularly when patients engage in behaviors that are detrimental to their health (Fox & Chesla, 2008; Jasmine, 2009; Martin-Rodriguez et al., 2005; Mol, 2008). These circumstances can challenge the development of personal caring relationships between nurses and their patients.

Working within a modern care environment requires healthcare professionals, such as nurses, to maintain their professional awareness and reduce the impacts of economically based and commercially driven approaches to healthcare (Kälvemark et al., 2004; Parker, 1999). Nurses follow a professional, ethical code that requires

---

2 The patient empowerment movement started in the early 1970s to improve patients' self-determination and self-regulation and aimed to establish the capacity for patients to serve as active participants in their healthcare, share in clinical decision-making, extend their perspectives in the healthcare system, and accept responsibility for their health (Funnell et al., 1991; Paulsen, 2011; Powers, 2003; Spiers, 2003; Tol et al., 2015).

them to act responsibly in ensuring patient safety and creating benefits for their patients; however, they are limited in the ability to make medical decisions and often lack the time necessary to engage in additional caring activities. (Kleppe et al., 2016). This type of moral distress[3] constantly challenges nurses during daily practice. How nurses experience and cope with moral distresses, which care situations are likely to induce conflicts and ethical dilemmas, the nurses' understanding of these care conflicts and ethical dilemmas, and whether they are reflected by or influence nursing practice are all questions worthy of consideration.

Healthcare delivery in Germany is highly fragmented (Schlette et al., 2009), with poor vertical and horizontal integration, and the system is characterized as being more focused on curing acute illnesses or single diseases than on managing patients with complex or chronic conditions or managing the health of specific populations (Schlette et al., 2009). A focus on medical treatments over holistic approaches and unequal power among physicians, patients, and nurses are noticeable in the German healthcare system (Daiski, 2004; Kramer & Schmalenberg, 2003). In Germany, diabetes care is typically led by physicians, who hold regulatory power.[4] Nursing is often viewed as an occupation or as a semi-profession rather than as an independent professional entity (Salloch, 2016; Thompson et al., 2006, p. 9; Wilkinson & Miers, 2003). In the hierarchy of health professions, physicians traditionally maintain professional autonomy and independence due to a higher professional status, which is typically accompanied by more power within their relationships with other healthcare workers (J. McDonald et al., 2012).

A strong professional identity and the maintenance of distinct boundaries between medical professions are viewed as the primary obstacles to collaborative practice among German healthcare teams (Martin-Rodriguez et al., 2005). Nurses, physicians, and other related professionals involved in diabetes care, such as nutrition consultants, know little of the practices, expertise, responsibilities, skills, values, and theoretical perspectives of professionals from other disciplines (Martin-Rodriguez et al., 2005). A lack of interprofessional collaboration often results in each professional performing only the necessary actions that they are legally or institutionally required to perform, which can result in certain responsibilities being relegated to other professionals or neglected entirely. Which professionals

---

3   Jameton (1984) defined moral distress as occurring "when one knows the right thing to do, but institutional constraints make it nearly impossible to pursue the right course of action" (p. 6). Fourie (2015) expanded the meaning of moral distress to define a psychological response to morally challenging situations, such as those of moral constraint, moral conflict, or both.

4   In the structure of the German healthcare delivery system, patients are covered financially by healthcare insurance, which pays the family doctors who perform disease management (Busse & Blümel, 2014).

are responsible for the care activities that fall outside of these regulations can, therefore, become unclear.

The hierarchies that exist between different professions affect whether professionals feel empowered to act on their moral positions (Kälvemark et al., 2004). Scholars have observed that disagreements and conflicts regarding the roles and associated boundaries of the members of a healthcare team and a lack of shared decision-making[5] can result from uneven power and authority distributions in professional relationships (Kälvemark et al., 2004; Rosemann et al., 2006; E. H. Wagner, 2000). These power disparities may also be sources of care tensions or ethical dilemmas, and understanding these sources of tension and how nurses respond to these disparities is important for optimizing nursing care.

A gap exists between the extensive theoretical reflections on diabetes care and the current lack of practical solutions for healthcare professionals to facilitate the management of chronic diseases in day-to-day care situations. The development of alternative methods of diabetes care that allow for the demands of the body to be met while reducing tension in daily living is crucial.

Caring for chronic diseases, including diabetes, involves a complex combination of private actions, which refer to those involved in the patient's healthcare, such as performing medical tests and providing medications; public interactions, such as those between patients and healthcare professionals and those between patients and society, which often does not consider the care needs of chronically ill individuals; and moral and ethical activities. The logic of care, which was conceptualized by Annemarie Mol, may serve as an adequate framework for diabetes care.

The logic of care theory is characterized as a nursing theory due to its encouragement of patients to share in caring actions with the healthcare team during disease management (Kohlen & Kumbruck, 2008; Mol. 2008). The logic of care emphasizes assessing situations, focusing on current events, and centralizing potential actions with real-world relevance. Using the framework of the logic of care to perform an in-depth analysis of the nature and function of diabetes care may provide a firm conceptual and empirical base for defining good care in the context of nursing science (See Chapter 2 and Chapter 3).

Mol views the logic of care and the concept of care as being related constructs that appropriately support the relationship between patients and the healthcare system while considering aspects of hospitality, care, and ethics (Mol, 2008; Mol & Law, 2004). However, the logic of care is co-existence, interdependent, and incorporated

---

5   Shared decision-making refers to a collaborative process in which patients and clinicians work together in a deliberative dialogue to identify reasonable management options that best fit and addresses the unique situation of the patient, with considerations for each individual's personal, social, and biomedical context and their values and reasons for valuing specific available options (Miers, 2003a; Serrano et al., 2016; Tamhane et al., 2015).

with other types of logic depending on the practical care situation (Mol, 2008, pp. 12, 106). Whether the caring and nursing activities described by the logic of care can be observed and identifying other types of care logic that may coincide with the logic of care during German diabetes care practice warrants further investigation and analysis.

Research Purposes and Questions

The research purposes were derived from the scope of the logic of care theory and aimed to explore care demands, the difficulties associated with care implementation, and emerging ethical dilemmas in German diabetes care. The goals of this research were to establish a logical care pattern that opens a dialogue between the theoretical needs and practical obstacles associated with diabetes care and nursing and support healthcare workers in addressing the care tensions and ethical dilemmas encountered during daily practice.

Based on the assumption that the concepts underlying the logic of care could be instilled into the German healthcare system to support care improvements for patients with diabetes, the logic of care theory introduced by Mol was applied as the framework of this research. To reach the research purposes, three themes were identified: understanding the disease and patients' needs, the logic of care and other types of care logic, and care tensions and ethical dilemmas.

The first research theme sought to understand the disease, identify the goals associated with disease management, and define the requirements for providing good care to patients with diabetes from the perspectives of both patients and healthcare workers. To address the first research theme, the following research questions were asked to both patients and healthcare workers: What are your thoughts about having diabetes? What are your care goals for diabetes management? What do you require when caring for patients with diabetes? What difficulties do you encounter in diabetes management? Do you have different opinions from other care actors regarding the process of disease management? What is your idea of good diabetes care?

The second theme addressed how this theory could be enacted in current care practice. To address this theme, the research aimed to analyze the following questions: How has the logic of care been applied to diabetes care practice? Is the application of the logic of care sufficient to promote good care in diabetes care practice? If the logic of care is insufficient, what is missing? What elements beyond those addressed by the logic of care should be addressed in care practice? How can we define the various types of care logic that may be active when we talk about good care?

The third research theme focused on the experiences of different types of healthcare professionals regarding the care tensions and ethical dilemmas encountered in the context of diabetes care. The research asked the following questions: What roles do healthcare professionals, such as nurses, play in German diabetes care? What types of care conflicts and ethical dilemmas have been encountered by a care team? How are these difficulties revealed? How do healthcare professionals react to care tensions and ethical dilemmas? How do they view situations in which care tensions and ethical dilemmas occur?

The issues central to nursing care were examined through the perspectives of each theme, and each theme was also analyzed separately, with inputs from other healthcare professionals during this research. The research structure can be summarised in the following figure, which captures the important aspects of the research purpose.

Figure 1: Flow diagram showing the research aims.

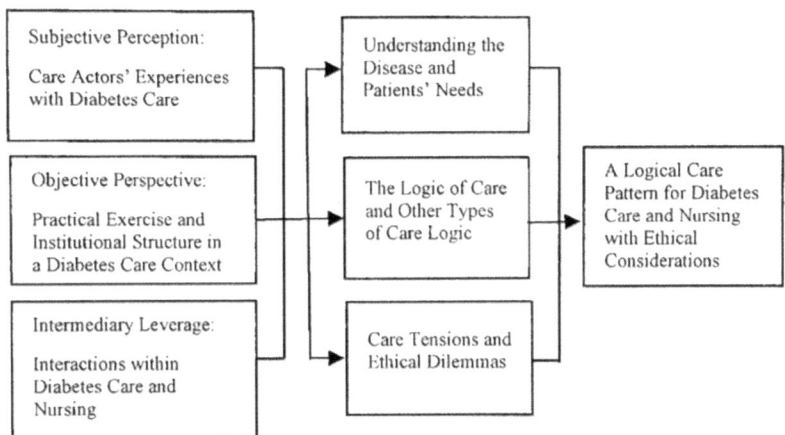

Taking different perspectives on the research questions, the left columns of the flow diagram present how the research data were collected (See Chapter 2). By analyzing the theoretical and empirical research data, three categories listed in the middle columns of the flow diagram were identified (See Chapter 3, Chapter 4, and Chapter 5). After summarising the research findings, a logical care pattern for diabetes care and nursing with ethical consideration was established. This research goal is shown in the right column of the flow diagram (See Chapter 6).

Chapter 2: Methodological Approach

State of the Art in Social and Nursing Science Research

In the past few decades, new approaches to the study of chronic care and nursing care have emerged. First, how healthcare workers make decisions when caring for patients has changed. The caring approach has shifted from a body-object approach, in which caring was practiced based solely on healthcare workers' professional judgments regarding the needs of the body, to a body-subject approach, which focuses on the needs of the body within the limits of the patient's subjective perceptions, to a final body-in-practice approach, which offers care suitable for real-world situations (Bury, 2001; Holm & Severinsson, 2014; Mol & Law, 2004; Stock et al., 2014; E. H. Wagner, Austin et al., 2001). Second, a debate regarding relationships has emerged in both social and nursing literature, especially the building of trust-based relationships between patients and healthcare workers and among various healthcare professionals (Bury, 1982; Charmaz, 1983; Gilligan, 1982; Lawton, 2003; Mol, 2008; Vanlaere & Gastmans, 2011). Third, a growing ethical concern has developed within the complex healthcare environment, especially in the care fields of diabetes care and nursing care (de Casterle et al., 2008; Gastmans, 2002; K. V. Smith & Godfrey, 2002). The increased performance and reporting of qualitative research, such as case studies, has allowed for the exploration of the complexities involved in caring for chronic illnesses and the concerns of the individual living with chronic disease (Baxter & Jack, 2008; Van Wynsberghe, 2007; Yin, 2009). Qualitative data analysis allows the underlying motivations of health behaviors to be established (Baxter & Jack, 2008; Yin, 2009). Current trends in social and nursing science offer a foundation upon which to build the framework for this research.

Shifting From Body Centralisation to Care Situations.

The first tendency that can be observed from studies of chronic care and nursing care is the shifting of care from a body-centralized approach to one that considers care situations. Early studies often applied a bodywork perspective, in which the body was viewed as a public body object, passively waiting to be observed (Bury, 1982;

Mol & Law, 2004). Observers, such as physicians, were tasked with understanding how the body was meant to work and making diagnoses when the body functioned incorrectly. However, living with a chronic illness means living a life that is hovering between enduring and suffering and often requires the patient to reformulate their self-identity (Ohman et al., 2003). The perspective of the body as an object fails to consider or seriously address the concerns of the patients without tailoring care to the patients' perceptions of illness or lived experiences, which is particularly problematic when caring for patients with chronic disease (Bury, 1982; Kodner & Spreeuwenberg, 2002; Mol & Law, 2004).

When caring for bodies with chronic conditions or complex illnesses, professionals that attempt to utilize object judgments may be missing valuable information (Bury, 1982; Mol & Law, 2004). Healthcare workers' primary tasks when managing patients with diabetes are based on objective clinical indicators, which lead to a view of diabetes as a pathophysiological problem that focuses on the physical impacts of the disease (Clark, 2005). By contrast, patients emphasize the difficulties they experience in the social domain and the impacts that diabetes has on their daily lives (Bury, 2001; Clark, 2005; Holm & Severinsson, 2014; Pols, 2005; Stock et al., 2014; E. H. Wagner, Austin et al., 2001). When patients' wishes are not fulfilled, patients sometimes develop negative perceptions of caring behaviors, which can significantly influence overall patient satisfaction[1] (Papastavrou et al., 2011; Scott et al., 2014).

Chronic care is not an activity that a single person passively undergoes but instead represents a collective endeavor in which all care actors play decisive roles in the interpretations and evaluations of care needs and actions (Gastmans et al., 1998; Mol, 2008). Understanding the similarities and differences in the approaches to disease management between healthcare workers and patients is an important issue in chronic care. The patients' life experiences and their approaches to disease management and care decision-making were considered in this research, and the differences between healthcare workers and patients in terms of both understanding the disease and their perspectives on what constitutes good care were also examined.

Real-world practice situations can be unpredictable. The application of certain qualification criteria to determine necessary treatment responses used at current healthcare institutions often fails to adequately consider the appropriateness of care. When caring for patients with chronic diseases, dichotomies during daily practice can arise between treating the patient as a subject and treating the patient as an object. A focus on the body-in-practice that considers the body as a whole

---

[1] The term patient satisfaction is derived from a marketing perspective and are often applied to the healthcare agenda. Patient satisfaction has also been explained in terms of adding value and creating a service exceeding or meeting patients' expectations (Torpie, 2014).

human person when practicing care becomes essential. The logic of care, as introduced by Mol, addresses how each micro-action that occurs in every moment must occur with concern for the needs of bodies and the particular situations in which care takes place. The conceptual framework outlined by the logic of care requires empirical examination. In Germany, the perspective of the logic of care theory has not yet been applied to either diabetes care or nursing science; therefore, the logic of care was selected as the theoretical framework for this research.

Focusing on Relationships

Relationships have been identified as an important foundation for caring (Bury, 1982; Charmaz, 1983; Lawton, 2003). According to the literature, caring for chronic illnesses involves relationships among the patient and various healthcare workers and different aspects of the illness experience have the potential to reinforce and amplify these relationships (Bury, 1982; Charmaz, 1983). In contrast to the individualistic views of people and communities, people sometimes opt not to follow their personal choices and instead conform to the desires of those with whom they are involved in complex networks of relationships. Care, therefore, fundamentally serves as a method that weaves people into a network of relationships, and caregiving represents a concrete form of interpersonal relationship (Gastmans, 2002; Mol, 2008; Tronto, 1993).

In healthcare, professional relationships are considered powerful tools, with socio-political dimensions that can influence the performance of caring (Tronto, 1993). However, professional care relationships are often role-oriented, focusing on a patient's specific needs in the context of health and illness (J. McDonald et al., 2012). Differences in the perceptions of clinicians and patients can result in the development of ethical conflicts in terms of patient autonomy, informed consent, and privacy, especially in the long-term care context (Rees et al., 2009; Rowe & Calnan, 2006). Professionals may, therefore, aim to maintain a sufficient distance, to avoid the need to restrain emotions and remain as objective as possible (Van den Hooff & Goossensen, 2014). Exploring the types of care relationships that can be observed in real-world care practice, how these relationships are developed, and how these relationships influence the performance of care activities becomes essential.

The successful management of chronic diseases requires the formation of a partnership between patients and healthcare workers (Rowe & Calnan, 2006). A trusting relationship is also considered a core component of effective therapeutic relationships, which may contribute to the successful management of chronic diseases (Nortvedt et al., 2011). Unfortunately, the ability to build a trust-based relationship with patients in healthcare practice is often limited by a lack of time and an excessive concern with task performance (Nortvedt et al., 2011). The delivery of primary and community-based health services that cross organizational boundaries can also add a layer of complexity to interprofessional relationships (J. McDonald et al., 2012). This research aimed to perform a detailed evaluation of the relationships that form during care practice, including the impacts of the multiple and complex actions and interactions that occur among various healthcare professionals and patients.

Growing Ethical Challenges in Care Practice

Awareness of the various ethical dimensions associated with healthcare practice is increasing, including in the field of nursing practice. Nursing is often viewed as a naturally moral endeavor, and nurses are expected to practice in an ethical manner (de Casterle et al., 2008; Gastmans, 2002; Kohlen, 2019; K. V. Smith & Godfrey, 2002). The discourse of nursing ethics is focused on the well-being of patients (Gastmans et al., 1998), the nurses' understanding of what makes a good nurse, and how nurses decide to make ethical choices (K. V. Smith & Godfrey, 2002). Joan Tronto (1993) and Elisabeth Conradi (2003) addressed nursing ethics as a social practice, with considerations of public and political issues, such as nurse-led diabetes management (Tronto, 1993; Conradi, 2003).

However, nurses are constantly confronted with ethical issues during care practice. Based on reports in the literature, the ethical dilemmas that nurses often confront derive from challenges associated with reflecting on how they can contribute to their patients' well-being, which requires high-level professional competence and ethical maturity (de Casterle et al., 2008; Gutierrez, 2005; Kitson, 1996; Kohlen, 2019). Although nurses often make compromises to provide competent care out of a sense of responsibility, the invisibility of nursing work, the limited training nurses receive for chronic care situations, heavy workloads, insufficient time for care practice, legal regulations, organizational and financial constraints, and staffing problems often create obstacles for nurses who aim to prioritize ethically-based decisions in their practice (Gutierrez, 2005; Kälvemark et al., 2004).

Nurses may, therefore, resolve their daily ethical predicaments by using a conformist approach, guided by conventional workplace rules and norms rather than relying on creativity and critical reflection (de Casterle et al., 2008; Gutierrez, 2005; Kohlen, 2019). These challenges can result in a sense of powerlessness among nurses, leading to emotional scarring and producing an environment in which nurses are hesitant to speak out against what is perceived to be an impenetrable and hierarchical system of care (Ulrich et al., 2010).

Unfortunately, most nurses appear to be ill-prepared to address ethical dilemmas (de Casterle et al., 2008). Implementing ethical decisions in more challenging contexts in nursing care practice is becoming increasingly important; however, studies that take an ethical approach to German diabetes care are rare, particularly in the context of nursing care. Therefore, exploring the underlying ethical issues associated with diabetes care practice was a principal component of this research.

Constructing a Qualitative Design

In this research, a qualitative case study was designed to explore the questions associated with the research purposes for the following reasons. First, comprehensive diabetes care should involve social, psychological, and biographical dimensions; however, these aspects are rarely considered by studies examining the German healthcare delivery system. In Germany, care delivery for patients with chronic illnesses, including diabetes care, emphasizes medical care based on clinical evidence (Busse, 2004; Hasseler et al., 2010; Stock et al., 2010). Identifying alternative methods of healthcare delivery and innovative approaches for nursing in the context of chronic care represent valuable contributions.

Second, qualitative research is recommended by the methodological literature for researching chronic diseases, such as diabetes (Polit & Beck, 2004; C. Pope & Mays, 1995). Qualitative research enables researchers to explore the complexities of the illness and the meanings of complicated relationships from the perspectives of both the individuals living with the disease and the healthcare workers who care for those individuals. Applying a qualitative research approach and qualitative data analysis to German diabetes care settings allows for the generation of rich and detailed information using a small number of cases, obtaining insights through detailed study to gain a better understanding of the interpretations and meanings that are ascribed to health behaviors (Polit & Beck, 2004).

Third, case studies can help researchers assess the story-like rendering of a problem, especially in the context of caring for patients with diabetes. Case studies enable researchers to obtain answers to "how" and "why" types of questions and to discuss how a phenomenon is influenced by the context within which it is situated (Baxter & Jack, 2008; Yin, 2009). With an iterative construction process, a case study can be congruent with an interpretive paradigm, able to delve deeply enough to provide the analysis (Van Wynsberghe, 2007).

In this research, diabetes care was defined as the research case. To obtain a comprehensive view of how diabetes care occurs within the context of the German diabetes care system, both primary and long-term care settings for diabetes care were considered as the context for this case study. These settings were selected because patients' knowledge and attitudes regarding diabetes management, their care actions, and interactions with others are often developed and utilized in these settings.

The challenges of living with disease accumulate for patients over time. Thus, the collection of diverse voices from both healthcare workers and patients is important. Understanding the patients' demands makes it possible for healthcare workers to support the patients' abilities to follow the principles of disease management without letting the disease dominate the patients' lives (Dwarswaard et al., 2016; Mol & Law, 2004). In addition, involving patients' voices in research can break down hierarchical relationships that exist between healthcare professionals and patients, facilitating the formation of partnerships in healthcare (Lawton, 2003). Therefore, the voices of both healthcare workers and patients were collected during this research to explore and represent the entire spectrum of chronic care.

Research Method

The study was designed within the scope of the logic of care introduced by Annemarie Mol to explore the care demands of patients diagnosed with type 2 diabetes. This research aimed to identify a logical care pattern with ethical considerations and put a focus on multi-professional teamwork in diabetes care and nursing care practice. Grounded in a qualitative case study, research data were collected through an integrative review and a practical investigation involving in-depth interviews with both patients and healthcare workers, in addition to field observations, which occurred in both primary and long-term care settings at the University Hospital Freiburg in south Germany. For this study, primary care refers to inpatient hospital admissions and diabetes consultations (including individual and group consultations), whereas long-term care refers to outpatient visits by hospital physicians, diabetologists, and family physicians and home-care visits by nurses.

Data Collection

Research data was collected through two methods: an integrative review and a practical investigation, which included field observations of participants in German diabetes care settings and in-depth interviews with patients and healthcare workers.

Integrative Review[2]

An integrative review allows for an exploratory and substantive approach to a phenomenon (Whittemore & Knafl, 2005). Therefore, the first data collection method performed for this research was an integrative review. An integrative review can be considered a type of literature review (Christmals & Gross, 2017).[3] In this research,

---

2 An integrative review is a non-experimental design in which the researchers objectively critique, summarise and make conclusions about a subject matter through a systematic search, categorization and thematic analysis of past qualitative and quantitative research studies on the subject (Christmas & Gross, 2017; Whittemore & Knafl, 2005).

3 The nursing scholars Christmals and Gross (2017) saw an integrative review as a type of literature review. They named this methodology illustrated by Whittemore and Knafl as integrative literature review.

the integrative review was performed using the process described by Robin Whittemore and Cathleen Knafl (2005). I began the integrative review by gathering clinical and qualitative evidence to expand on the definition of diabetes; the prevalence, mortality, and complication rate associated with diabetes; and the system of diabetes care delivery, including the factors that impact care outcomes and possibilities for care improvement. Then, a thematic, data-driven analysis was performed, referring to the defined research purposes, including a literature review of caring and ethical perspectives. The findings of identified studies were summarised and analyzed according to various thematic headings. Finally, four thematic headings and their associated concepts and theories were defined: the field of diabetes care, the care theories applied to the subject, the logic of care theory, and the ethics of care.

To perform the integrative review, a comprehensive, computer-assisted search was undertaken. The two databases[4] that were searched were the Cumulative Index of Nursing and Allied Health Literature (CINAHL) and PubMed.[5] To combine keywords and different databases, Boolean operators, such as "and", "or", and "not", were used as recommended by Regina Freitas (2008). Reviewed sources included primary sources, secondary sources, conceptual and theoretical papers, and anecdotal or clinical resources. In particular, journals or books that were specifically related to the topic of interest or those that were likely to cover the topic were identified.

All resources were first gathered and reviewed for their relevance to the overall purpose. Once the initial review was completed, the identified materials were read in-depth to perform a more systematic and critical review of the contents. After writing a summary of each source, including key thoughts, comments, and the strengths and weaknesses of each publication, a final appraisal was performed using the computer program Citavi. The initial searches were limited to articles published in the last ten years but were later expanded to include relevant literature with any date of publication when the earlier literature was evaluated as being important and relevant for this research. Papers were excluded if they were not published in English or German because the most important global studies are typically published in English, and the research setting took place in Germany.

Practical Investigation

The data collection method was a practical investigation performed in German diabetes care settings. During this step, participants were subjected to field observa-

---

4   Based on the guidelines established by Whittemore and Knafl (2005) for performing systematic reviews, the use of two to three database sources is recommended.
5   Keywords were developed with reference to the defined research questions and the research purpose. The keywords used for this study were as follows: Diabetes Care, Care Delivery in Germany, Chronic Disease Care, Nursing Roles, The Logic of Care, Ethics of Care, Ethical Dilemmas, and Moral Distress.

tions, and in-depth interviews were performed to obtain empirical data to nourish and expand the concepts identified in the integrative review.

Field observation was selected because observing practices in real-world, daily-life situations with specific characteristics allow people to enact or restrain from enacting appreciation, allowing for the observation of how patients live their specific and diverse daily lives (Bury, 2001; Lawton, 2003; Pols, 2005). To help a researcher to structure the research questions and record details during the field observation process, field notes were utilized in this research, following the guidelines established by Anne Mulball (Mulball, 2003).[6] I often made field notes during observations and conversations or shortly after these events, which were recorded in greater detail upon leaving the field site. When observers permitted it, care encounters and conversations are recorded. I experienced countless conversations with observers, in addition to many silent understandings and misunderstandings, which were recorded in the field notes.[7]

Narrative and thematic interviews were utilized in this research.[8] To clarify situations that occurred in the field during observations, I asked healthcare workers questions to improve my understanding of how various issues are addressed and which principles were guiding their actions. To further explore the factors underlying the behaviors of patients and healthcare workers, I interviewed both patients and diabetes care workers, including physicians, diabetes consultants, diabetes assistants, and nurses. An interview guide was implemented, which covered topics including the experience of diabetes management (disease development, the meaning of the disease, coping with and living with diabetes), the experience of working together with a multi-professional team (including physicians, nurses, other related healthcare professionals, and the surroundings where they live), and the needs for the diabetes care.

---

6   The field notes used in this research included the followed scheme: structural and organisational features (e.g. what does the environment look like and its intended use), people (e.g. how do they behave, interact, dress, and move), the daily process of activities, special events, dialogue, a daily diary of events as they occur chronologically, and a personal reflective diary (including the thoughts of the researcher regarding field observations and reflections on their own life experiences that might influence observation).
7   The field notes contain all notes that were made during the individual consultations (BE–B1–01, BE–B1–02, BE–B1–03, BE–B2–01, BE–S1–01, and BE–S2–01) and during the group consultations (BG–DA2–01, BG–DA2–05, BG–DB1–01, BG–DS2–02, BG–DS2–03, BG–DS2–04, BG–DS2–07, and BG–FA2–06).
8   Based on the literature, a dialogical process in qualitative research can provide researchers with animated descriptions of the concerns, meanings, and practices of patients in their daily lives, allowing for their lived experiences to be transformed into a textual expression that is reflexive of reliving the experience (Lawton, 2003; Van Manen, 1990).

Sampling and Participants

The Department of Diabetology and the home-care center at the University Hospital Freiburg in South Germany were the settings used for this case study. The interview participants were divided into two groups. One group consisted of patients with diabetes and their families. The other group consisted of healthcare professionals who work in diabetes care practice. A half-year of fieldwork was conducted in these two German diabetes care settings simultaneously. I observed and participated in daily activities, including in the outpatient department, diabetes patient education courses, and individual counseling for diabetes patients, at the Diabetes Outpatient Centre at the University Hospital Freiburg. I also accompanied home-care nurses on visits to patients with diabetes and was present during team meetings with other team members, such as doctors, nurses, and diabetes consultants.

Interviews with patients were performed in multiple settings, including the diabetes care center, in the community, or at patients' homes. Ten patients (I-PP-01, I-PP-02, I-PP-03, I-PP-04, I-PP-05, I-PP-06, I-PP-07, I-PP-08, I-PP-09, I-PP-10, and I-PP-11) were identified as fulfilling the inclusion criteria for study participation: older than 18 years, with type 2 diabetes diagnosed for at least one year. Patients with dementia or other severe psychiatric or physical diseases were excluded. The patients' family members, particularly the main caregivers, were also invited to the interviews. Of the ten patients (four women and six men) interviewed, three included the participating of family members. Although only one official interview was conducted with each patient, when the content was unclear, I contacted the patients to obtain clarification.

The perspectives of healthcare professionals were collected by interviewing eleven healthcare workers, including two diabetes specialists (physicians) (I-FA-01 and I-FA-02) two diabetes consultants (I-DB-01 and I-DB-02), one diabetes assistant (I-DA-01), and six home-care nurses(I-NN-01, I-NN-02, I-NN-03, I-NN-04, I-NN-05, and I-NN-06). Except for one male physician, all other healthcare professional participants were women. All participating professionals had a diabetes care education or experience with diabetes care and had held their current position in the German diabetes care center or the home-care center for at least two years.

All eligible participants were asked to join the study via oral invitation and were provided with an official invitation by letter, which included information regarding the aim of the study and confidentiality protocols. They were asked to inform me of their interest in participation. The participants who expressed interest were contacted by telephone or in person to determine a time and place for the interview. All participants were requested to sign a declaration of participation when they agree to be involved in this research.

Two pilot interviews (one with a patient and one with a healthcare professional) informed the development of an interview guide, but these interviews were not included in the analysis. From April to November 2012, ten structured face-to-face interviews with patients (three of which included the patients' main caregivers) and eleven interviews with healthcare workers occurred via face-to-face interviews.[9]

Interviews and feedback sessions were audio-taped and transcribed verbatim for the thematic analysis of the content. All interviews proceeded in German and were later transcribed by an independent German speaker. Some recordings of the original reactions and situations during interviews were recorded in my native language and later translated into German. The audio-recorded interviews lasted from 40 to 90 minutes. After coding ten interviews for each group, the additional information did not add new meaning, and the same issues were raised in most of the interviews, which indicated that the samples had reached a point of saturation, as described by Janice Morse (1991).

All references to interviews and field notes are designated using a combination of letters and numbers, which consist of three components: the first component of each code refers to the type of documentation (I: interview, BE: individual consultation [Einzel Beratung in German], BG: group consultation [Gruppe Beratung in German]); the second component of each code refers to the identity of interviewed participant (DA: diabetes assistant [Diabetes Assistentin in German], DB: diabetes consultant [Diabetes Beraterin in German], FA: diabetes specialist [Facharzt in German], PP: patient), the location where individual consultations were performed (B1 and B2: in consultation rooms [Beratungsraum in German], S2: in the ward [Station in German]), or the person moderating the group consultations (DA2: nutrition assistant [Diät Assitentin in German], DB1: diabetes consultant [Diabetes Beraterin in German], DS2: diabetes assistant, FA2: diabetes specialist [Facharzt in German]); the third component of each codes uses a number to identify the participants of interviews, the times of individual consultations, or the course numbers of group consultations.

Data Analysis

A two-level coding scheme using Creswell's (2007) thematic analysis[10] was applied to this research, and data management was facilitated by a computer program (NVivo

---

9   Eight patient interviews occurred in the participants' homes, and two occurred in the diabetes education centre. All eleven interviews with healthcare workers occurred in their workplaces.

10 Thematic analysis was used to categorical establish themes or patterns. It starts with a provisional list of codes based on selected concepts identified in the literature, with new codes added according to the empirical data (Creswell, 2007; Miles et al., 2013; Yin, 2009).

10). During the first level of the coding scheme, an integrative review and literature analysis were performed according to the steps outlined by Whittemore and Knafl (2005). In this phase, the sources that met the inclusion criteria were coded and subsequently clustered into groups after initial data abstraction. Data were then extracted and entered into a literature review matrix to reach the phase of data display.

In an iterative process of coding and condensing the data, three recurring themes emerged: understanding the disease, including the demands of diabetes care and the general concepts for practical care; the logic of care, in which a comparison of theoretical and practical activities is fostered; and care tensions and ethical dilemmas, which focuses on the ethical activities that occur in care practice. During the second level of coding, empirical sources were added to offer a comparison of the theoretical data and provide additional meaning to the themes.

After analyzing the research data using the two-level coding scheme, according to Creswell's thematic analysis, three main themes containing the underlying meanings and expanded subthemes were gathered from the integrative literature review, and the empirical data were structured. The issues central to nursing care were examined through the perspectives of each theme, and each theme was also analyzed separately, with inputs from other healthcare professionals during this research. By analyzing the research data and constructing emergent themes, a logical care pattern for diabetes care and nursing with ethical considerations was established to achieve the research purpose.

Trustworthiness

To establish the qualitative criteria for trustworthiness and rigor for the research, some strategies that were recommended by Andrew Shenton in 2004 were applied to this research (Shenton, 2004). In addressing credibility, I consulted related documents, visited the settings, and introduced my study to develop an early familiarity with the culture of the participating organizations before performing any data collection. To ensure the honesty of the informants when contributing data, each participant was allowed to refuse participation, ensuring that the data collection sessions only involved individuals who were genuinely willing to participate and were prepared to offer data freely. Probes were used during this research to elicit detailed data, and iterative questioning was applied, in which I repeatedly returned to issues that were raised by the informant to extract related data through rephrased questions.

Frequent discussions regarding the research occurred with my superior and colleagues at colloquiums, in addition to team conferences in the context of diabetes care settings, such as the home-care center and the Department of Diabetology.[11] The vision of a researcher may be broadened by others who contribute their experiences and perceptions. I have presented some of this work at international conferences in Utrecht, Freiburg, Amsterdam, and Leuven, in addition to the campus doctoral conference in Vallendar. Field notes, including detailed descriptions, were used in this research during data collection to promote credibility by conveying the actual situations. Engaging in a thick description of the research process is important because detailed descriptions allow others to determine whether the insights can be transferred to their local contexts and settings (Nimmon & Stenfors-Hayes, 2016). I attempted to provide sufficient detail regarding the field in which the research was performed to allow readers to decide whether the prevailing environment is similar to other situations and whether the findings can be justifiably applied to other settings.

Finally, to achieve dependability and conformability,[12] some selected interview transcripts were discussed with and coded by colleagues at doctoral colloquiums to identify additional insights. I used a data-oriented approach to data analysis, which involved demonstrating how the data led to the formation of recommendations as it was gathered and processed throughout the study. I sometimes recoded the same datasets and compared the results after a while. Having multiple researchers independently code the same set of data and then reaching a consensus regarding the emerging codes and themes can prevent a researcher from reaching conclusions based on their predispositions rather than from the data.

Ethical Considerations

The Ethics Committee and the Staff Council of Alber-Ludwigs-University Hospital Freiburg (EK-Freiburg 43/12) approved this study, and all participants received the usual assurances regarding anonymity, confidentially, and the right to withdraw at any point during the study, without prejudice. Any names that appear in quotes are pseudonyms.

Limitation

To establish a logical care pattern for diabetes care and nursing, this research puts focus on nursing activities in diabetes care practice. In Germany, most of the multi-

---

11 To ensure the accuracy and availability of codes categorised from the empirical data collected in 2012, the meanings of the codes were presented and discussed at team conferences held at these two care settings in September 2018.
12 The strategies used to achieve dependability and conformability were applied according to the guidelines established by Baxter and Jack (2008) and Shenton (2004).

ple diabetes care services are offered in the Department of Diabetology and home-care center. The care actors who are working in these settings, including patients, nurses, diabetes consultants, and diabetes specialists, were selected as the interview participants for this research. In my field investigation, however, the roles of family physicians within a care team and their influence on patient care were frequently mentioned. Adding the voices of this occupational group into practical analysis becomes valuable and is recommended for further research.

Chapter 3: Literature Review and Theoretical Framework

The Field

Diabetes is one of the largest global health emergencies of the 21st century. Each year, an increasing number of people are diagnosed with this condition, resulting in life-changing complications that are associated with a high financial burden for the patients, their families, society, and the country. Improving care for patients with diabetes is considered both a challenge and a high priority for healthcare policy worldwide, including in Germany.

In this research, the context of diabetes care settings in Germany was examined as the research case. Understanding the suffering associated with diabetes, the terms used in care practice, the structure of German healthcare delivery, and the barriers and challenges encountered during diabetes care served as the foundations for further discussion. Investigating the professional roles of healthcare workers in care practice can help us to identify problems and offer possibilities for care improvement.

The Suffering of the Disease

Diabetes mellitus, referred to here as simply diabetes, is a chronic condition that occurs when the pancreas is no longer able to produce insulin or when the body cannot make good use of the insulin it produces (IDF, 2019). Over time, the resulting hyperglycemia causes damage to many organs in the body, which can result in disability and life-threatening health complications, such as cardiovascular disease, blindness, kidney failure, and lower limb amputation (IDF, 2019). In 2019, an estimated 4.2 million people worldwide died due to diabetes-related complications (IDF, 2019).

In recent years, the prevalence of diabetes has increased at a worrying pace worldwide. In 2019, the global diabetes prevalence was estimated at 9.3% (463 million people), which is expected to further increase to 10.2% (578 million) by 2030 and to 10.9% (700 million) by 2045 (Abdul et al., 2020). Approximately 232 million people with diabetes are estimated globally to be undiagnosed (IDF, 2019). The proportion of people with type 2 diabetes,[1] in particular, is increasing in most countries. Approximately 462 million individuals were affected by type 2 diabetes globally in 2017, corresponding to 6.28% of the world's population (IDF, 2019).

In the European Union (EU), over 66 million people live with diabetes, corresponding to an average EU prevalence rate of 9% of the adult population, which is expected to grow to over 10% by 2040 (Abdul et al., 2020). Germany has the highest prevalence of diabetes in Europe. A prevalence rate of 6,059 cases per 100,000 people in 2017 was reported in Germany, and among the German adult population, 15.3% were living with diabetes in 2019 (Abdul et al., 2020; IDF, 2019). In Germany, 95% of people diagnosed with diabetes have type 2 diabetes, but more than 2.5 million adults are estimated to have undiagnosed diabetes (DDG, 2020). According to a survey by IDF, Germany also had the highest number of diabetes-related deaths in the EU, with over 50,000 diabetes-related deaths reported in 2019 (IDF, 2019). The mortality rate for people with documented diabetes aged 30 years and older was approximately 50% higher than that for age-matched individuals without diabetes in Germany (Robert Koch Institute [RKI], 2019).

Patients with diabetes experience physical and psychological distress, in addition to constant socioeconomic pressure, during their day-to-day lives. The costs associated with diabetes include the increased use of health services, the loss of productivity, and disability (DDG, 2017). The German government reduces the pressures associated with high expenditures by offering diabetes care. On average, the German healthcare insurance (Krankenkasse) spends four times as much to care for a patient with diabetes as for an insured person without diabetes due to the costly complications associated with diabetes, such as strokes, amputations, and renal failure (DDG, 2020; Stock et al., 2010). According to disease-related cost calculations released by the Federal Statistical Office, diabetes care in Germany cost EUR 7.4 billion in 2015 (RKI, 2019).

Similar to other chronic illnesses, diabetes affects the psychosocial dimension of a person's life, often combined with feelings of fear, anxiety, uncertainty, and decreased self-esteem, in addition to complicating family and social relationships (DDG, 2020; Callaghan & Williams, 1994). Diabetes impacts the individual through physical, psychological, social, and economic dimensions. Caring for patients with diabetes is, therefore, complicated, and multiple aspects must be considered.

---

1 Three main types of diabetes have been identified: type 1 diabetes, type 2 diabetes, and gestational diabetes. Type 2 diabetes is the most prevalent form of diabetes and has increased alongside cultural and societal changes (IDF, 2019). People with type 2 diabetes can often initially manage their condition through exercise and diet. However, over time, most people with type 2 diabetes will require oral medications or insulin (IDF, 2019).

Terms Used in Diabetes Care

In the literature, various terms, including client, customer, patient, diabetic, and people with diabetes, are used in the context of diabetes care. All of these terms are used to describe relationships between individuals who provide care and social services and the individuals who receive these services. However, each of these terms describes relationships with different nuances and implies different assumptions (McLaughlin, 2009). To improve the overall understanding of the relationships that exist among various healthcare actors, the terms used in diabetes care practice must first be defined and clarified in the context of the research being performed.

The use of the term client focuses on care workers' roles and tasks, with connotations of an agency relationship, in which one individual purchases the professional services of another (Deber et al., 2005; C. McDonald, 2006; McLaughlin, 2009). Within this type of relationship, the client represents an individual in need of assistance due to a lack of necessary abilities or capacities. The term client suggests the hierarchical power position of the care worker as an individual with the necessary specialist knowledge and skills to affect a situation and who is accountable to the client, the care profession, and their organization (McLaughlin, 2009). However, the notion that the patient is a client represents the care relationship that suggests that the professional has the power to identify what the passive client needs. (C. McDonald, 2006; McLaughlin, 2009; Wing, 1997).

With the increasing conceptualization of medical services as a commodity, the term client has slowly been replaced with the term customer, which was originally used to describe relationships in business and commerce and has been extended to the practice of healthcare (Shevell, 2009; Torpie, 2014). The term customer is embodied by the ideas of freedom and choice, in contrast to a citizen's passive reliance on professionalism or expert knowledge, which diminishes the professionals' power and increases the customer's power (C. McDonald, 2006; McLaughlin, 2009; Torpie, 2014). In effect, welfare has come to be viewed as a commodity to be bought or sold (C. McDonald, 2006; McLaughlin, 2009; Torpie, 2014).

Although the term customer is associated with freedom and choice for care receivers, some doubts and criticisms of this perspective have emerged. First, care workers are required to provide their services, even when those services are costly, cheaper alternatives are available, or the assessments of the professionals do not match the customers' view of their needs (C. McDonald, 2006; McLaughlin, 2009). Second, the discourse of customers is rarely discussed comprehensively when describing a vulnerable group (C. McDonald, 2006). Third, an individual's ability to make rational choices that do not necessarily serve their immediate interests but are in the best interest of improving their overall health conditions has been questioned (Entwistle et al., 2010; McLaughlin, 2009; Reach, 2014; Wing, 1997). Fourth, the terms customer and client may be associated with potentially objectionable overtones and imply that medical services are commodities that should be managed by a market (Deber et al., 2005; Torpie, 2014). For these reasons, the terms client and customer are not appropriate for use in this research, which aims to describe the relationships among healthcare actors.

The term patient is broadly implied in healthcare. The term patient includes limited scope for the concept of a patient's right to choose, which implies the weakness and helplessness of a patient who requires the support of healthcare professionals who know what is best for the patient (Butts & Rich, 2008; Shevell, 2009; Thompson et al., 2006). The construct implied by the term patient devalues the intrinsic autonomy of the individual and describes a healthcare relationship with a focus on the acute recognition of disease and disease management, which might represent essential factors for successful diabetes care.

The term diabetic is often used in diabetes care; however, the term diabetic is often viewed as a stigmatizing word that labels the individual as a medical condition rather than as a whole person. Hugh McLaughlin (2009) warned that some populations of people exist who meet the criteria for services but do not access these services because they fear the associated stigmatization and are not honest about their disease. This hidden and invisible consequence of stigmatization may also result in dangerous care delivery situations in which care services are replicated or repeated (McLaughlin, 2009). The term person with diabetes is, therefore, considered the best option for describing care receivers with diabetes in care practice.

However, research by Jane Ogden and Kirstie Parkes (2013) revealed no difference in patients' perceptions of their condition when they were referred to using the terms diabetic and person with diabetes. These terms did not generate significantly different positive or negative stereotypical attitudes (Ogden & Parkes, 2013). The important issue is, therefore, not which words we use but how these words are used, whom they are used to describe, and when and in what situations these terms are used while respecting users' languages and perspectives.

In describing this research, I was careful to retain and analyze the terms used by the various care actors in the research field, but my personal preference is to use the term patient to describe care receivers because a patient is an individual with diabetes who is ill and receiving healthcare from caregivers. As described in the logic of care, patients have few choices when dealing with their disease and living with diabetes (Mol, 2008). The term patient used in this research, however, is not meant to imply a passive position relative to their care activities. Instead, this research emphasizes the role of active patients,[2] who share in the responsibilities for their care with healthcare workers.

Diabetes Care Delivery in Germany

The increasing prevalence of chronic diseases that require long-term care, such as diabetes, has led the German government to consider new methods of offering healthcare. New forms of German healthcare, such as disease management programs (DMPs), that integrate various healthcare professional groups have been created (Schlette et al., 2009; Ulrike et al., 2008). However, because patients in Germany are traditionally afforded a high degree of free access and choice regarding their care providers and healthcare insurance,[3] several problems have emerged within the German healthcare system, such as the overuse of healthcare services, a customer-oriented approach, and segmented care (Busse & Blümel, 2014; Lenzen et al., 2016). In this section, the structure of German diabetes care is discussed.

In Germany, statutory health insurance (SHI, Gesetzliche Krankenversicherung) represents the major source of healthcare financing, covering 71 million people and insuring approximately 90% of the nation's population (Busse & Blümel, 2014). In the SHI scheme, regional associations of SHI physicians are required to deliver healthcare services as defined by law and contracts with health insurance providers (Busse & Blümel, 2014).

German healthcare maintains a relatively strict separation between the ambulatory care sector and the hospital sector. The hospital sector focuses on inpatient care, whereas ambulatory care is focused on office-based and often single-handed physicians, who do not work with other healthcare providers. (Busse & Blümel, 2014; Maynard, 2006). To cope with the increasing prevalence of chronic disease, the Federal Ministry of Health in Germany has passed several laws since 2000, establishing new forms of care that are aimed at improving care coordination and strengthening the function of primary care within the German healthcare system. These new care

---

2   The term active patient is based on the logic of care theory described by Mol in 2008. According to Mol, patients need to be freed from passivity and be able to construct a better characterisation of an active patient (2008, p. 92). Further discussion regarding active patients and related concepts are presented later, in Chapter 3: The Logic of Care.

3   In Germany, general laws, such as the Patients' Rights Act (Patientenrechtegesetz; 2013) and the Charter of Rights for People in Need of Long-term Care and Assistance (2003), regulate the rights of patients to choose their physicians and hospitals freely, receive information and qualified medical treatment, determine the type of treatment undertaken, receive medical procedures only with their legal consent, obtain individual advice from their health insurance provider, receive care that fulfils all legal quality and safety requirements, receive their medical records, and have their confidentiality remain protected (Busse & Blümel, 2014).

entities include integrated care contracts on the contractual side and new care programs, such as gatekeeping,[4] medical care centers, and DMPs, on the delivery side (Lisac et al., 2010; Schlette et al., 2009). Among these care programs, DMPs play especially important roles in diabetes care.

In Germany, DMPs for type 2 diabetes were first introduced in 2003, following new legislation that aimed to improve the quality of care and foster competition among health insurance providers (Nagel et al., 2008; Schlette et al., 2009; Stock et al., 2010; Szecsenyi et al., 2008; Ulrike et al., 2008). Participation in DMPs is voluntary for both patients and physicians. Approximately 30% of all diabetes patients in Germany are enrolled in DMPs, representing 1.2 million individuals insured by national health insurance (DDG, 2017).

Some studies have demonstrated the positive effect of DMPs in diabetes care, such as strengthening patients' abilities to perform self-management (Gensichen et al., 2006; Szecsenyi et al., 2008) and improving teamwork among multiple healthcare providers (Gensichen et al., 2006; Stock et al., 2014; Szecsenyi et al., 2008). Other studies have indicated that German DMPs in diabetes care often perform in a fragmented manner (Gensichen et al., 2006; Stock et al., 2014). In the next section, the barriers and challenges encountered during German diabetes care are explored further.

Barriers and Challenges to Diabetes Care

The healthcare situation of patients with type 2 diabetes is frequently viewed as problematic in Germany, particularly in primary care settings. Patients are described as being too passive or complaining of receiving little effective support (Gensichen et al., 2006). The social and biographical aspects of the lives of patients with diabetes are rarely considered in German diabetes care (Hasseler et al., 2010). An individual- and setting-oriented concept of diabetes management in primary care is missing, despite the majority of diabetes patients being cared for in the primary care setting (Hasseler et al., 2010). In addition to the lack of coordination among members of the healthcare professional team, the increased workload and time pressure associated with primary care can considerably increase the challenges associated with diabetes care (Möller et al., 2004; Taylor et al., 2005).

---

4   Gatekeeping depends on primary care physicians and was introduced in 2000 to enhance the quality of care and reduce costs by preventing unnecessary specialist visits. In Germany, patients are free to choose their family physicians, who serve as gatekeepers. Once a patient has subscribed to a gatekeeping programme, specialists can only be seen upon referral from the primary care provider (Lisac et al., 2010; Schlette et al., 2009). However, some studies have revealed that patients who enrol in gatekeeper contracts are not associated with better health outcomes than patients who are not enrolled, and the numbers of specialist visits are not significantly reduced (Lisac et al., 2010; Schlette et al., 2009).

Although some studies have described the successful implementation of DMPs for diabetes care in Germany, many healthcare workers are hesitant to join DMPs and require additional reassurances that participation in DMPs will not compromise their professional status or prestige (Magnezi et al., 2013; Schlette et al., 2009; Szecsenyi et al., 2008; Taylor et al., 2005). Organizational factors, such as the lack of funding, limitations on the personal budget, the lack of time with patients, and the lack of organizational support for caregivers, are also viewed as barriers to participation in DMPs (Busse, 2004; Busse & Blümel, 2014; Magnezi et al., 2013).

Another difficulty in German diabetes care is the increasing need for psychosocial care among patients with diabetes (DDG, 2017). Healthcare professionals are often focused on the goals and expectations of diabetes management, whereas patients are more concerned with reducing the impacts of diabetes on their lives, which often include a loss of spontaneity, feeling forced into adaptation and submission, feeling worthless, feeling ignored, feeling unsafe, lacking confidence, and a general sense of uncertainty (Lenzen et al., 2016).

An effective diabetes care management program aims to alter the patients' lifestyles and can be quite time-consuming. Unfortunately, high workloads and time pressures are major problems in German care practice (Hasseler et al., 2010; Lenzen et al., 2016; Möller et al., 2004; Taylor et al., 2005). The economic pressures associated with the current healthcare system increase the difficulties encountered by healthcare workers attempting to offer their patients individual-centered care. Although a fee-for-service system can control expenditures, it does not improve the efficiency of diabetes care nor prevent the delivery of care with little or no health benefits[5] (Maynard, 2006). With a budget cap, German fee-for-service payments can create fragmentation and inefficient practices.

Caring for patients with chronic conditions, including diabetes, requires multiple healthcare professional groups across different care settings to work together (Martin & Landgraf, 2010; Schlette et al., 2009). Unfortunately, coordination between the ambulatory sector and the hospital sector is lacking within the German healthcare system (Martin & Landgraf, 2010; Schlette et al., 2009). The invisible influences associated with power and trust can affect the strategic choices made by healthcare workers regarding whether to collaborate, with whom, and at what level (J. McDonald et al., 2012; Schlette et al., 2009). These impacting factors and their effects on German healthcare sectors are explored in Chapter 4 and Chapter 5.

---

5   In Germany, most diabetes patients receive the majority of their diabetes care from their family physicians (Hausärzte), who typically work within a fee-for-service system in which physicians are encouraged to see more patients and perform more complex procedures due to the relative reward structure of the fee schedule (Maynard, 2006).

Roles of Nursing in German Diabetes Care

How the roles of the healthcare professionals are developed and deployed within a healthcare system can change the management and delivery of healthcare in daily practice (Hasseler et al., 2010; Manski–Nankervis et al., 2014; Stock et al., 2010; E. H. Wagner, Austin et al. 2001). Numerous studies have demonstrated enhanced roles for nursing in the management of chronic diseases, and the development and maintenance of practice environments can promote high-quality care (Albine, 2008; Carey et al., 2009; Havens et al., 2010; Lindh et al., 2007; Renders et al. 2001; Siminerio et al., 2007). Nurses represent the professional group with the most regular patient contact, but they are frequently mentioned as a group that other team members have less trust in, which is especially apparent in the relationships between nurses and physicians. Fatima Sayah and her colleagues (2014) viewed this discord as the result of a lack of clear role descriptions and divisions of labor, indicating the importance of clarifying each healthcare actor's roles and what those roles entail.

In many countries, including the United Kingdom and the Netherlands, diabetes specialist nurses (DSNs) play important roles in providing specialized, long-term care for chronically ill patients with diabetes (Lindh et al., 2007; Mary, 1989; Moser et al., 2006; Manski-Nankervis et al., 2014).[6] Recently, diabetes nurse educators have been increasingly employed by community health centers and private practices to coordinate multi-professional care to improve collaboration, problem-solving, and communication in diabetes care (Manski-Nankervis et al., 2014). Nurses serve as consultants in diabetes care, particularly for care issues that involve lifestyle changes, including nutrition and motivation to engage in physical activity (Rosemann et al., 2006; Young, 2016).

In Germany, diabetes care is usually led by physicians. Family physicians manage all ambulatory diabetes care. The involvement of other diabetic care groups in patient care, including diabetologists and endocrinologists, diabetes consultants, diabetes assistants, wound assistants, nurses, and other professionals, such as psychologists, are coordinated by family physicians based on need (DDG, 2020). Only some diabetes professionals are certified by DDG because state-recognized vocational training has not yet been implemented for certain professionals, including diabetes consultants and diabetes assistants (DDG, 2020).

---

6   In the Netherlands and the United Kingdom, DSNs work independently with their patients and are responsible for their care activities. In this nurse-led, shared-care program, DSNs who are tasked with providing direct patient care, organising and coordinating care (including medical care) for individual patients, and providing advice and health education to patients and other care providers (Carey et al., 2009; Moser et al., 2006).

In German primary care practice, nurses support the physicians in performing administrative tasks, such as arranging appointments for patients, answering telephone calls, and preparing and providing patient files (Schlette et al., 2009). However, the traditional structures and infrastructures of diabetes therapy and management are neither sufficient nor effective in German primary care settings. Technological and societal changes in healthcare have raised the possibility of expanding nursing roles in Germany (Rosemann et al., 2006; Schlette et al., 2009).

Recently, nurse-led diabetes care within primary care settings was introduced in Germany, structured around the concept of regular preventive home visits (Möller et al. 2004; Taylor et al. 2005; Van den Berg et al., 2009). A pilot study exploring the effects of home visits by community nurses in 2005 showed positive improvements in German diabetes care. Unfortunately, the implementation of this new nursing role within the limited financial budget available for ambulatory care remains a major obstacle (Schlette et al., 2009). Nurse-led education is criticized in the literature as time-consuming, and ambivalence toward this change by physicians and a lack of motivation among nurses to play this role are not encouraging (Rosemann et al., 2006). Not all patients and physicians are willing to accept a change in nursing roles, even if nurses are willing to play new roles (Rosemann et al., 2006).

The expansion of nursing roles in German diabetes care continues to face major barriers, such as deficiencies in the professional knowledge and clinical skills of nurses due to a lack of medical training in German nursing education (Callaghan & Williams, 1994; Magnezi et al., 2013; Manski-Nankervis et al., 2014; Rosemann et al., 2006; Young, 2016). The organizational hierarchy of German healthcare society makes the expansion of nursing roles difficult (Magnezi et al., 2013). Most nurses are trained to follow protocols, focusing on medical management and disease-specific medical outcome indicators (Lenzen et al., 2016), despite the desire of many nurses to offer a care- or relationship-oriented focus rather than a disease- or cure-oriented service (Kleinman, 2004). Nurses are, therefore, disinclined to offer holistic care, which does not align with their professional training and can result in ethical dilemmas in care practice. Research is required to offer an in-depth examination of the roles of nursing in care practice, explore the factors that influence care relationships, and identify emerging care and ethical issues that do not align with established professional identities.

Summary

Diabetes is one of the largest global health emergencies of the 21st century. In Germany, the increasing prevalence of diabetes and the associated high mortality rate results in a high burden of disease for individuals, their families, the national healthcare system, and society as a whole. Patients with diabetes suffer from physical ailments, psychological distress, and socioeconomic pressures during their day-to-day lives. Therefore, this disease group is worthy of additional attention.

The term patient was determined to be the most appropriate term for care receivers in the context of this research because the word patient is not associated with the hierarchical power associated with the words client or customer and minimizes the confounding issues of freedom and choice. In the context of this research, the term patient refers to an active state for care receivers, who participate in their care activities and share responsibilities with their healthcare providers.

Caring for patients with type 2 diabetes is viewed as problematic in primary care settings in Germany. The current German policy uses chronic DMPs, in which patient self-management is encouraged to reduce the burden of chronic disease. However, German diabetes care is also described as fragmented. Patients rarely receive systematic care that includes consultation and education. The social, psychological, and biographical aspects of patients' experiences with diabetes are rarely considered. Patient's willingness and abilities to participate in decision-making are often questioned. Rather than a care- and human-oriented focus, German diabetes healthcare often takes a cost- and task-oriented approach, which may result in an undesired care consequence associated with power and trust.

Nurses are increasingly involved in caring for patients with chronic diseases, such as diabetes. Nursing-led care is defined by the literature as feasible and can positively improve diabetes care. However, the current role of nurses and the nursing profession in Germany is trivial and seldom discussed. Nursing professional competence is often doubted by physicians, patients, and even nurses themselves. Medical hierarchy and economic expenditures within the German healthcare system are guided by healthcare insurance policies and play an important role in influencing nursing activities. Consequently, nurses may often experience a struggle between the sense of offering a commercial service when following organizational guidelines and their professional awareness of their responsibility to provide holistic care, resulting in ethical dilemmas in their daily work. Further research clarifying nursing roles, identifying the positions of nursing professionals, and investigating the factors that influence relationships and emerging ethical issues in practice remain essential.

The Theoretical Nursing Care Approaches to the Subject

This section analyses the theoretical nursing care approaches described in the literature from the perspective of patients' bodies, which focuses on individuals' perceptions, and the perspective of collaboration, which focuses on the interactions among various healthcare actors and patients.

Patients' Bodies

Three theoretical nursing care approaches, including the trajectory model, self-management, and body-work, focus on individuals' bodies and are often applied to the context of chronic disease care to improve care outcomes. All three of these theoretical nursing care approaches center around the careful observation of changes in patients' bodies and offer various methods for monitoring the disease trajectory, with a focus on patient self-management and the social aspects of caring.

The trajectory model, also referred to as the Corbin-Strauss model, is a nursing model for the care of patients with chronic diseases, especially in the outpatient setting (Corbin & Strauss, 1988, 1998). The trajectory model identifies nine stages[7] associated with chronic diseases and describes a holistic, case-accompanying nursing system, in which a permanent caregiver considers the patients' biography and their social aspects during the chronic and serious courses of the disease (Corbin & Strauss, 1988, 1993).

The application of the trajectory model into practice involves healthcare workers accomplishing different tasks to care for different types of disease and patients actively contributing to addressing their health, prevention, disease, and rehabilitation conditions (Corbin & Strauss, 1993). Within the trajectory model, the self-help and self-determination of patients are important, as is the involvement of patients' families and the overall environment (Corbin & Strauss, 1998). To address an unpredictable chronic disease, a dynamic and flexible approach are essential to the application of the trajectory model (White et al., 2002).

Self-management is used extensively in the literature as a method for improving chronic illness outcomes and is recognized as an essential component for the treatment of patients with chronic illness, including diabetes care (Bury 1982; DDG, 2017; Hinder & Greenhalgh, 2012; Holman & Lorig, 2000; Koch et al., 2004; Udlis, 2011; Wilde & Garvin, 2007). Self-management studies aim to encourage individuals to be aware of their bodies and disease by developing self-monitoring, self-efficacy, and self-care abilities to address their chronic diseases (Udlis, 2011; Wilde & Garvin, 2007). Patients are encouraged to shift from a passive to an active role in disease management (Hasseler et al., 2010; Holman & Lorig, 2000; Mol & Law, 2004; Peel et al., 2004).

Numerous studies have explored methods for improving self-management in chronic care.[8] However, the cost-cutting focus of European healthcare systems does

---

7   The nine stages of a chronic disease course are the initial phase, pre-trajectory phase, trajectory onset phase, crisis phase, acute phase, stable phase, unstable phase, downward phase, and dying phase (Corbin & Strauss, 1988, 1998).

8   For example, normalising the process of self-management is thought to result in positive outcomes, balancing the limitations and demands of daily disease management (Callaghan &

not prioritize teaching Self-Management skills (Elissen et al., 2013). This can minimize the holistic potential associated with self-management due to a focus on clinical outcomes and healthcare expenditures in care practice (Udlis, 2011).

An increasing number of healthcare scholars have focused on the body-work for diabetes care, which was initially described by Mol and Law (2004) and later expanded by Julia Twigg et al (2011). Body-work studies ask questions about how the human body can be interpreted or known and how it may be handled, transformed, and understood (Twigg et al., 2011). Body-work researches emphasize paying attention to bodily symptoms, learning to monitor an implanted device, or performing periodic measurements, as necessary, to care for bodies with chronic diseases (Mol & Law, 2004; Wilde & Garvin, 2007).

The components of body-work involve assessing, diagnosing, handling, treating, manipulating, and monitoring bodies and emphasize not only the embodied action and enacted bodies but also on the embodied emotional experience that produces changes or modifies bodies (Gimlin, 2007; Mol & Law, 2004). The application of emotional contexts can make body-work meaningful and rewarding but can also represent a source of frustration and vulnerability (Twigg et al., 2011). Healthcare professionals who practice body-work not only focus on the bodies of their patients but also manage their bodies and bodily performances. The values, pleasure, or authority of healthcare workers may add to their embodied work (Twigg et al., 2011).

Power relies on forms of expertise and organizational authority that can specify how the body is treated. Therefore, the implantation of body-work may represent the corporeality of power relations between healthcare workers and patients in the form of corporeal interdependence interactions (Twigg et al., 2011; Wolkowitz, 2002). Body-work occurs in domestic spaces and can extend commoditization and simultaneously remove waged labor from direct managerial control, embedding body-work within extra-economic social, spatial, and temporal relationships (Twigg et al., 2011). As a result, trust relationships become difficult to build, and becoming attuned to one's body becomes difficult due to limited time and practice (Twigg et al., 2011).

The theoretical nursing care approaches from the perspective of patients' bodies stress how the care actors understand their sick bodies and disease, emphasize a dynamic and flexible caring process, put focus on emerging healthcare restrictions,

---

Williams, 1994; Ouwens et al., 2005). Improving the knowledge and care skills of patients is considered to represent an essential component of self-management (Holman & Lorig, 2000; Taylor et al., 2005; Udlis, 2011). Adding a biopsychosocial perspective improves the understanding of a patients' beliefs and values, which can help professionals guide patients in expressing their self-management goals and taking responsibility for their care activities (Holman & Lorig, 2000; Hunt et al., 1998; Koch et al., 2004; Lenzen et al., 2016; Udlis, 2011). The establishment of a reciprocal partner relationship is encouraged between patients and healthcare workers (Holman & Lorig, 2000; Udlis, 2011).

with concern on revealing ethical issues. Caring for patients with diabetes, caring activities involve more than coping with a complex body; caring involves connecting with society, which is frequently influenced by the economy, culture, and policy (Corbin & Strauss 1991; Wilde & Garvin, 2007). However, many researchers have reported that patients with chronic illnesses do not receive sufficient assistance or support from medical care professionals in coping with the physical, psychological, and social demands of their illnesses (Barr et al., 2003; Bodenheimer et al., 2002; Matthews, 2007; Ulrike et al., 2008; E. H. Wagner, Grothaus et al., 2001). In the next section, professional collaborations are explored, in which relationships are formed, and interactions are examined.

Professional Collaboration

A body does not work alone. Instead, a body tinkers with others (Mol & Law, 2004). In the literature, focusing on illness experiences in the collaborative sense extends beyond the life and biography of the individual experiencing the illness. Collaborative care integrates micro sectors that seek to better understand how an illness is lived and negotiated in patients' daily lives (Barr et al., 2003; Bodenheimer et al., 2002; Gittell, 2009; Lawton, 2003; Ville et al., 1994; E. H. Wagner, 1998; E. H. Wagner, Grothaus et al., 2001). In this section, three theoretical nursing care approaches are reviewed from the perspective of professional collaboration: integrated care, chronic care model (CCM), and relational cooperation (RC).

Integrated care, also referred to as shared care for chronic disease, was developed to unify medical inputs and the delivery, management, and organization of care services to improve care access, quality, and efficiency and enhance user satisfaction (Gröne & Garcia-Barbero, 2001). Within this care model, healthcare systems focus on the coordination of multi-professionals to foster complete and comprehensive healthcare delivery (Gittell et al., 2013; Kodner & Spreeuwenberg, 2002; Temmink et al., 2000; Way et al., 2000). The application of integrated care typically occurs within the context of chronic diseases, such as diabetes, but is increasingly becoming population-oriented, with a focus on health promotion and prevention (Hickman et al., 1994; Schlette et al., 2009).

In the literature, the successful implementation of integrated care requires the integration of resources, continuous and comprehensive delivery of medical care, pooling of information, application across the primary-secondary care interface, and coordination with insurance systems (Carry et al., 2001; Szecsenyi et al., 2008; Ulrike et al., 2008). Within integrated care, a collaborative process is built voluntarily and necessarily implies negotiation (Martin-Rodriguez et al., 2005; Szecsenyi et al., 2008; Ulrike et al., 2008;). Integrated care, from the perspective of professional collaboration, results in the delivery of continuous and comprehensive medical care by multi-professionals, during which patients are informed and agree to care, and all actors communicate with each other.

However, the sources of power differences between professionals can prohibit the development of team collaborations in care practice (Martin-Rodriguez et al., 2005). The hierarchical process driven by organizations is often described as a barrier to the optimization of integrated care (Kodner & Spreeuwenberg, 2002). The process of professionalization is often characterized by domination and control, rather than collegiality and trust, which can disrupt collaborations within a care team (Clark, 2005; Martin-Rodriguez et al., 2005).

Healthcare delivery systems are often reported as fragmented, lacking the ability to share information between different types of medical providers, prone to duplication of services, and poorly designed for the coordinated delivery of chronic care (E. H. Wagner, Grothaus et al., 2001). Edward Wagner's CCM is based on the planning of coordinated actions by multiple caregivers within overlapping domains in the context of chronic care.

In the CCM, chronic care occurs within three overlapping domains: the entire community, the health care system, and the provider organization (Bodenheimer et al., 2002). The essential elements of the CCM include community resources and policies, the health system organization, self-management support, delivery system design, decision support, and clinical information systems (Rothman & Wagner, 2003). In the CCM, all patients with chronic illness are encouraged to be active and develop new relationships with relevant medical specialists (E. H. Wagner, Grothaus et al., 2001). Healthcare workers are increasingly called upon to respond effectively to diverse cultural and linguistic needs among patients by enhancing their sensitivity. Within the CCM, treatment decisions are based on explicit guidelines, which are discussed with patients to allow patients to understand the principles underlying their care (E. H. Wagner, Grothaus et al., 2001).

However, the CCM does not reflect the diversity and complexities of disease prevention and health promotion (DDG, 2017; Jacobsen et al., 2012), and the narrow perspective, which is focused on information and community, has been criticized (Barr et al., 2003). An expanded CCM featuring five additional themes has been introduced to incorporate health promotion and public policy (Barr et al., 2003).[9]

In diabetes care practice, many clinical studies have indicated that patients with type 2 diabetes enrolled in CCM-based practices were more likely to receive patient-

---

9   The five added concepts are patient safety (in health systems), cultural competency (in delivery system design), care coordination (in health systems and clinical information systems), community policies (in community resources and policies), and case management (in delivery system design; Barr et al., 2003). In the *Expanded Chronic Care Model*, the fields of health promotion work with the broader determinants of health (e.g. housing, income, and social supports), and public policy is considered (Barr et al., 2003).

centered and collaborative care compared with patients who received routine care (Barr et al., 2003; Bodenheimer et al., 2002; Gensichen et al., 2006; MacLead et al., 2004; Nutting et al., 2007; S. A. Smith et al., 2008; Stock et al., 2014; Siminerio et al., 2004; Szecsenyi et al., 2008); however, barriers to CCM implementation have also been reported, especially at the clinic level and the organizational level (Hroscikoski et al., 2006). Reimbursement policies and insurer contracts with care plans often prohibit the implementation of improvements for chronic care (Hroscikoski et al., 2006; E. H. Wagner, Grothaus et al., 2001). The professional power of physicians to shape care processes and their general stance of neutral autonomy can also result in resistance to changes in chronic care (Hroscikoski et al., 2006; E. H. Wagner, Grothaus et al., 2001). A mistrusting relationship towards a care team can develop when team members do not understand why they cannot influence the care process (Holm & Severinsson, 2014). Feelings of fatigue and apathy can develop, both among healthcare workers, which can result in poor care delivery and antagonistic interactions with the patients, and among patients, which can result in negative feelings towards healthcare workers, lack of trust in the healthcare workers, and further exacerbate negative interactions (Holm & Severinsson, 2014).

Improving care relationships may improve the delivery of collaborative care. RC, which explores the relational dynamics of coordinating care work, is reviewed. RC is defined in the literature as "a mutually reinforcing process of communicating and relating for task integration or more simply as coordinating work through relationships of shared goals, shared knowledge and mutual respect" (Gittell et al., 2013). RC researchers call for organizations to replace traditional bureaucratic structures with more relational structures, such as hiring and training to promote cross-functional teamwork, cross-functional conflict resolution, cross-functional performance measurement and rewards, and cross-functional boundary spanners,[10] protocols, and information systems (Gittell et al., 2013). Promoting connections across workgroups rather than reinforcing existing professional silos[11] is important (Havens et al., 2010). By enabling participants to effectively perform their work and providing social support to enable resilience in response to a stressful situation, the application of RC can improve job satisfaction (Cramm et al., 2011; Gittell et al., 2013).

However, some problems continue to be observed in care practice. Although nurses and physicians engage in highly interdependent tasks, due to contested

---

10 Boundary spanners are staff members whose primary task is to integrate the work of other people around the needs of a particular project, process, or customer (Gittell, 2009).
11 Professional silo refers to healthcare professions that share common core values, knowledge, and skills but typically act in isolation. Professional silos often foster relationships based on power, competition, and hierarchies, resulting in inadequate preparation for teamwork (Margalit et al, 2009).

boundaries between their practice status and power differentials, efficient collaboration is often lacking (Gittell et al., 2009; Havens et al., 2010). Patients' voices are historically less powerful than the voices of professionals, and patients are often required to navigate the fragmented healthcare system and coordinate care on their own (Callaghan & Williams, 1994; Gittell, 2009). Social psychological foundations, personal relationships, and participants outside of the focal organization were added to expand the focus of RC networks (Gittell, 2011).

RC researches seek to support healthcare professionals and promote teamwork in daily practice. Healthcare workers are meeting resistance at the individual level, practice level, and organizational level. Unequal power distribution and the fragmentation of healthcare delivery in the current German healthcare system can make constructing relational partnerships in care settings very difficult. This lack of relational partnerships can increase uncertainty regarding care responsibilities among healthcare actors. The theoretical nursing care approaches from the view of professional collaboration, the concepts referring to ethical issues, such as mistrust relationships and unequal power relationships, become increasingly important for care practice. In the section on the logic of care and the ethics of care, the emerging concepts developed for research purposes are explored and analyzed.

Summary

When coping with a complex, chronic disease, the theoretical nursing care approaches from the perspective of the body focus on self-awareness in response to each individual's body. The trajectory model offered support for understanding the variety of care tasks that depend on the disease trajectory. The application of self-management emphasized each individual's ability during the management of physical symptoms and treatment, in addition to psychosocial concerns associated with adapting life to the continued experience of a chronic condition. Body-work studies focused on the understanding and interactions of practitioners with patients' bodies through the careful monitoring of bodies to address physical changes while respecting the psychosocial biographies that form the individual's self and interacting with all surrounding factors.

Caring activities necessary for chronic disease care involve not only one's own body but also interactions with other persons, healthcare professionals, care organizations, and society, and care can be influenced by economics, culture, and policy. From the perspective of professional collaboration, an integrated care model was developed to combine inputs, delivery, management, and the organization of care services. Collaborative, multidisciplinary teams are advocated by the CCM to repair a fragmented delivery system that lacks clinical information capabilities, duplicates services, and is poorly designed for the coordinated delivery of chronic care. The application of RC offers the possibility of understanding relational dynamics associated with coordinating work through a mutually reinforcing process of communication and task integration through relationships based on shared goals, shared knowledge, and mutual respect.

Although these theoretical nursing care approaches are suggested by the literature to increase the efficiency of chronic care delivery, continued difficulties and barriers exist in care practice. Ethical concerns in care practice continue to grow concerning a vulnerability in decision-making, unequal power distribution in the healthcare system, and mistrust within relationships. A further review of these issues and a discussion of both theoretical and practical approaches to ethical considerations are warranted. The logic of care theory, which was chosen to serve as the theoretical framework for this research, is reviewed and analyzed in the following section.

The Logic of Care

The logic of care is a philosophical theory that was first proposed by Mol in 2008. Mol analyzed diabetes care and explained why patients require care services that follow the logic of care. Using various methods, including ethnographic observations, field research, and interviews with patients and medical practitioners in a hospital in the Netherlands, Mol examined chronic diabetes care as her research case. Mol (2008) used the term logic in her theory because the term logic helped her in practice when she examined whether an action was appropriate or logical for specific circumstances (Mol, 2008, p. 10). By comparing the logic of care with the logic of choice, which can be used to describe the organization of most current healthcare activities, Mol addressed how the care activities occur in individual situations at the momentary, micro-level.

Debate on Situation and Collection

By asking questions[12] regarding the issues of force, choice, and care, Mol compared and contrasted two methods through which people provide care to address disease. One method was the logic of care, which is considered an alternative care practice, and the other method was the logic of choice. According to the logic of choice, care is guided by patients, and patients are treated as customers; therefore, care services are provided in response to patients' desires (Mol, 2008, p. 16). The identification of patients as customers was not considered a good idea for diabetes care by Mol.

---

12 The questions proposed by Mol were as follows. When compared with force, choice is more often than not a great good. But what about comparing it with care? Is care a softer form of force, or might something entirely different be going on? (Mol, 2008, p. xii)

Although respecting patient autonomy is important, not all patients with diabetes are capable of making their own choices (Mol, 2008, p. 7). Due to the uncertainty of disease development, patients often have difficulty weighing the advantages and disadvantages of treatment options. Often, patients use fear as their adviser or allow emotions to cloud their judgments during decision-making (Mol, 2008, p. 7).

Instead of requesting that patients make decisions, paying more attention to the conditions in which choices must be made can be valuable. Compared with the logic of choice, which emphasizes the abilities of patients and asks who should make such choices, the logic of care focuses on the practices and situations that result in choices being necessary (Mol, 2008, p. 8). For Mol, the crucial question in care practice was not how many activities are performed but what types of activities are being engaged in. As Mol stated, "The logic of care is not preoccupied with our will, and with what we may opt for, but concentrates on what we do" (Mol, 2008, p. 9).

The logic of care does not start with the individual but with the collective (Mol, 2008, p. 68). According to the logic of care, good care focuses on the conditions where people live, and caring is a matter of attending to the balance inside the body, the intricate surroundings, and the interactions between bodies and the outside environment (Mol, 2008, pp. 39, 79). An individual's activities are influenced by collectives (such as families or friendship groups) in unexpected ways,[13] and supporting patients in disentangling themselves from collectives and creating a nourishing surrounding[14] that encourages patients to engage in moderating and health-promotional behaviors is an important goal for healthcare workers (Mol, 2008, pp. 68, 72). For patients, becoming someone different and knowing how to act differently from others are tasks they must learn when coping with their disease (Mol, 2008, p. 70).

To apply the logic of care to care practice and offer the possibility for comparisons between theory and practice in the current research, the concepts described in the logic of care are summarised and categorized into three themes that depend on engaging with an active patient: responding, shared caring, and ongoing. Responding describes the attentiveness of the patients to their bodies, enabling them to be aware of their care needs, in addition to being active in identifying their care needs and performing care. Shared caring means that patients must work as a team with

---

13   In diabetes care practice, Mol (2008) notes that families are relevant for therapy. However, family habits do not always help patients with diabetes control. When a patients' surroundings have negative effects on patients' disease management, patients should be encouraged to insist on caring for themselves. Sometimes, they must remove themselves from situations harming their health and create circumstances that cater to their needs (Mol, 2008, p. 69).

14   Mol (2008) highlights the importance of creating achievable care interventions, such as providing access to a swimming pool, a cooking course, stricter food legislation, or suitable types of agriculture. For Mol, offering patients acceptable care services may improve the collectively shaped conditions in which patients live rather than telling individuals what pathways to choose (Mol, 2008, pp. 80–81).

their healthcare professionals and share caring with them. Care is a dynamic activity. Ongoing refers to care actions that are iterated through attempting one solution, paying attention to outcomes, adapting to the response, and trying again using an improved approach.

Core Concepts

The healthcare system is organized such that healthcare professionals must wait for patients to present themselves, and care is not provided if patients do not visit their healthcare professionals (Mol, 2008, p. 95). An active patient is a prerequisite of the logic of care in practice, and successful care depends on patients' activities (Mol, 2008, p. 95). According to Mol, "people who take care of themselves get care" (Mol, 2008, p. 83), and "it is impossible to take care of people who do not take care of themselves" (Mol, 2008, p. 94).

Based on the assumption of an active patient, the first classification in the logic of care is defined as responding. To receive care tailored to their specific situations, active patients are encouraged to respond to their own needs and engage in activities that are good for their bodies. Being attentive to patients is especially important. Patients who live with diabetes frequently used the term control to describe stabilizing their blood sugar levels through outside interventions, such as the use of insulin injections. But for Mol, the term control is usually misleading in care practice. She said, "Learning to achieve metabolic balance is not a question of strengthening one's muscles and hardening one's will, but of learning to be attentive" (Mol, 2008, p. 36). To be sensitive, to address the situation, and to respond in time, patients must monitor and receive sufficient information. Within the logic of care, information is not applied linearly during the care process. Instead, information is used to determine a sensible course of action (Mol, 2008, p. 52).

Responding results in abstinence being replaced with balance and the use of adaptive calculations rather than relentless restrictions in diabetes care (Mol, 2008, p. 55). In cases where patients engage in pleasures that are likely to lead to complications but that the patients are unable or unwilling to give up, these activities should not be viewed as sins (Mol, 2008, pp. 41–42). Rather than feeling guilty when something goes wrong, patients are encouraged to identify a counterbalance between the demands and desires of daily life. The logic of care is not focused on repression but rather emphasizes cherishing our bodies (Mol, 2008, p. 42). The logic of care describes a learning process involving the gathering of knowledge to define bearable ways of living with reality or living in reality (Mol, 2008, p. 53). All healthcare actors should consider what can be achieved within the limits of the real world.

When living with a chronic illness, day-to-day care responsibilities fall most heavily on patients and their families. Although support from healthcare workers is crucial, offering support does not represent fulfilling the patients' wants or achieving the healthcare professionals' needs. Instead, a counterbalance should be identified that responds to, respects, and shares in each other's experiences and values to perform suitable care practice (Mol, 2008, p. 28).

The second conceptual classification in the logic of care is shared caring, including the meaning of shared doctoring and nursing. The original term used by Mol (2008) was shared doctoring. Based on the logic of care, engaging in care is a matter of doctoring. Mol said that "doctoring depends on being knowledgeable, accurate and skillful. But doctoring is not something that only doctors do. It also involves being attentive, inventive, persistent and forgiving" (Mol, 2008, p. 64). The term 'nursing' was not directly mentioned by Mol, implying that nursing is included in her description. Care not only describes the activities of medical treatment but also involves all activities of daily living, which also describes nursing. To avoid confusion regarding the term doctoring, which is traditionally used to describe the activities only doctors engage in, and to clarify what doctoring describes based on Mol's assumption, I add the meaning of nursing to this concept and use the term caring to refer to the combination of doctoring and nursing for my research.

According to Mol, healthcare receivers should be treated as patients instead of customers. Based on the logic of choice, patients are viewed as customers who choose a product to their liking because they often play a managing role, and caregivers offer to implement care associated with the patients' wishes. However, management and implementation can be difficult to separate when caring for patients (Mol, 2008, p. 8, 13). Care involves more than engaging in a transaction to provide a product selected by the patient but involves interactions between the healthcare provider and the patients and the moderation of various actions during patients' lives (Mol, 2008, pp. 13–14).

Shared caring is one method for preventing a monopoly on expertise by professional groups because everyone's concerns and contributions should be taken seriously (Mol, 2008, p. 65). All members of the care team should respect each other's experiences and values, each individual's strengths and limitations should be considered, and an achievable care target should be established (Mol, 2008, pp. 53–56). According to Mol (2008), patients' values should be considered because values affect the patients' lives and can have major and long-lasting impacts (Mol, 2008, p. 50). In practice, healthcare professionals should ask patients about their experiences and attend carefully to what they are told, what difficulties patients experience, and attune to these descriptions. The role of healthcare providers should be to serve as inventive mediators (Mol, 2010, p. 56).

Within the logic of care, all actors work together, and no one needs to act alone. Patients and healthcare professionals are encouraged to constantly seek ways to improve the experience of living with the disease. The third classification identified by the logic of care is ongoing. According to the logic of care, care is an interactive, open-ended process that may be shaped and reshaped depending on the results

(Mol, 2008, p. 23). Actions and responsibilities can shift; as described by Mol, "one moment you care for and the next you are taken care of" (Mol, 2008, p. 92).

Time is an indispensable element of the logic of care. When dealing with a chronic disease, such as diabetes, "the caring process is chronic, too. It ends only on the day which one dies" (Mol, 2008, p. 22). Continuing to try, modify, and retry care approaches is essential. Day-to-day care for chronic disease introduces stress for both patients and their healthcare providers, and being able to let go is sometimes necessary for diabetes care (Mol, 2008, p. 95). The importance of being tenacious and adaptable in practice is emphasized (Mol, 2008, p. 61). For Mol, care does not depend on how much we do but on how long we pay attention. Care is not a product that changes hands but is the product of various hands working together over time toward a result (Mol, 2008, p. 21).

The logic of care emphasizes care situations rather than the making of choices; however, patients' autonomy and rights in decision-making situations may be questioned. Although the logic of care advocates that patients must be active, the responsibilities of healthcare professionals are not addressed. The logic of care encourages healthcare actors to avoid the feelings of guilt and sin associated with enjoying pleasurable activities, but the judgment of care outcomes encountered during daily practice represents a constant source of patient stress. The logic of care encourages healthcare actors to let certain issues go unaddressed in certain situations, but professional care awareness and goals for patient outcomes may cause healthcare workers to experience moral distress. The logic of care does not separately address the moral sphere because moral activities and moral communication represent separate aspects of care (Mol, 2008). In the following section, the ethical issues discussed in the logic of care regarding independence, patient autonomy, responsibility, and judgment are discussed.

Morality Concern

From the perspective of the logic of choice, choice offers individuals autonomy, and all individuals should have equal opportunities to make their own choices. However, patients with diabetes rely primarily on medicine and the actions of healthcare professionals (Mol, 2008, pp. 84, 94). Therefore, many patients with diabetes might feel as though they have no choices. However, Mol argues that patients feel a lack of freedom due to the nature of the disease itself rather than because they have been forced to submit to authority (Mol, 2008, p. 46). Encouraging patients to identify mechanisms through which they can live well with diabetes by trying different strategies is, therefore, more important than allowing patients to make choices that appear to respect their autonomy but damage their lives (Mol, 2008, p. 47).

When a patient makes a choice, the outcome of that choice, for better or worse, is their responsibility (Mol, 2008, p. 92). In the logic of choice, patients must take responsibility for their healthcare decisions and the ensuing outcomes. However, responsibility within the logic of care works differently. Although the logic of care does not offer security or self-satisfaction, a wrong choice is not associated with blame or guilt for the decision-maker (Mol, 2008, p. 60). Within the logic of care, failures are allowed, and finding fault in oneself or others is not necessary. Guilty people are viewed as deserving punishment, not care (Mol, 2008, pp. 87, 91). Instead of making judgments or administering punishments, addressing the situation and identifying what went wrong are viewed as the best resolutions within the framework of the logic of care. Mol views living as more important than life, and life should be treated as a task (Mol, 2008, p. 94) that patients remain active in. Rather than engaging in judgment and punishment, letting people feel safe enough to examine what is going wrong and why is more important (Mol, 2008, p. 60).

Within the logic of care, good and bad are never defined. Diabetes care is complex, and the disease trajectory is often unpredictable. Rather than defining what actions are good, Mol suggests that caring practices entail a specific modality of handling questions to do with the actions (Mol et al., 2010, p. 13). Defining distinctions between good and bad can make readjusting care more difficult, particularly in diabetes care. Instead of introducing dichotomies, discussions should focus on what is working to facilitate the creation of flexible interventions, address difficult situations, and respond by adjusting the approach to care (Mol, 2008, p. 101). In care practice, asking questions, such as "What is it difficult to do?" or "What can be done?" may help both patients and healthcare professionals to rethink the care problems when something fails to work instead of instilling feelings of guilt (Mol, 2008, p. 101). Focusing on the situation, considering what can be done next, and acting without giving up on the patient are emphasized by the logic of care.

In the literature, ethical issues, such as decision-making, autonomy, responsibility, and judgment, are often discussed in the context of diabetes care. Reviewing morality concerns in the logic of care can help me to better understand the related ethical issues in the field and offer theoretical support to the analysis of ethical dilemmas that emerge during field research.

Summary

The care theory of the logic of care, first presented by Mol in 2008, offers a theoretical framework for this research. Based on a comparison with the logic of choice, which centralizes the patients' rights in decision-making situations, the logic of care focuses on daily practice and care situations. The logic of care encourages paying attention to the types of activities being engaged in without judgment or creating the feeling of sin. Failures are allowed, and healthcare workers and patients are encouraged to continue trying new approaches to care management. The logic of care describes the care that occurs among a collective of individuals that includes healthcare professionals, the patient's families, and society, all working closely together.

The core concepts described in the logic of care can be divided into three classifications: responding, shared caring, and ongoing. According to the logic of care, patients are active, and the care process is continuous, specific, and adaptable. Patients are empowered to take care of their bodies and to cooperate with healthcare professionals. The duties of professionals lie in encouraging patients to take care of their bodies and empowering them to improve their self-caring abilities and skills. Within the logic of care, patients and their healthcare professionals share caring and care responsibilities.

The logic of care is concerned with what patients need and how they act. Therefore, making choices is not the mission for either patients or healthcare professionals. Advocating for patients' rights in decision-making and autonomy is not suitable under the scope of the logic of care. Care activities should focus on what has been attempted, and care represents a task that can be improved upon in daily practice. Feeling guilty or determining who is responsible for failed approaches is not necessary. Instead of making a judgment, the logic of care advocates for all healthcare actors to continue trying, adapting, and retrying new strategies and approaches to care.

Nursing practice is grounded in ethics, and nursing ethics is understood as a part of care ethics (Conradi, 2003; Kohlen & Kumbruck, 2008; Kunyk & Austin, 2011; Vanlaere & Gastmans, 2011). The next section explores the ethical concepts that often arise in the context of diabetes care and nursing, in some depth.

The Ethics of Care

Based on the previous literature review, various ethical issues encountered in diabetes care emerged. In this section, the foundations of the ethics of care are reviewed, with a specific focus on the relational and situational care that occurs in nursing. By comparing the benefits and drawbacks of individual autonomy and relational autonomy, the role played by autonomy in healthcare practice is discussed. From the perspective of relational power, how power and empowerment within a care team are established and the interaction between power and trust interacted are explored. Finally, the issue of professionalism, especially for the nursing profession, is examined, with a focus on professional obligations, vulnerability, and ethical sensibilities.

Foundations

The evolution of the ethics of care can be defined in three versions. The first version was established by Carol Gilligan in 1982. In her book In a Different Voice, Gilligan defined care as a specifically female virtue or disposition. Moral theorizing moves from a position where selves are viewed as independent to a position where selves are interconnected and interdependent throughout the discussion, with a focus on the context of the situation, and an impartial deliberation of ethical issues is viewed as an element of justice-based moral deliberation (Gilligan, 1982; Lachman, 2012). Expanding upon Gilligan's argument, Margaret Little turned her attention to the concept of relationships and emphasized the response to needs in terms of the responsibility of an individual in a situation rather than merely displaying an equal level of respect and refraining from unduly interfering with others (Little, 1998). To complement the description of care relationships in Gilligan's work, Vicki Lachman denoted different levels of emotional involvement among the individuals in caring relationships (Lachman, 2012).

The second version of the ethics of care is grounded by Tronto's contributions to the arena of political philosophy in 1993. Tronto, as a political scientist, demonstrated caring through the use of four phases associated with four ethical elements: caring about, which refers to attentiveness; caring for, which involves taking responsibility to meet a care need; caregiving, which requires care competence; and care receiving, which is associated with responsiveness (Paulsen, 2011; Tronto, 1993, 2010). For Tronto (2010), all of these phases of caring for patients involve physical, cognitive, and emotional actions. For Tronto, identifying power in the care relationship, recognizing the need for the politics of care at every level, finding methods for care to remain particularistic and pluralistic, and having well-defined and acceptable purposes of care can improve the understanding of relational practices (Edwards, 2009; Tronto, 2010).

The third version of the ethics of care was proposed by Chris Gastmans (2006), who considered the ethics of care to represent a moral orientation from which action emanates. Focusing on nursing practice, Gastmans (2006) saw that a moral vision may exist but may not develop fully because individuals may suffer from moral blindness caused by institutional obstructions and personal limitations, which prevents them from being sufficiently moved by the suffering of others to take action. For Gastmans, this moral blindness can threaten both the nurse-patient relationship and the nursing profession itself (Gastmans, 2006).

The delivery of healthcare is a highly complex process. Care ethics starts from a relational view of the human person and fundamentally weaves people into a network of relationships. In the past, scholars have focused on relational and situational care to explain the normativity of care in care practice, especially in nursing care practice (Lachman, 2012; Nordhaug & Nortvedt, 2011; Pettersen, 2011; Tronto,

1993; Vanlaere & Gastmans, 2011). The boundaries of these relationships transcend the private or individual field and expand into the public and collective world (Maio, 2018). Therefore, these relational webs involve not only daily and long-term care contexts but also involve institutional care, which requires moral considerations of relational interdependence and the moral judgments necessary to harmonize competing interests (Nortvedt et al., 2011; Pettersen, 2011). To achieve this type of care in practice, relational ontology[15] was introduced by Tove Pettersen in 2011. According to Pettersen (2011), the values of care can be better understood through the sharing of the human experience and transforming relationships when relationships are being built.

However, the conditions for fully-fledged relational care are often undermined within institutional and role-oriented settings (Pettersen, 2011; Torpie, 2014). Even though relational ontology appears able to offer healthcare workers a method for applying relational and situational care, many problems continue to be encountered in nursing care practice. The clinician-patient relationship is often viewed as a therapeutic relationship, in which patients are passive objects who receive formulated care activities, the medical profession holds a leadership position in healthcare, and hierarchical relationships dominate clinical freedom in decision-making (Gastmans et al., 1998; Rowe & Calnan, 2006; Torpie, 2014).

The building of professional relationships and trust relationships is articulated in care practice but has boundaries (Maio, 2018; Nortvedt et al., 2011). Patients may have no desire to enter such a relationship, preferring to simply make use of services (Maio, 2018). The limited time available and a general concern for accomplishing tasks over developing relationships, combined with varying priorities within professional healthcare settings, can result in different degrees of consequentiality, depending on the calculation of needs and the effectiveness of relationship-building across different patients (Nortvedt et al., 2011). This prioritization of tasks over relationships has become increasingly problematic as various professions, including nursing, are evaluated and perceived to represent an economically driven management model of service delivery. As a consequence, institutional and healthcare professionals may diminish or turn a blind eye to the experience of anxiety and vulnerability in their relationships with patients (Ramvi, 2015).

According to the literature, a good care relationship is defined as a relationship in which the individuals' responsibilities towards each other are established (MacDonald, 2002a; Nortvedt et al., 2011). In the ethics of care, professional responsibility is an important element that emphasizes the individuality, autonomy, and rights of

---

15   Relational ontology is the philosophical position that what distinguishes subject from subject, subject from object, or object from object is mutual relation rather than substance (Pettersen, 2011).

the patient (K. V. Smith & Godfrey, 2002) and includes respect for the unique otherness of the patient as a person (Nortvedt et al., 2011; Van den Hooff & Buijsen, 2014). Thus, the social alliances that connect people are frequently aimed at care capacities and relational powers, which can impact the development of individuals or their autonomy (Vanlaere & Gastmans, 2011), resulting in care and ethical conflicts. Highlighting insights regarding autonomy can leave room to understand and re-conceptualize the meaning of autonomy in relationships.

Autonomy in Healthcare

Autonomy often refers to trusting one's ability to make judgments and decisions and exercising autonomy involves reflecting on one's beliefs, values, and desires (McLeod & Sherwin, 2000). According to the literature, different types of autonomy including hermeneutic autonomy[16], therapeutic relationship[17], relational autonomy[18], and conscientious autonomy[19] have been defined. However, the notion of individual autonomy from a care perspective is frequently criticized as fundamentally individualistic and is considered a type of self-sufficiency defined by self-governance (Boldt, 2018; MacDonald, 2002a; Van den Hooff & Buijsen, 2014; Varelius, 2006; Verkerk, 2001).

The first critique of autonomy is that the emphasis on independence may lead to the neglect of certain values, such as trusting, caring, and responsibility, within the moral discourse (Ells, 2001; Kukla, 2005; Varelius, 2006). The second critique is that the right to autonomy can be viewed as the right of defense in healthcare, in which respecting autonomy includes a patient's right to refuse any medical treatment, even those that are necessary to restore health or save the patient's life (Boldt, 2018). The third critique refers to the consumer view of autonomy. Autonomy in healthcare is often guided by market assumptions about offering services to consumers identified as autonomous, capable of making a choice, and pursuing customer satisfaction (Torpie, 2014; Tronto, 2010; D. Wagner & Bear, 2009). The fourth

---

16   Hermeneutic autonomy stresses the procedural and inter-individual character of will-formation and decision-making (Boldt, 2018).
17   Within a therapeutic relationship, laypeople are encouraged to rely upon the expertise of healthcare professionals, who have a duty to guide, mediate, and manage healthcare to compensate for the inadequacy of a patient's medical understanding, which can prevent an inappropriate choice (Kukla, 2005; Varelius, 2006).
18   Relational autonomy was introduced, based on the understanding that humans are socially situated, deeply interconnected, and interdependent (Donchin, 1995; Entwistle et al., 2010; MacDonald, 2002; MacDonald, 2002b; Paulsen, 2011).
19   Conscientious autonomy was introduced as a type of concrete, limited autonomy that is especially relevant to the ethical assessment of healthcare practices (Kukla, 2005).

critique regarding autonomy is that paternalism, which has customarily been exercised throughout organizational and medical hierarchies within healthcare systems, is recognized as a direct threat to autonomy (Cole et al., 2014; Hedman et al., 2015; McLeod & Sherwin, 2000). The fifth critique is the feasibility of autonomy. The exercise of autonomy in healthcare is not always possible, and many situations exist in which patients have problems with autonomy due to weakness of will or limited executive functions, which can impair an individual's ability to enact their preferred behaviors to achieve their health-related goals (Entwistle et al., 2010; Reach, 2014). Self-distrust may additionally limit autonomy due to a lack of information for decision-making, limitations inherent to the circumstances in which decisions are made, or the values and desires that inform one's decisions (Cole et al., 2014; Entwistle et al., 2010; McLeod & Sherwin, 2000).

Professional autonomy is articulated for healthcare professionals, who identify as both professionals and as individuals. In healthcare systems, society often offers professionals the privilege of setting their standards of both technical and ethical excellence (MacDonald, 2002b). This relative freedom from outside scrutiny and control constitutes an important type of autonomy. Within this scope, respect for professional autonomy means allowing professionals to exert substantial control over their professional practices, allowing significant room for the exercise of judgment when performing their responsibilities (MacDonald, 2002b).

In nursing care, developing a practice that ensures both patients and professionals the ability to retain autonomy is important but difficult. First, patients have a high degree of autonomy in decision-making within a commercial medical delivery system; in particular, patients have the right to choose their healthcare services (Busse & Blümel, 2014; Lenzen et al., 2016). Second, nurses regulate activities according to their own will but are deeply influenced by the profession's relationship with other segments of society, including the executive, legislative, and judicial branches of government (MacDonald, 2002b). Third, institutional rules and budgetary constraints can greatly limit the delivery of healthcare services (Maynard, 2006).

Practically, professional autonomy justifies nurses who act according to their professional judgment rather than simply being told by physicians what to do. When a physician's orders conflict with nursing standards or with a nurse's expert judgment, the nurse's professional autonomy implies a right to object. However, a hierarchical medical society places physicians in a position of power relative to other healthcare workers (Kälvemark et al., 2004; Rosemann et al., 2006). Nurses do not generally have the autonomy to engage in the range of practices granted by legislation to physicians, and regulation may facilitate or limit individual nurses' autonomy (MacDonald, 2002b).

Nurses often lack the freedom to decide certain issues according to their professional judgments due to the power imbalance that exists between clinicians and patients and among other professionals. In the review of the literature, by examining the foundations of the ethics of care and the ethical issues of autonomy in healthcare, the dynamics of power within relationships were revealed.

Relational Power

Ethics refers to the relationship between power and responsibility and the occurrence or lack of power-sharing among all healthcare workers, including nurses and physicians, in hospital and community settings (Thompson et al., 2006). Recently, scholars have explored the empowerment of active participants in decision-making processes associated with care activities, especially among patients with chronic illnesses (Paterson, 2001; Powers, 2003). However, empowerment is restricted when the patient is vulnerable to the acts of power performed within a relationship (Hardy et al., 2000). In this section, the approach to power issues is explored by examining the nature and dynamics of power within relationships. The concepts of empowerment and shared decision-making, which are often mentioned in the context of diabetes care, are discussed. Finally, how trust forms within relationships characterized by unequal power distributions are elaborated.

Power is a matter of authority and control (Hardy & Phillips, 1998; Palviainen et al., 2003). Power has been explained by theorists as a process of domination in terms of individual wants, needs, choices, and real interests (Gergen, 1995) and represents a relational co-constructed process that is interwoven in all social relations (Nimmon & Stenfors-Hayes, 2016; Palviainen et al., 2003). The consequences of power can be influenced by language, executive positions, the value systems of local realities, and the local ontology of groups. For instance, physicians can exert power by drawing on the legitimized institutional language of medicine under their qualifications and training (Nimmon & Stenfors-Hayes, 2016).

In professional medical relationships, physicians' power has frequently been equated to paternalism (Porter, 2003). An unequal power relationship between patients and physicians is often observed in healthcare practice because physicians possess legitimized, referent, and expert power, and patients rely on physicians to provide necessary care and services (Nimmon & Stenfors-Hayes, 2016). Although the exercise of power in some situations can increase safety (Palviainen et al., 2003), paternalism may entitle physicians to ignore or override patients' choices that are deemed to be in opposition to their medical ethos (Schei, 2006).

Within interprofessional relationships, unequal power distributions can also be observed due to the sources of power differentials, which impact interprofessional relationships (Martin-Rodriguez et al., 2005; J. McDonald et al., 2012). Often, the physician-nurse relationship is based on a hierarchical relationship, with physicians occupying the position of the superior, limiting nursing power (Butts & Rich, 2008).

In effect, the dominance of medical authority and nursing subservience in physician-nurse interactions can leave nurses feeling oppressed and powerless.

Although empowerment and shared decision-making have been demonstrated to be effective for disease management in the context of diabetes care (Funnell et al., 1991; Lemay, 2010; Meetoo & Gopaul, 2005; Miers, 2003a; Serrano et al., 2016; Spiers, 2003; Tamhane et al., 2015; Tol et al., 2015), some barriers continue to exist in care practice. Doctoring entails and generates power, and the physicians' possession of expert knowledge is characterized as powerful in a physician-patient relationship (Joseph-Williams et al. 2014; Nimmon & Stenfors-Hayes, 2016; Schei, 2006). The blind trust of patients in healthcare providers may enable abuses of power in the form of exploitation or domination (Bachmann, 2003; Laugharne et al., 2011). Healthcare agencies generally organize the workloads of healthcare workers in a manner that restricts the amount of time available to interact with patients with chronic illnesses (Paterson, 2001; Wikblad, 1991). As a consequence, physicians often become the decision-makers (Paterson, 2001), and an individual's capacity to participate in a decision-making encounter is limited, particularly when a covert contract[20] exists within the patient-physician relationship (Joseph-Williams et al., 2014).

When patients are unaccustomed, unwilling, or unable to take responsibility for their healthcare, they may willingly transfer decision-making power back to healthcare professionals or empower healthcare professionals to make decisions on their behalf (Meetoo & Gopaul, 2005). However, this choice should remain with the patients, even when the choice is to decline power. Patients, who choose to remain passive recipients of care, are responsible for that choice and its consequence (Funnel et al., 1991). Powerful physicians dominate the decision-making process in healthcare contexts, and patients are often unable to be empowered during a caring process. Nurses often experience powerlessness when attempting to offer healthcare services according to their professional judgments, which can impact the trust relationships among physicians, nurses, and patients.

Trust is identified as a core facet of effective therapeutic relationships and serves as the foundation of relational power (Calnan & Rowe, 2006; Robinson, 2016; Schei, 2006). However, trust is also described as fragile, ambiguous, and dependent, particularly relative to the inherent vulnerability of patients (Dinc & Gastmans, 2013). In a consumerist type of relationship, patients are asked to guide their healthcare and take responsibility for problem-solving and decision-making. Healthcare relationships refer to the receipt of the desired care with a high level of patient control

---

20 A covert contract can develop between patients and clinicians, especially physicians, which are not typically acknowledged openly. Many patients enter into an unspoken contract with their clinicians, adopting the role of a good patient, characterised by passivity and compliance (Joseph-Williams et al., 2014).

(Robinson, 2016). This type of economic power may lead to feelings of powerlessness and neglect among patients at the prospect of living in a community with little support and the threat of neglect (Palviainen et al., 2003).

In nursing practice, trust is conceived as an internal good and as a normative ethical concept (De Raeve, 2002b; Sellman, 2007). A trusting relationship also allows nurses to undertake painful procedures with minimal distress (Dinc & Gastmans, 2013). Unfortunately, distrust relationships can form between nurses and patients during the process of nursing care practice due to the lack of necessary knowledge and skills for performing nursing procedures; ineffective communications, often associated with the overuse of medical rather than layperson terminology; failure to anticipate or understand the information needs of patients; the depersonalization of patients; neglect of responsibilities, and emotional distance (Dinc & Gastmans, 2013; Laugharne et al., 2011). Moreover, work-related factors (e.g. busy workload and inadequate time), emotional challenges (e.g. lack of understanding and value or power conflicts between nurses and patients), and social structures (e.g. a commercial organization or a hierarchical medical system) can hamper the development of a trusting relationship in nursing care practice (Dinc & Gastmans, 2013; Laugharne et al., 2011).

Working within this type of care environment can affect how the nursing profession and nursing roles are conceptualized and enacted and determine the views held by nurses regarding their professional identities in response to their organizational and social surroundings. A nurse's professional identity promotes awareness of their professional duties relative to the ethics of care (Nortvedt et al., 2011; Paulsen, 2011; Ramvi, 2015). In the next section, professional identity in nursing is explored.

Professional Identity in Nursing

Both the general public and nurses themselves identify the nursing profession as being strongly associated with caring for patients (Hoeve et al., 2014; Paulsen, 2011; Salloch, 2016). In German healthcare society, healthcare duties and commitments to patient autonomy, public accountability, power, and scientific excellence frame the concept of nursing professionalism and ethics, which can limit the roles of nursing (Davies et al., 1999; Gunnarsdóttir & Rafferty, 2006; Hoeve et al., 2014; MacDonald, 2002b; Salloch, 2016). In this section, the role of the nursing profession and the factors that impact the identity of a nursing professional are investigated.

The recognition of nursing as a profession has grown as nursing roles have changed. Based on the international literature, nursing is a licensed, self-regulating profession with professional standards (Kangasniemi et al., 2015; Porter, 2003, p. 100). In recent years, regulations have increased in German care practice to provide a unified legal framework and create legitimate participants in the decision-making process, obtaining the commitment of participants to coordinate their actions and to contribute to the common public interest (Busse & Reisberg, 2000; Dryzek et al. 2002; Gunnarsdóttir & Rafferty, 2006; Salloch, 2016).

However, regulation can also be ambiguous; although regulations can be powerful for guiding contributions to the social good, professionalism remains an ideology or belief system within the medical community that is used to defend the inherent values of the professional's ethos[21] (Nortvedt et al., 2011; Salloch, 2016). The professional echo, the obligation of professionals to be independent of those who empower them legally (Freidson, 2001), may be impaired, resulting in professional vulnerability in nursing.

Nursing scholars have attempted to explain the vulnerability of the nursing profession. First, the nursing profession continues to suffer from the influences of traditional values and cultural and social norms for sex, gender, and professional status (Hoeve et al., 2014; Miers, 2003a). Nursing's functional importance derives from its interdependence with the medical profession and other professional groups. Nursing remains a predominantly feminine and domestic activity, accorded a low social status that is often discredited by society (Ramvi, 2015). Nursing's subordinate position, the reduced importance of their work relative to physicians' work, and the dependence on medicine reduce the full professional status of nursing (Miers, 2003b, p. 84). Nurses feel that their jobs are vulnerable (Miers, 2003b, p. 93). Even establishing a shared care relationship can result in vulnerabilities being revealed within care relationships (Ramvi, 2015; Van Heijst, 2011), as the differences between various professions can become potential sources of conflict, hindering the development of truly collaborative practice (Clark, 2005; Martin-Rodriguez et al., 2005).

The accountability for care work is placed exclusively on nurses due to their responsibilities and obligations to the institutions at which they work, although nurses have individual vulnerabilities (Kunyk & Austin, 2011; Thompson et al., 2006). As a consequence, nurses' passivity and deference in work performance can minimize their influence on physician-nurse relationships. Nurses' work can, therefore, become subordinate to doctors or fall within the doctors' shadow (Miers, 2003b; Hoeve e al., 2014; Ramvi, 2015). Nurses can constantly experience frustrations regarding their relationships with patients, in addition to limitations on professional pride and development due to nursing vulnerability and compassion fatigue, resulting in feelings of irritability, anger, and negativity (Austin et al., 2009; Ramvi, 2015). To overcome professional vulnerability, the concepts of ethical sensitivity and moral courage were introduced to support nurses, reflect emerg-

---

21   Professional echo is similar to professional ideology. Freidson (2001) identified professional echo as being concerned with justifying the privileged position of occupational institutions in a political economy and the authority and status of its members.

ing care conflicts and ethical dilemmas, and create a practice that allows for the development of moral responsibility[22] within the nursing profession.

In the nursing literature, ethical sensitivity is described as the capacity, ability, and response of nurses to care situations that allow them to recognize, understand, and evaluate each situation (Milliken, 2016; Nortvedt, 2001; Nortvedt, 2003; Thorup et al., 2012; Weaver, 2007; Weaver et al., 2008). If nurses lose some of their sensitivity to recognize patients' problems over the years, they may overlook the patient's experience and begin to view their jobs as routine and may begin to work for their good rather than for the patients' good (Gjengedal et al., 2013; Milliken, 2016; Weaver, 2007).

In clinical nursing, a practical understanding of ethical sensitivity is critical because professionals who work with vulnerable human beings are challenged by the need to make decisions amid uncertainties that are often not accounted for in established protocols or policies (Milliken, 2016; Weave, 2007). Through the lens of clinical knowledge and awareness, ethical sensitivity may be transformed into careful decision-making in professional practice (Nortvedt, 2001; Weaver, 2007); however, nurses merely performing a job, addressing the situation from a solely technical perspective, or presenting with an ethical issue identified by others may not know how to respond to these situations (Weaver et al., 2008).

Affective sensitivity (or emotional sensitivity) plays an important role in clinical observations, allowing clinicians to identify clinically relevant clues (Nortvedt, 2001; Weaver, 2007). However, the corresponding negative consequences associated with emotional sensitivities, including signs of stress, discomfort, pain, exhaustion, anxiety, emotional overload, exploitation, personal loss, and moral distress, are often ignored (Nortvedt, 2001; Weaver, 2007). Although emotional sensitivity and expressivity are the necessary characteristics of medical care, they are often conceived of as being unprofessional and threatening to the abstract system of medicine (Twigg et al., 2011).

Nurses' emotions inform their cognition and reasoning skills and are often reflected in caring activities (Kunyk & Austin, 2011; Thorup et al., 2012; Weaver et al., 2008). In the literature, the personal and professional life experiences of vulnerability and suffering influence nurses' ethical formation and shape their courage about care (Thorup et al., 2012; Weaver et al., 2008). This embodied understanding and values towards a situation can determine how nurses present their caring behaviors, even in situations that require them to act in contrast to nursing standards or codes of ethics (Kunyk & Austin, 2011).

---

22 Moral responsibility was interpreted as a relational way of being good, which involves guidance by one's inner compass, comprising ideals, values, and knowledge, which translates into a striving to do good. Ethical challenges arise when one experiences being unable to act in a good enough manner (Holm & Severinsson, 2014).

To support the ability to stand alone for what is right without compromising in the face of injustice and threats, the concept of moral courage was defined as a positive and empowering tool (Kunyk & Austin, 2011; Numminen et al., 2017; Rahman & Myers, 2019). Courageous behavior in nurses refers to their ability to stay person-centered, admit their vulnerabilities and mistakes, face unpredictable care situations and risks, respond to moral distress and ethical uncertainty, bridge personal and professional values, encourage patients and preserve their dignity, feel empowered, stand against criticism, and manage their anxiety and ambivalence (Numminen et al., 2017; Rahman & Myers, 2019).

The fulfillment of moral duties towards patients represents an ongoing challenge for nurses. Courageous nurses must be aware of their professional boundaries and have the strength to reject demands from others (Numminen et al., 2017); however, nurses do not bear the responsibility of those making demands of them. Even when healthcare professionals do their best to care for patients, not all patients will recover, especially patients with chronic diseases. Labeling this situation as the professional's defeat should be avoided, as Mol (2008) indicated, a more tolerable way to cope with misery and suffering should be identified rather than creating sin or placing blame.

Summary

Working in a multifaceted care practice, nursing care constantly ranges between basic and complicated levels, subjective and objective, and rational and emotional. Care problems may emerge in response to a hierarchical and commercial medical society because nurses tend to emphasize the interpersonal and relational importance of their practices while simultaneously attempting to deliver an objective or evidence-based service, resulting in ethical dilemmas. The ethics of care increases the concerns about relationships and actions in a care situation. The foundations of ethical care support nurses in understanding emerging care tensions and ethical dilemmas.

In the literature, nurses are often reported to care about their patients based on their acceptance of their inherent moral commitments to care for patients and their responsibilities for care activities. Nurses are compelled to address threats to the delivery of safe, competent, and ethical nursing care. Although care ethics have been criticized for not sufficiently safeguarding personal autonomy, care ethics contains a critique of autonomy, which views the self as free and independent.

Ethics describes the relationship between power and responsibility rather than subjective attitudes and feelings. Power-sharing within an interprofessional team is advocated to improve collaborative care. Patient empowerment and shared decision-making might be useful for developing the patient's inherent capacity to act responsibly for their own lives. In healthcare, trust is identified as a core facet of effective therapeutic relationships and serves as the foundation of relational power. Beyond building trust and reorganizing the interdependent power environment, an ethical relationship in healthcare requires mutual respect, embodied knowledge, and professional competencies.

The nursing professional identity supports nurses to become conscious in self-understanding their professional work. Increasingly, nursing professionals secure nursing positions and ensure the continued present balance of responsibilities for accountability, regulation, and the management of professional activities. By enhancing ethical sensitivities and moral courage, nurses are enabled to recognize and respond morally to patients' suffering and their professional vulnerabilities.

In the context of healthcare, the process of professionalization is characterized by the achievement of domination, autonomy, and control rather than collegiality and trust. Although several duties, such as a commitment to patient autonomy, public accountability, or scientific excellence, are used to frame the perspectives of professionalism and ethics, establishing an ethical practice for nursing professionals is difficult. Autonomy in healthcare is often guided by market assumptions involving the offering of consumer services to individuals who are capable of making a choice and pursuing customer satisfaction. Physicians are often drawn to wielding power instead of sharing power. Compassionate interference does not appear in caring relationships. The imbalance of power within care relationships increases patients' vulnerability and dependency. Nursing work is limited by time and organizational regulations, making the building of trust relationships with patients difficult.

Through a review of the literature, the borders and limits for role-related nursing involvement and partiality are not always clear, particularly in German nursing practice. How do nurses identify their professional nursing roles? How does the care policy influence practical nursing care? How do nurses experience their vulnerability in care relationships? How do nurses reflect care conflicts and ethical dilemmas in practice? When applied to the German healthcare system, these questions become more problematic for nurses because the nursing profession in Germany is progressively becoming defined by an economically driven management model of service delivery. In the empirical section of this research, these ethical issues are continually investigated in the context of diabetes care.

Chapter 4: Practical Arena Analysis

Grounded by the thematic analysis approach described by Creswell, the research data were analyzed following a two-level coding scheme, and three themes were established. To support a better understanding of the meanings associated with each theme, quotes[1] were selected as references for each theme. All quotations and observations from the empirical data are presented based on a coding scheme. The first theme, understanding the disease, was divided into the following subthemes: meaning and goal of having diabetes, and patients' needs in diabetes care. The second theme, care logics in diabetes care, contains two subthemes: the empirical study of the logic of care, and other care logics in practice. These two themes categorized from the research data are illustrated and analyzed in Chapter 4. The third theme, care tensions and ethical dilemmas, includes the subthemes of autonomy in a vulnerable body, responsibility without authority, and professionalism around care boundaries are later described and discussed in Chapter 5.[2]

Understanding the Disease

Diabetes is an ongoing chronic disease that cannot be cured and results in the suffering of the whole body. Caring for patients with diabetes requires more than metabolic control; diabetes care requires adjusting to how the illness interacts with the real world. Understanding patients' priorities and concerns can help caregivers become engaged in caring and contribute to building a trusting relationship with

---

1 The quotes were collected from transcriptions of the interviews and the observation notes, which were made and documented in German. The selected quotes presented in this section were translated from German to English.
2 Lied of the theoretical basis for the empirical work, Chapter 4 and Chapter 5 were constructed with the presentation of the research findings, the theoretical discussion based on the literature, and the critical reflections on the current diabetes care and nursing care practice.

the care team.³ Thus, the definitions and understanding of the disease reported in the literature can be diverse, and how patients and their healthcare professionals understand the meaning of having diabetes must often be clarified. How do they set their care goals, and what do they view as necessary for good diabetes management?

Meaning and Goal of Diabetes Management

> For me, the care goal of diabetes care is that patients can someday accept their disease, live well with it, and integrate it into their daily lives. I believe the goal of diabetes care is the manner in which the patients understand how their bodies act and react and how should they take care of their bodies. (I–NN–02, 488–506)

Many patients characterize diabetes management as being difficult because the disease is often both invisible and painless (BG–DS2–07, p. 2; I–PP–03, 491–493; I–PP–09, 213–215). Without the ability to sense changes occurring within their bodies, patients' bodies may suffer from undetected damage that is often irreversible by the time patients recognize the complications associated with diabetes (BG–DS2–07, p. 2; I–NN–01, 143–153).

For patients, diabetes can be experienced as an undramatic disease with slow progress due to their increasing age (I–PP–01, 246–248; I–PP–09, 288–299) or as a serious and life-threatening health problem (BG–DS2–07, p. 2; I–PP–02, 120–128; I–PP–09, 288–299). Patients generally recognized that diabetes is a chronic disease that cannot be cured (I–PP–05, 14–28). To manage diabetes, both patients and healthcare professionals recognized that patients must be aware of their bodies, face and accept the disease, and act in a manner that is beneficial for their bodies (I–DB–02, 25–27; I–NN–02, 488–506).

When discussing their views of good diabetes care, however, many patients quickly focused on medical treatments and physical values. In many cases, the patients set their goals for diabetes management based on achieving acceptable blood sugar levels.⁴ If the patients break the rules and bad things happen to their bodies, the patients may feel guilty (I–PP–03, 432–433; I–PP–11, 205–206).

Doris Callaghan and Anne Williams (1994) assumed that an imbalance in blood sugar levels could result from lapses in management rigor, and patients' responses were forthright in accepting responsibility for these lapses. Anne Rogers et al. (2005)

---

3   The relevant discussion is presented in Chapter 3 and the related references can be found in the literature by Butts & Rich (2008), Lemay (2010), Miers (2003a), Mol (2008), and Snow et al. (2013).

4   Concern about blood sugar levels was often observed in the consulting room, where patients frequently displayed their blood sugar values from the past few days as their first action upon entering the room. Blood sugar values are deemed by many patients as being the most important issue when visiting diabetes consultants.

saw that self-management is interpreted narrowly as compliance with medical instructions. Mol and Law (2004) argued that patients need not turn into accurate number-guessers within their bodies but should instead learn to feel their bodies from the inside and train their bodies to practice self-awareness.

Living with a chronic disease represents an endless process associated with various stresses (I–NN–01, 323–330; I–PP–02, 210–211; I–PP–05, 66–68). Conflicts, compromises, persistence, and adaptations may occur in response to these stresses. Based on the empirical data collected in this research, the psychological loads that patients with diabetes experience can be identified as feelings associated with the loss of freedom, discomfort, fear, uncertainty, a loss of control, unnaturalness, abnormality, and being alone and helpless.

Many strict guidelines exist for diabetes management. Patients feel as though they have lost their liberty. Many patients reported strongly experiencing limitations to their freedom and feeling as though they were controlled by the processes associated with disease management, reducing their enjoyment of life (BE–B1–01, p. 5–6; I–NN–01, 354–360, 368–371; I–PP–02, 120–128; I–PP–11, 139–145). According to Janie Butts and Karen Rich (2008), patients with chronic illnesses frequently feel as if their illnesses are controlling them, rather than feeling that they are in control of their own lives. For many patients, living with diabetes represents something arduous and endurable. Patients recognized that they could not get rid of their disease but had to endure it and accept it. Tiredness or fatigue has been elaborated in the literature as a significant impact of living with a chronic illness (Hedman et al., 2015). Consequently, as one patient said, "I am surely getting more depressed because everything becomes more difficult with diabetes" (I-PP-01, 253–254).

In care practice, the patients often complained that they experienced the feeling of being forced (I–PP–05, 53–54). Moreover, the loss of freedom can result in the loss of passion for life (I–PP–02, 120–128, 446–448, 453–455). The feeling of being forced into adaptation and submission has been reported in the literature. In the study by Asa Hörnsten et al. (2005), patients talked about unsatisfactory encounters, which they characterized as professionals' efforts to reshape them into adopting a healthier lifestyle. In the current research findings, the patients realized their obligations to adapt their lifestyles and their duties as patients to obey strict care principles, but they also perceived this duty as a type of emotional load.

Another emotional pressure that patients often mentioned was their uncertainty regarding the development of the disease and its complications (I–PP–09, 197–201; GB–DB1–01, p. 2), the complicated medical treatments (I–PP–09, 599–603), and the impacts of the disease on their normal lives (BG–DB1–01, p. 1). Patients often worry about the negative outcomes that could occur if they failed to follow the principles of diabetes treatment (GB–DB1–01, p. 2). They were afraid of doing something wrong during their disease management processes (I–PP–04, 17–18; I–PP–11, 139–145).

If their blood glucose became unstable, some patients would experience anxiety (I-PP-04, 17-18; I-PP-11, 139-145).

The presence of uncertainty, the feeling of being unsafe, and the lack of confidence in caring for themselves were also described by patients in other studies (Callaghan & Williams, 1994; Hörnsten et al., 2004, 2005). Callaghan and Williams (1994) claimed that uncertainty was evident in participants' expressed concerns regarding their illness trajectories, with the threat of long-term complications being prominent (Hörnsten et al., 2005).

The feeling of being unnatural and abnormal was also reported by patients in this research as a type of psychological load (GB-DB1-01, p. 5; BG-DS2-04, p. 1; DB-S2-01; I-PP-05, 84-90). In care practice, patients often avoid injecting insulin in a public area because "I am ashamed of myself. I felt that I am abnormal like I have a handicap" (GB-DB1-01, p. 5). Based on the literature, the feeling of abnormality may lead to decreased self-esteem (Callaghan & Williams, 1994) and may cause the patients to experience a loss of self, which has been identified as a fundamental form of suffering among chronically ill persons due to a failure to develop new, equally valued self-images (Hörnsten et al., 2004).

A recognition of the emotional aspects caused by this chronic condition is inseparable from diabetes care. The research data highlight that patients may wish to be able to express feelings and share emotions with healthcare professionals (I-DB-02, 82-90, 152-153). Working with psychologists is also becoming increasingly necessary in diabetes care practice, especially when the care problems are associated with the cognitive and emotional dimensions of the patients (I-DB-02, 218-222).

Recently, studies have begun to focus on patients' real-life experiences because the notion of self-care is likely to include psychosocial and everyday elements of health (Costantini et al., 2008; Dwarswaard et al., 2016; Kendall et al., 2011; Rogers et al., 2005). This trend in diabetes care was observed in the data gathered during this research. Instead of criticizing the patients' blood sugar values, viewing patients as whole human beings and helping them live normally has become an essential goal of diabetes management (I-NN-01, 19-22; I-NN-02, 488-506, 542-543; I-DB-01, 236-240).

For both healthcare professionals and patients, being able to live normally without being labeled as a person with diabetes who no longer enjoys life represents the primary care goal of diabetes management (I-NN-02, 542-543; I-PP-04, 155-157). As a nurse said, "Patients want to be able to take part in a normal life instead of being stamped as a diabetic with the insight of no joy in life anymore" (I-NN-02, 542-543). Or as one patient said, diabetes care is "not necessary to be successful in health promotion, but having a good life should be addressed" (I-PP-04, 155-157). This goal is especially essential for patients who manage their diabetes outside of the clinical setting (I-PP-04, 164-166; I-PP-05, 138-140; I-PP-06, 324-329; I-PP-08, 333-334).

Based on the data collected in this research, patients wish to be independent (I-PP-04, 164–166; I-PP-05, 138–140; I-PP-06, 324–329; I-PP-08, 333–334). They want to be free of the limitations asserted by the disease in their daily lives. However, many patients were unable to fully separate themselves from their healthcare team. For situations in which the patient's care abilities are limited or when patients desire guarantees regarding successful disease management, the support provided by a professional healthcare team is welcome (I-PP-02, 210–211; I-PP-08, 18–20, 387–391). Kerstin Nyhlin (1990) called this type of independence "dependently independent", which was described as a form of ambivalence.

The meaning of having diabetes in care practice is full of contradictions. The patients wish to have freedom and independent life, but they also realize their dependence on medical treatment and that following diabetes management principles represents an inseparable part of life. Although obeying the prescribed caring principles and receiving medical therapy are expected to provide a cure, a chronic disease is never fully cured. Viewing the disease as something simple may reduce the feeling of burden, whereas treating the disease seriously may motivate patients to better control their disease. Patients have difficulty separating themselves from the healthcare professionals who treat them, and healthcare professionals desire to offer their patients care services that are tailored to the patient's care goals; therefore, understanding the patient's needs in terms of diabetes care is important.

Patients' Needs in Diabetes Care[5]

In this section, patients' needs for diabetes care are explored from the perspectives of both patients and healthcare professionals. Based on the research data, patients' needs in diabetes care start with the participation of patients who are active and well-informed. Participation encourages patients to enhance their attentiveness to their bodies and their motivations when acting. Integrating patients' care activities into their normal lives is described as the key to good patient care. To successfully integrate disease management into daily life, patients and healthcare professionals must cooperate to identify balance when care conflicts arise. Supportive medical care, involving medical treatments, nursing care, and the professional competencies of healthcare workers, serves as the foundation for diabetes care. Care can be shaped by families, society, healthcare insurance, and public health policies, which can determine not only how healthcare is delivered but also how individuals act and interact with collective society.

---

5   This research focuses on patients' needs rather than exploring the patients' interests. According to Tronto (2010), to say "I have a need" is less indisputable from the care perspective and invokes a different response than the notion of "I have an interest" (p. 164).

Participation

> A doctor tries to help his patient. When he has the feeling that his patients participate in care activities, then he will have an interest in working with them. I have received this message from my doctor, who said to me, "Phillip, let us do this!" (I–PP–11, 269–272)

The first need identified for diabetes care is participation because care starts when the patient is willing to act. Both patients and healthcare professionals agreed that patients, as key actors within a care team, must participate in care activities (I–FA–01, 84–88; I–FA–02, 679–682; I–PP–05, 274–276; I–PP–09, 658–660; I–PP–11, 269–272). They stated that diabetes management involves "much self-work" (I–PP–09, 658–660). To manage diabetes, "there is no one who can help you unless you do it by yourself" (I–PP–05, 274–276), and "the only thing patients have to do is learn to know their bodies" (I–PP–03, 307–311).

A care process cannot be started without the participation of patients. From the view of healthcare professionals, the disease can only be diagnosed when a patient visits their physicians and tells them about their health problems (I–FA–2, 679–682). Even if the patients visit their physicians once if they do not follow their treatment plan or do not visit their physicians for follow-up, the physicians will lose their patients (I–FA–02, 199–203). Many healthcare professionals can better help patients who are ready to take an active role in maintaining their health, such as obeying the principles of diabetes management and changing their lifestyles (I–DB–02, 661–670; I–NN–03, 299–310).

Disease management represents a day-to-day and moment-to-moment issue. Patients have autonomy over their bodies and make decisions regarding whether or not to engage in care activities. Corresponding to this finding, the literature proposed that care can only be improved when patients are attending to engagement in all efforts to improve the effectiveness of care. Patients who are active participants in care plans can assist in the development of a more realistic and easier approach to diabetes management (Hibbard & Greene, 2013; Van den Hooff & Goossensen, 2014).

According to the research data, being active involves the additional meaning of patients taking responsibility for their health (I–FA–01, 84–88; I–PP–03, 438–440; I–PP–11, 205–206). Patients are also aware that they cannot expect healthcare professionals to do everything for them. Patients have a responsibility to do good things for their bodies and view the consequences of neglect as a form of self-guilt (I–PP–03, 432–433; I–PP–11, 205–206). When patients can commit themselves to a care plan and are actively involved in it, the positive consequence of good care is expected. As the literature described, allowing patients to assume some responsibility for the management of their diabetes is noted by many healthcare teams as an efficient way to help patients set goals for self-management (Lemay et al., 2010; Hasseler et al., 2010).

To encourage patients to participate in care, the patient's motivation must be recognized. Diabetes management strategies, such as adjusting a patient's lifestyle, require the patient's willingness. As one patient said, "I have good diabetes care because I want it and because it is working" (I–PP–05, 321). Based on the research data, patients' motivations are often built on the patients' desires to live longer and maintain well-being in life (I–PP–02, 156–163; I–PP–03, 316–317; I–PP–04, 136–137). When patients experience the advantages of participating in their care activities or when they receive more attention from their healthcare professionals, they gain increasing confidence and motivation for performing self-care (BG–DA2–05, p. 3; I–PP–08, 255–257; I–PP–11, 207).

Sometimes, negative feelings, such as the fear of long-term complications (BG–DS2–04, p. 5; BG–DS2–07, p. 2; BE–B1–02, p. 1; I–PP–01, 320–321; I–PP–02, 167–176; I–PP–05, 76–79; I–PP–07, 331–335) and the fear of uncertainty (I–PP–07, 331–335), can be viewed as a type of motivational push to convince the patients to do things for their bodies. The desire to avoid any further development of the disease trajectory into a worse stage can help motivate patients to manage their diabetes.[6] The fear of complications and the uncertainty of disease development affects not only the patients themselves but also their families because patients with serious complications cannot be cared for at home (I–PP–02, 167–176). This fear can represent a source of motivation for both the patients and their families to become involved in caring activities.

Therefore, warning patients about potential long-term complications can be viewed by healthcare professionals as a useful strategy in diabetes care practice (I–NN–06, 75–83; I–DB–02, 240–243, 469–474; I–DB–02, 353–355; BG–DB1–01, p. 4). Motivating patients through the use of warnings, however, is not a comfortable method for many healthcare professionals. This approach can also cause patients to leave their healthcare professionals and the outcome of these patients is unknown. One diabetes consultant told me about her experience:

> So, for the patient who was sitting there, I still had a bit of a bad feeling after I told her about what will happen in 20 years because she began to cry. I felt a little bit sorry for that. I looked at the computer later and found that she visited the nutrition consultant quite often and always asked for a follow-up appointment. This story happened at the beginning of this year; since then, I didn't see her anymore. (I–DB–02, 478–483)

---

6 For example, among patients who only require oral pills to control their diabetes, the disease has less impact than for patients who require regular insulin injections. Maintaining current conditions can motivate patients to engage themselves in doing good things for their health (BE–B1–02, p. 1).

Identifying and avoiding unpleasant symptoms associated with the disease and fearing long-term complications could sometimes motivate the patients to act (Callaghan & Williams, 1994; I–PP–02, 167–176). However, too much focus on the negative aspects of the disease can also lead to diabetes management failures. Rather than merely creating fear, focusing on the facts and delivering essential information about the disease is preferable in diabetes care, based on the research data and the reports in the literature (I–NN–06, 80–83; Mol, 2008).

In care practice, the boundaries between administering warnings and providing information are often blurred, and care responsibility can be difficult to place on a single party within a close care relationship. As one nurse said:

> I avoided creating fear, but I have to tell the patients about the complications caused by diabetes. I think it is important to give patients information by telling them what will be happened if they don't do it so that they don't later say that "I know nothing about it" when something happens. (I–NN–06, 80–83).

In this case, the nurse highlighted the importance of giving her patients information so that her patients can be to make decisions. The questions that were raised from examining this case were as follows: Which types of information do patients need? How is information delivered? How do patients experience informed decision-making during disease management? How do well-informed patients act in care practice? Who is responsible for an informed care decision?

Patients, as laypeople, usually have no idea what the disease means, which consequences may follow, how treatment goals are formulated, and which principles have to be followed. One nurse indicated that it is impossible in diabetes care to merely tell patients with the words "now, do it" without any explanation (I–NN–03, 539–548). From the view of healthcare professionals, ensuring that patients are well-informed is important in the context of diabetes care, especially for nursing care (I–NN–01, 15–21; I–NN–02, 260–275; I–NN–04, 43–47; I–NN–03, 709–716; I–NN–05, 825–832). According to the research data, offering patients information can decrease the patients' uncertainty and improve their motivation and confidence in caring, especially for patients who are newly diagnosed with diabetes (BE–B1–01, p. 2; I–NN–03, 539–548; I–PP–03, 8–17; I–PP–08, 273–274; I–PP–11, 369–373).

In care practice, the information that patients require involves issues associated with understanding the disease, disease treatment, and the caring process (BG–DS2–02, p. 5; I–NN–01, 15–16; I–NN–02, 260–275; I–NN–03, 20–23). For healthcare professionals, information delivery aims to answer the questions raised by their patients (I–NN–03, 711–712), enlighten the patients on the path that patients should follow (I–NN–03, 710–711), and support the patients in achieving the capacity for self-care (I–NN–01, 15–21; I–NN–02, 260–265; I–NN–03, 11–12, 420–431). Unfortunately, not all patients receive sufficient information in diabetes care practice (BG–DS2–04, p. 4; I–PP–03, 33–84). One patient complained, "I got the needles, but I didn't know when I had to change the needles. I asked my family doctor, but he just answered 'Oh, you will know it.'" (BG–DS2–04, p. 4). Moreover, the information contents and the information delivery mechanisms supplied by healthcare workers are often criticized as being inappropriate and not tailored for the individual (I–NN–06, 489–495).

Without proper information, patients experienced uncertainty and helplessness in disease control (BG–DS2–04, p. 49). In the worst-case scenario, uninformed patients may fall into a life-threatening situation (I–PP–03, 33–84). As a patient described:

> My family doctor gave me an injection syringe when I had to use insulin therapy. He gave me no other information. Only the word 'inject'! At home, I sat next to my table and did not know what I had to do. I felt helpless as a child. (BG–DS2–04, p. 4)

Nurses also reported their need to obtain clear information, especially basic knowledge related to diabetes care, such as the type of diabetes, complications, related treatments, guidelines for diabetes care, and resources that can be consulted (I–NN–04, 589–596; I–NN–06, 461–466). According to the CCM, treatment decisions need to be based on explicit guidelines, but these guidelines should be discussed with patients to allow patients to understand the principles underlying their care (E. H. Wagner, 1998). The problem that emerges in care practice is how the guidelines for diabetes care are constructed and utilized in care practice. The information needed can differ from one patient to another. When information is delivered, patients' interests and their disease trajectories must be examined. If healthcare professionals do not understand the conditions of their patients, including their needs and interests, the information they offer could be inefficient (I–PP–05, 349–351).

The concept of attentiveness is necessary to offer patients a level of individual care that integrates their thoughts, feelings, and actions into their daily lives. In this research, both patients and healthcare professionals agreed on the importance of watching and responding to the changes in the patients' bodies during diabetes management (I–DB–02, 688–692; I–FA–02, 679–682; I–PP–01, 75–77; I–PP–08, 71–74). In care practice, healthcare professionals often told their patients to learn how to notice and respond to symptoms of hypotension (BG–DB1–01) or to visit their doctors when they have health problems (I–FA–02, 679–682).

From the view of healthcare professionals, a patient who is attentive, articulate, and able to express his complaints to his healthcare professionals is likely to obtain better therapy and treatment (I–DB–02, 688–692). For patients, monitoring the changes in their bodies helps patients to accept their sick bodies (I–PP–08, 71–74) and to discover various factors that might improve their well-being but might not be noticed by their healthcare provider (I-PP-01, 75-77; I-PP-03, 271-273; I-PP-07, 106-108, 165-166). By being aware of the changes inside their bodies, the patients were ready to act (I-PP-07, 165-166).

Attentiveness and bodily control are not the same things in care practice. Although patients are aware of their duties to care for their bodies, maintaining an acceptable blood sugar value and following principles can be exhausting for patients. Even though patients are told they should be able to enjoy their lives, they encounter a great deal of uncertainty and limitations due to their disease. In the next section, how patients applied their resources to the daily practice of diabetes management and those places where patients feel they can improve in their approach to diabetes management are further explored.

Integration

> The wish for the patients who visit us is to get good therapies so that they can live well in their daily life, go to work, play sports, to carry out the whole concept of therapy without the feeling of being limited too much. (I-DB-01, 236-240)

A patient who can normalize his care process and integrate it into his everyday life has a better chance of living well with his disease. Once disease management becomes just another part of one's life, patients often feel free from the need to adhere to strict principles. Patients must identify a counterbalance in which both disease management and their personal values and life experiences are acknowledged. Typically, successful integration requires patients to cooperate with their healthcare teams until an appropriate compromise can be identified. Nurses represent the healthcare professional group that spends the most time with patients and, therefore, have the best chance of understanding their patients. Nursing professional roles are expected to be multifaceted within the care team. In this section, the concept of integration in diabetes care practice is explored, and how the care team works together and the roles played by nurses in German care practice are discussed.

Maintaining desirable outcomes in diabetes management remains challenging for patients, particularly when disease management requires sustained willingness over a long-term period. Based on the research data, patients must often balance their desires with the limitations that are necessary for effective disease management (I-PP-06, 389-390; I-PP-05, 239-242; BG-DA2-05, p. 3). In care practice, some patients reject their desires and strictly adhere to care principles (I-PP-11, 110-116). However, most patients attempt to identify alternatives that allow their desires to be partially fulfilled (BG-DA2-05, p. 3; I-PP-01, 130-138; I-PP-05, 239-242). Patients may begin to focus on what their bodies can tolerate rather than attempting to achieve perfect blood sugar levels (I–PP–03, 293–303; I–PP–09, 669–670).

Caring for a sick body during day-to-day life is never easy. Patients must be able to continue enjoying life to remain willing to invest in their care over a long-term period (I–DB–01, 236–240). According to Mol et al. (2010), "care offers no control. It involves living with the erratic" (p. 10). In care practice, patients are allowed to break the rules to continue experiencing pleasure in their stressful lives (I–PP–09, 669–678). Sometimes, patients learn from their mistakes (I–PP–09, 228–234). Many patients viewed finding a balance as a learning process, in which they learned from their failures, adjusted to mistakes, and modified their lifestyles in daily practice (I–PP–08, 265–282; I–PP–09, 228–236; I–PP–11, 130–137).

In the consulting room, the patients described their original lifestyles as prohibitive factors for diabetes management (BG–DS2–07, p. 7). Offering alternatives may help patients to modify their lifestyles within the framework of diabetes management. In care practice, healthcare professionals treat the process of modifying lifestyle as habits that must be relearned and re-established. As one nutrition consultant told patients: "People are habitual animals, and their tastes can also be changed" (BG–DS2–07, p. 7).

However, changing one's lifestyle can be difficult, especially for older patients who have maintained their lifestyles for as long as 80 years. Patients may sometimes continue living their inappropriate lifestyles when they do not feel these lifestyles to be life-threatening. One patient expressed, "I am passionate about these cook-ready soups. I still like to eat them, although I know that's not so good. But I don't make myself crazy" (I–PP–08, 85–88). Healthcare professionals must recognize that motivating the patient to make acceptable changes can sometimes make more sense than trying to convince the patients to make the best changes. A nurse described her experience as follows:

> I think it works only by way of finding a common point with the patients with whom you can work. It is also necessary that both sides are ready to get rid of their own opinions. Sometimes, you may see that "okay, it is not the best way but still possible for the patient". (I–NN–03, 696–699)

Respecting patients' life experiences and making compromises can help healthcare professionals identify successful methods for caring for patients with chronic and stressful diseases. Unfortunately, the literature tends to focus on the patients' narratives of the illness experience, and less emphasis has been placed on nursing practice (Fox & Chesla, 2008). The duality of self-management[7] may also occur, in which healthcare professionals cannot offer care services without consideration of their patients' daily lives (Kendall et al., 2011).

Diabetes care requires teamwork and involves various types of hands working together. In the literature, effective collaboration has been shown to strengthen and support self-care in diabetes, ensuring that effective medical, preventive, and health maintenance interventions are implemented (Heisler et al., 2003; Lenzen et al., 2016; Miers, 2003a). In this research, almost all of the healthcare professionals agreed that good diabetes care requires regular and intensive teamwork that includes the participation of patients, their families, and other related healthcare professionals, such as family physicians, diabetes specialists, foot care specialists, nutrition consultants, psychologists, and pharmacists (I–DA–01, 94–96, 170–175; I–DB–02, 638–652, 218–222). A multi-professional team working together provides both patients and healthcare professionals with access to expertise and support when they encounter difficulties in caring (I–DB–01, 118–122; I–NN–01, 518–521; I–NN–02, 138–143).

A good network involves various healthcare professional groups and patients (I–DB–01, 15–17). Often, family doctors are viewed as the diabetes care team leaders who organize disease management (I–PP–04, 87–92; I–PP–11, 378–387). A patient explained to me how his care team works:

> The family doctor decides my disease treatment. He asks the diabetes specialist how my insulin dosage should be set. The home-care nurses send the doctor's prescription to the pharmacy and order the insulin for me. The post carrier brings the insulin to me, and I put it in the refrigerator. (I–PP–04, 87–92)

A good network forms when patients understand what they should do and follow the care principles, and healthcare professionals execute their duties to assess the patient's abilities for self-care. If healthcare professionals recognize that their patients are not able to care for themselves, they have a responsibility to take care activities from the patients' hands into their own hands (I–NN–01, 121–127).

Nurses are viewed as the professional group that spends the most time with patients and has the best understanding of patients relative to other healthcare professionals, especially in the context of the home-care setting. Home-care nurses visit patients regularly and frequently. Nurses used the following terms to describe their roles in caring for patients with diabetes: "care-doer", "guidance", "companion", "supporter", "mediator", "advocator", and "care manager". Nurses view

---

7   The duality of self-management means that patients may appear to accept advice from healthcare professionals but continue to manage their health and their lives as they deem fit (Kendall et al., 2011).

themselves as care-doers who implement medical treatment in line with the physician's orders, such as blood sugar measuring and insulin injection (I-NN-03, 6-8; I-NN-05, 7-14; I-NN-06, 133-138). Ensuring the implementation of the correct care plan is the responsibility of a care-doer (I-NN-05, 9-12).

Many nurses mentioned that they act to guide patients, meaning that they accompany their patients and offer them support. The tasks that nurses perform when providing guidance include informing patients about their disease and treatment, accompanying patients during the process of disease management, and encouraging their confidence in self-care until they can perform it alone (I-NN-01, 419-426; I-NN-05, 28-32; I-DB-02, 6-8). If the patients feel uncertain about their abilities to perform self-care, particularly when the issue pertains to medical treatment, nurses will accompany them and offer them support. When nurses recognize that their patients are unable to care for themselves, they will take over the medical treatment completely (I-NN-01, 441-447).

When acting to provide guidance, nurses regulate medical treatments and offer their care services depending on each patient's level of confidence and skills. In the literature, the provision of guidance is often mentioned in healthcare to describe someone who ensures skill, offers safe spaces for learning or action, follows plans, controls surveillance, and prevents mishaps. Due to the vulnerability of patients, whose physical conditions are often restricted and whose care competencies are limited, healthcare professionals, such as nurses, are necessary to coach patients and improve their security during disease control (DDG, 2017).

Working as a mediator was often identified by nurses as a component of their professional roles in this research. For many nurses, working as a mediator means more than simply delivering messages or information from the patients to the physicians; mediation involves communicating with the care team and advocating for patients, especially when they view the physicians as being inactive (I-NN-01, 452-461; I-NN-03, 6-8; 589-598; I-NN-06,133-138). Often, the nurses inform their patients' family doctors when the patients' health conditions become poor or when patients are experiencing difficulties communicating with their doctors. When nurses recognize that the family doctors of their patients fail to respond to patients' requests for improvement, nurses will pressure the physicians to act. Nurses act as advocates for their patient's health. A nurse spoke about her experience as follows:

> I give a little pressure on the family doctor when I have the feeling that nothing is happening. I believe that our presence can give the physicians enough pressure. When they notice that someone is calling every week, then they will realize that they have to respond to it now. (I-NN-03, 595-598)

Working as a mediator often means that nurses serve as care managers. When patients receive care services from various healthcare professionals, nurses serve as managers who coordinate teamwork (I–NN–03, 76–83; I–NN–06,133–138). For example, when patients visit diabetes specialists or consultants, nurses often help their patients arrange appointments (I–NN–06,133–138). This care manager role is often visible. By contrast, home-care nurses work in the area of care transition.[8]

In the literature, nurses' roles as advocates are highlighted. Patient advocacy consists of empathizing with and protecting the patients, which represents the values and beliefs used by nurses during moral reasoning and influences the nurse-patient relationship (Barlow et al., 2018; Butts & Rich, 2008; Davoodvand et al., 2016). In German healthcare practice, the role of an advocator is rarely mentioned by nurses because of limited competencies and time. In practice, nurses view diabetes consultants as the experts who are best able to act as patient advocates.[9] Unfortunately, only a small number of diabetes consultants are active in outpatient care practice, and diabetes consultants and home-care nurses rarely work together.

This research finding indicates that a huge gap exists between the theory and the care practice. The nurses interviewed here realized their multiple roles in diabetes care, and although they attempted to offer care tailored to their nursing identification, institutional and social restrictions often prohibited these activities. This issue will be further explored in Other Care Logics in Practice.

Medical Care

A family doctor should give his patient the right insulin and the right injection scheme so that his patient can achieve a blood sugar value in an acceptable range that the family doctor also accepts. (I–NN–05, 844–850)

Medical care is an inseparable component of diabetes care. Patients with diabetes need medical treatment to maintain their health at a stable level. Patients also need a professional healthcare team, including nursing care to accompany them through

---

8   A care transition [Pflegeüberleitung in German] is structured to ensure post-hospital care and is often performed by nurses. The tasks of care transition include patient consultation and the management of post-hospital care. The goal of care transition is to ensure that each patient who requires post-stationary care or has medical requirements receives individualised discharge management involving continuous, on-demand care. In the home-care centre where this research was performed, some home-care nurses work simultaneously on care transition. The care transition department is an independent department within the organisational structure of the hospital, located directly near the home-care centre.

9   In German diabetes care practice, diabetes consultants are well-educated professionals who care for diabetes patients. However, the official occupation of a diabetes consultant remains uncertified in most German federal states (except for in the federal state of Rheinland-Pfalz). Their job title is typically defined by hospitals as nurses, and they are paid as nurses. This research found that diabetes consultants hope that the occupation of diabetes consultant will eventually become certified, well paid, and independent (I–DB–02, 495–510).

the rigorous challenge of disease management. Based on this research, proper medical treatment, an advanced technique for insulin therapy, and a cooperative healthcare team can significantly impact the outcome of diabetes care. Professional competencies serve as the foundation for trusting relationships with the care team.

Living with diabetes requires patients to maintain their blood glucose levels within an acceptable range to prevent complications and promote well-being. Therefore, glucose control is often viewed as a fundamental component of diabetes management by both patients and healthcare professionals (I–PP–07, 326–327; I–PP–11, 196; BE–B1–01, p. 5; I–NN–03, 655–663; I–NN–05, 844–850). Physicians are responsible for prescribing their patients a suitable insulin treatment to allow the patients to maintain their blood sugar values within an acceptable range (I–PP–04, 241–243; I–PP–06, 423–426; I–NN–02, 477–484; I–DB–01, 149–150). Appropriate medical treatment is both prescribed correctly and can be correctly executed by patients (I–DB–01, 149–150). To ensure that patients can execute their medical treatments, a medical plan must be devised with input from both the physician and the patient (I–PP–08, 129–132).

Attainable medical care is essential in care practice. According to patients, attainable medical care means that they can schedule an appointment in time (I–PP–09, 618–621), the family physicians' practices are nearby (I–PP–01, 148–149), the physicians make home visits when the patients are unable to reach the clinic (I–PP–04, 96–97; I–PP–06, 191–195; I–PP–09, 414–419), and good communication occurs with the physician (I–PP–09, 414–419). In addition, good diabetes care also includes providing the patients with sufficient medical materials (e.g. blood sugar test strips and insulin pens) to ensure that the correct level of care is sustainable for patients and does not further hinder their quality of life (BE–B1–01, p. 5; I–DB–01, 639–653; I–NN–01, 554–561; I–PP–07, 103–106; I–PP–09, 505–507).

However, organizing attainable medical care is not an easy task in the outpatient sector. In the German healthcare system, healthcare insurance plays a key role, deeply influencing how healthcare is delivered. Usually, this active interference by health insurance limits what services can be offered (I–PP–02, 419–423, 456–466, 501–510; I–PP–07, 103–106). Patients are often required to wait for days to receive a prescription after they visit the doctor (BE–B1–01, p. 5). Patients complained about reductions in healthcare services and insufficient medical materials, such as testing strips (I–PP–02, 359–361, 371–376, 419–426, 501–510; I–PP–07, 103–106) or injection pumps (I–DB–01, 240–245). The reduced budget for diabetes treatment, as determined by healthcare insurance, often restricts the care activities of patients (I–PP–07, 103–106). Patients and healthcare professionals working within a limited healthcare system describe a feeling of powerlessness during caring work (I–NN–01, 554–561; I–DB–01, 639–653). As a nurse illustrated: "The blood glucose test strips are often not paid for by healthcare insurance. The healthcare insurances have their rules and you cannot change anything. That's so! But, of course, this is bad" (I–NN–01, 554–561).

The issue of technology emerged in the discourse of diabetes management. In diabetes care practice, modern technological medical equipment, such as the insulin pen, helps patients to control their disease (I–PP–09, 685–689; I–NN–04, 290–303; BE–B1–03, p. 2). Nevertheless, professionals sometimes have difficulty keeping up with changes in technology. In the home-care practice, the nurses complained that they are not familiar with the various machines available for diabetes control, which can lead to feelings of uncertainty when the nurses are offering care (I–NN–04, 290–298).

In the literature, technology such as glucose monitors or insulin pumps serves as an integral component of diabetic therapy, providing patients with the necessary support for living well with their disease (DDG, 2017; Mol, 2009). Mol and Law (2004) stated that machines only become instruments if the body can manipulate them and incorporate them into its actions, and technology does not succeed or fail in and of itself. Rather, how technology integrates into care depends on people being willing to adapt their tools to specific situations and to adapt the situations to make the best use of the tools (Mol et al., 2010, pp. 14–15).

This research indicated that choosing a suitable machine was helpful for patients in addressing some care problems. Learning how to manipulate the machine and incorporate it into caring is a necessary task for both patients and healthcare professionals. In care practice, most patients are taught how to manipulate the machines they received in hospitals or practice. However, patients must also be able to manipulate these machines independently at home. If patients are unable to operate their machines alone, a home visit from a nurse may be established, but not all home-care nurses are able to manipulate the patients' machines. Technology, then, is not supportive of disease management in these situations. A professional who does not understand a patient's machine may have their care competence questioned, which can damage the trust relationship (Fox & Chesla, 2008).

In this research, many patients complained about the absence of professional knowledge regarding diabetes among their family doctors (I–PP–03, 72–78; I–PP–05, 127–133; I–PP–08, 102–106). As the leaders of diabetes care, if family physicians lack clinical competencies, their patients' health can be endangered. A patient claimed:

> I have a doctor who has no idea about diabetes. He had prescribed two kinds of insulin for me when I came back from the hospital. The consequence of this prescription is that I had to eat pure jam from the jar every night only because the man understands nothing about diabetes. (I–PP–08, 102–106)

In addition to patients, nurses also noted incompetence among family physicians (I-NN-01, 110-111; I-NN-03, 112-116). When a family physician's diabetes care competence is limited, the transfer of patients to a diabetes specialist or to diabetes consultants who have received a diabetes specialist education is essential to good diabetes care (I-DB-01, 671-673; I-DB-02, 84-87; I-NN-03, 52-55, 112-116; I-PP-02, 250-253; I-PP-03, 72-78; I-PP-08, 110-113). In care practice, some home-care nurses might attempt to serve in the role of a disease manager by transferring their patients to a diabetes specialist; however, nurses are often prevented from taking these types of actions by physicians who are unwilling to cooperate with other healthcare professionals (I-NN-03, 52-55; I-PP-08, 110-113).

Diabetes care should be offered by diabetes specialists with specialist training, but the capacity for appointments is often very limited (I-DB-01, 642-646). Patients who have health problems often must wait long times to get an appointment with a diabetes specialist or a diabetes consultant. In an emergency, their problems may be treated by healthcare professionals who are simultaneously caring for other patients. Whether patients can get appropriate care before they reach the point of being in critical condition remains uncertain, and even then, whether they can receive good care from healthcare professionals caring for multiple patients is also not clear.

In the current research, nurses reported that they sometimes lack clinical competencies, especially in the context of offering diabetes consultations (I-NN-03, 52-55). In home-care practice, nurses generally agreed that offering diabetes consultations for patients is essential, but they do not view this task as part of their work when caring for diabetes patients. As Thomas Rosemann et al. (2006) stated that examinations, explanations, and counseling could only be performed by physicians because practicing nurses lack adequate medical knowledge in this area. Patients may expect nurses to engage with them in discussions about non-medical goals (Lenzen et al., 2016).

The lack of competency among nursing professionals in offering diabetes consultations is due to the foundational training involved in becoming a nurse (McKee et al., 2006; Rosemann et al., 2006). In Germany, a nurse becomes qualified after receiving very basic training in specialized high schools, which provide nursing students with very basic care skills and a negligible scope for action independent of the medical profession. The knowledge nurses have is commonly acquired through work experience instead of from schooling (Rosemann et al., 2006). This research supports these assumptions, and the nurses mentioned that their diabetes-related training often occurred alongside other courses (I-NN-03, 607-620; I-NN-04, 350-353; I-NN-05, 467-513). The nurses elaborated that their medical knowledge regarding diabetes was minimal and that most of their technical skills were gained through practical experience (I-NN-03, 607-620; I-NN-04, 350-353; I-NN-05, 467-513).

Despite clinical competencies, such as medical knowledge and care skills, personal competence[10] influences patients' trust in healthcare professionals and their satisfaction with care services (I–PP–01, 338–339; I–PP–02, 241–246; I–PP–06, 218–219; I–PP–07, 402–404; I–PP–08, 313–315; I–PP–09, 334–345). The word professional is often associated with one who maintains a sufficient distance, restrains emotions, and offers objectivity. Therefore, personal competence can strengthen the bonds that form between patients and healthcare professionals, in addition to those among the care team (Robinson, 2016; Rørtveit et al., 2015;). As one patient said, "Even as a doctor, he has to know how to go with the people. Otherwise, he is out of place" (I–PP–06, 218–219).

When patients experience the personal competencies of their healthcare professionals, they are more willing to be open and discuss issues that might be embarrassing or shameful. They felt more comfortable asking questions, questioning advice, and disagreeing with their healthcare team. Patients are, therefore, enabled to continuously represent their true experiences within the care relationship (Fox & Chesla, 2008). As one patient described, "The diabetes consultants have compassion. They understand my pain. They do not just say, 'Yes, it is so.'" (GB–DB1–01, p. 4).

Every patient belongs to a broader social entity, and each care activity takes place within the scope of other interactions. Tronto (2010, p. 164) described that how one arrives at a need is a matter of social concern, and the surrounding influences associated with diabetes care are discussed in the following section.

Surrounding Support

My family gives me a lot of support. When I go for a walk, my daughter accompanies me. She also knows how to deal with hypoglycemia when it is happening. Another example is that my family eats the same meat as me. I used to cook two different kinds of food. But one time, my daughter tasted my food and said, "It tastes good. We eat it too. You do not have to cook two different kinds of food." (GB–DB1–01, p. 7)

All people, including outpatients with diabetes, live within a society that includes their family, friends, and colleagues. How society is structured, how healthcare is organized, delivered, and financed, how the residents within the society are educated, the attitudes with which they respond to disease, and how they act and interact within the collective must be considered components of the settings in which the daily activities of diabetes management occur. When patients and healthcare

---

10   Personal competence refers to whether a person is personable and reflects their interpersonal skills, such as listening, communication, friendliness, empathy, having a personal touch, and compassion (Laugharne et al., 2011).

professionals spoke about care needs in diabetes care, they regularly mentioned the need for medical and financial support. The impacts of healthcare insurance and public policies on German healthcare are worthy of exploration.

The patients' families offer various levels of support for patients during their diabetes management. The research data shows that family members often help patients detect symptoms of complications (GB–DB1–01, p. 7; I–NN–02, 302–305; I–PP–07, 265–269), follow the principles of their disease (I–NN–03, 227–230; I–NN–05, 253–267; I–DB–02, 175–178; GB–DB1–01, p. 7; I–PP–02, 332–341), and change their patterns of nutrition (I–NN–01, 384–392; I–NN–03, 227–230; I–DB–02, 161–165; I–PP–05, 227–230, 253–267). In many cases, family members serve as advocates, consult with patients when they have health problems, and accompany them on visits with physicians (I–PP–07, 265–269).

Family members, particularly those who live with patients, are expected to acquire diabetes-related knowledge and care skills and are expected to participate in diabetes training courses (I–DB–01, 306–318; I–DB–02, 161–165; I–NN–01, 384–392; I–NN–02, 302–305; I–NN–03, 227–230; I–PP–02, 332–341; I–PP–03, 419–423). The study by Martina Hasseler et al. (2010) reported comparable findings, demonstrating that the inclusion of the patient's families in diabetes training, education courses, and counseling were helpful for the patients' diabetes management, suggesting that families represent a very important social resource that should be considered. Hasseler et al. (2010) also highlighted that family support is often directed at emotional and physical/practical needs, especially for coping with disease, uncertainties in detecting symptoms, and changes in diet (Hasseler et al., 2010).

The patients' families can also represent a source of ethical dilemmas. Jenny Rees et al. (2009) suggested that ethical conflict often arose when gaps existed between the relatives' needs and the patient's needs. This finding was reflected in the current research, which revealed that healthcare professionals, patients, and patient's families have different understandings of the disease and the value of life, resulting in conflicts (I–NN–03, 367–371). When working with families, healthcare professionals have to avoid forming negative judgments and attempt to mirror the family's strengths or competencies (Robinson, 2016). Healthcare professionals should act as inventive mediators, able to adjust their practice to accommodate the family, try to compensate for those areas where the families lack competence, and balance the diversity of views across all involved parties (Mol, 2010).

According to Mol et al. (2010), the problems associated with care are not localized to a single individual but occur within life and as part of the collective (p. 17). The findings of the current research supported this assumption, suggesting that friendly surroundings in which the patients' activities towards health promotion are supported can help them to better deal with their disease (GB–DB1–01, p. 2). Sometimes, society can also offer patients with diabetes safety assurances, especially when patients suffer from hypoglycemia. The public can help patients detect the symptoms of hypoglycemia and address the symptoms quickly. Therefore, public awareness of diabetes and its symptoms is essential (I-DB-02, 386-394, 614-619). Diabetes consultants often remind patients in the consultation room that "as a diabetes patient, you should let your friends and colleagues know your diabetes disease and inform them about how to deal with hypoglycemia" (GB-DB1-01, p. 2).

According to the literature, self-help groups can be very effective for diabetes management,[11] but these have received little attention in Germany (Hasseler et al., 2010). In this research, healthcare professionals generally viewed participation in a self-help group as a positive contributor to diabetes management because patients might be motivated to participate in care activities after sharing their experiences, learning about successful, caring strategies, and sharing their feelings and difficulties with controlling diabetes with other people with diabetes (I-NN-06, 278-281).

The opposite perspective regarding participation in self-help groups was noted by the patients in this research (BE-B1-01, p. 4; I-PP-05, 355-358; I-PP-08, 355-358). These patients reasoned that the lack of individual focus in self-help groups prevented their participation (BE-B1-01, p. 4; I-PP-08, 355-358). The diversity of patients can also limit communication within a group because each person is focused on tailoring their responses to their specific disease trajectory (BE-B1-01, p. 4). In addition, the care knowledge, abilities, and motivations can differ across participants within any self-help group (I-PP-05, 355-358). Consequently, patients will stop attending self-help groups if they feel uncomfortable or not understood (BE-B1-01, p. 4).

How healthcare services are offered is often guided by health insurance policies. Unfortunately, diabetes care is often deemed unimportant within the German healthcare system. Both healthcare professionals and patients realize that the quality of diabetes care may be reduced due to the lack of financial support, time, and manpower in current caring practice. Consequentially, financial restrictions may either narrow the scope of diabetes care or reduce the quality of care. The willingness of healthcare professionals to engage in diabetes care may be withdrawn. A desire for improvements in the approach of the German healthcare system to diabetes was reported (I-DB-02, 401-404; I-NN-06, 530-536; I-PP-02, 501-510). Similar to this finding, Rosamund Snow's study proposed that patients are unsatisfied with their care when their budgetary demands. In effect, patients' care activities may be greatly discouraged or even forbidden by hospital policy (Snow et al., 2013).

The issues surrounding diabetes prevention were taken for granted by the people who were interviewed in this research. Many healthcare professionals suggested

---

11   The study by Hasseler et al. (2010) suggested that a self-help group can offer spiritual and instrumental support for patients with diabetes, enabling them to talk about their diseases and obtain reassurance (Hasseler et al., 2010).

that diabetes prevention should be included as part of the diabetes care system because prevention can decrease the prevalence of diabetes and associated complications (I-NN-03, 638-644; I-NN-06, 521-525; I-DB-02, 393-394, 401-408; I-FA-01, 468-470). Some healthcare professionals suggested that interventions targeted at prevention, such as teaching children about healthy nutrition and exercise at school, should be included in the diabetes care budget covered by healthcare insurance (I-NN-03, 638-644; I-NN-06, 521-525; I-DB-02, 393-394, 401-408; I-FA-01, 468-470). A German study by Hasseler et al. (2010) showed comparable findings and identified that offering preventive interventions and measurements regularly may support patients in coping with the disease; however, the same study also indicated that the care services offered by healthcare insurance were not clear for patients, even though they were aware that training courses were considered diabetes-relevant healthcare services.

A caring process can be long and stressful, and understanding the care goals and needs for diabetes care based on the views of both patients and healthcare professionals may be insufficient to achieve care improvements. The patients' motivations in caring, their physical limitations and psychological loads, and the limitations exerted by medical organizations and society contribute to the complexity and difficulty of diabetes care. In the next section, the scope of the logic of care theory will be used to examine diabetes care and care relationships in the context of German diabetes care

Summary

Patients who live with diabetes start by attempting to know the disease, followed by integrating their understanding of disease management into their daily lives. For patients, a caring process starts with "to know", which involves being attentive to their sick bodies and having the ability to respond to their illness by finding possible methods of practical implementation. Helping patients approach their bodies, offering sufficient information and attainable resources, and motivating patients to be more aware of their care duties and responsibilities represent the first steps that healthcare professionals should take when caring for patients with diabetes. Both patients and healthcare professionals should be involved in caring and sharing care responsibilities.

To know, however, is different than "to do". Many times, the patients indicated that they were motivated to perform diabetes management, but they recognized the difficulties of implementing disease management practices into their daily lives. Frequently, they experienced ambiguities. Caring situations are often full of contradictions. When patients are self-aware of their duties in caring for their bodies, day-to-day maintenance within the frame of care principles can be exhausting. Although the patients are told to enjoy their lives, their lives are full of uncertainty and limitations. Patients recognize their dependence on medicine and the need for a healthcare team, but they still desire freedom and independence.

Diabetes management is an endless and troublesome lifelong challenge. Patients who live with a sick body have difficulty integrating into a healthy society and often have to exclude themselves from society to maintain their health. Accompanying the patients during diabetes management is essential. Effective communication among the collective groups interested in a patient's health, aiming for a consistent target, may lead to success. Healthcare insurance and public policies should be improved in the context of German diabetes care. For instance, more financial support for caring time, staff, materials, and equipment is necessary. A friendly environment that encourages caring activities is recommended.

Motivating patients to do in diabetes care practice represents a vital issue. In practice, patients, healthcare professionals, healthcare insurance, and society have different values regarding healthcare. These divergent values can lead to care failures in diabetes management. The German healthcare system is strongly influenced by the values of healthcare insurance, which can result in doing more difficult to accomplish than knowing about diabetes care. The implementation of good care, based on the logic of care in the context of German diabetes care, is examined in the next section.

The Empirical Study of the Logic of Care

If, as Mol (2008) claimed, "care has its own logic", then what types of care logic exist in the real world, and do they fit our ideas of what it means to offer good care? If the logic of care is the best logic to apply when caring for patients with diabetes, then how are the care concepts formulated by the logic of care understood by care actors, and how are they expressed in care practice? In which care situations may prevent the implementation of the logic of care in care practice?

The Application of the Logic of Care by Mol

> Care is not a matter of size about how much we do, but a matter of how long we pay attention. Care is not a product that changes hands but a matter of various hands working together over time toward a result. Care is not a transaction in which something is exchanged but an interaction in which the action goes back and forth. (Mol, 2008, pp. 21)

In this section, I examined the logic of care as described by Mol through the following questions. How is the theory of the logic of care utilized in real-world practice? What are the difficulties encountered when applying the logic of care in care practice? Does this mean that something described in the Logic of Care is incompatible with diabetes care? How do difficulties encounter when applying the Logic of Care further influence healthcare in the context of German diabetes care? The quotes collected from practical cases are presented as either antithetical, transformed, or supportive of Mol's theory.

To compare the theory with the practice, the care concepts mentioned by Mol were categorized into three themes after the first coding process: responding, shared caring, and ongoing. The empirical data were classified into these themes to provide them with additional meaning during the second coding process. Finally, the themes were expanded and reidentified as responding and reflecting on health values, exchanging experiences and shared caring, and learning and ongoing.

The first identified theme was responding and reflecting on health values. Responding, based on the logic of care, refers to active patients who can be attentive to their bodies, reflect their care needs, show their interest in health improvement activities, and perform care activities (Mol, 2008). Responding draws on the duties of all care actors' activities and involves the bilateral activities between patients and healthcare professionals. The patients, as the care receivers, must be active in their disease management. They have to be aware of their bodies and be able to relay their care problems to their healthcare professionals (I–FA–02, 679–682; BE–S1–01; p. 2; I–NN–03, 299–310; I–PP–03, 438–440).[12] Healthcare professionals, as care providers, must also be aware of their patient's needs and be willing to respond to their patients when they call for help (I–PP–06, 225–227; I–PP–11, 356–358, 432–434).

Responding can be broadly described as caring with[13] a person's wholeness instead of only caring for a disease. According to the literature, patients desire to be valued as individual people and for their experiences and goals to be taken seriously when developing their care plans (Mol & Law, 2004). The findings of this research reinforce that patients and healthcare professionals recognize the importance of treating patients as human beings and that caring with the patients, using a holistic view is preferable to caring for sick organs (I–DA–01, 619–632; I–DB–01, 662–666). Thus, the use of the term 'diabetic' in care practice is inappropriate, and referring to patients using their names makes the patients feel respected (I–DA–01, 619–632; I–DB–01, 662–666; I–PP–09, 468–471).

---

12   Sometimes, active patients are described as "intelligent patients" in care practice. Intelligent, in this case, does not refer to the intelligence quotient; rather, this term is used to describe active patients who engage themselves in their disease management, such as searching for care information and resources. To avoid confusion with the accepted definition of the term intelligent, which typically refers to one's cognitive capacity, the term motivated patient may be preferable to intelligent patient.

13   Rather than 'care for', the term 'care with' emphasises that both the patient and the healthcare professional have duties that require active participation in care activities.

To be able to offer patients whole-person care, understanding how the patients live, what they want, and what they are capable of in their daily lives is necessary (I–DA–01, 87–91; I–DB–01, 93–105; I–NN–06, 194–199). Providing individualized care that is flexible and adjustable is essential (I–FA–01, 247–268; I–NN–05, 218–221). As one nurse explained: "Everyone is different, and their reactions are also different. Someone who reduces his body weight may do so because of experiencing stress from exams. You have to take a look at the whole situation" (I–NN–05, 218–221).

The literature defined whole-person care as focusing on the whole person rather than focusing on the disease, emphasizing personal strengths rather than deficits, analyzing failures as problems to be solved rather than as personal deficits, coaching patients through certain situations rather than critiquing them, and discovering and enhancing internal methods of reinforcement for behavioral change rather than external reinforcements (Funnel et al., 1991; Lenzen et al., 2016; Tol et al., 2015). In care practice, different care goals are often established by healthcare professionals depending on the patient's age (I–FA–01, 247–268; I–DB–02, 465–468; I–NN–03, 200–209; I–NN–05, 344–353), disease trajectory, or physical condition (BG–DB1–01, p. 4; I–NN–04, 133–138; I–NN–06, 229–238).

However, some fuzzy boundaries were identified between the theory and the practice. Although older people with diabetes are expected to be less capable of caring for their health and are allowed to fulfill their desires in daily life more than younger people because there is a limit to how long an older person's life can be prolonged, what determines the age at which patients should be allowed to be less active in caring for their health? Are older patients not responsible for improving their care? Do younger patients have to accept stricter rules and lose the ability to enjoy their lives? At what time and in what situations do patients' caring needs change?

Instead of categorizing all patients into a single collective, examining each case individually, focusing on the quality of life issues for each patient, and determining how to integrate diabetes control into each patient's life is important (I–DA–01, 87–91, 619–632; I–DB–01, 100–108, 662–666, 737–743; I–FA–01, 247–268; I–NN–06, 185–190, 194–199; I–PP–09, 468–471; I–DB–01, 100–108). Similarly, Mol (2010, p.13) argued that different 'good choices' reflect different values and involve different ways of ordering reality and should be addressed together. Within the logic of care, care implies a negotiation about how different goods might coexist in a given, specific, local practice (Mol et al., 2010, p. 13).

Reflection on health values was also classified as belonging to the same theme as responding in this research. Reflection can be viewed as a type of response that focuses on improving patients' motivations and reinforces their healthcare values when they encounter care difficulties in practical care circumstances. For example, when health becomes the most important value for patients, they can overcome situations in which their care activity might be delayed (GB–DB1–01, p. 6) or remain motivated to follow their care principles throughout the tedious and endless process of disease management (I-PP-03, 476–483). Reflecting on the care situation and values of patients allows patients to disclose their issues more openly and take ownership of the lifestyle changes they must pursue to be healthy (Schlette et al., 2009). Reflecting, as described here, refers to both an internal process, in which the patients consider their values and responses, and an external process, in which the healthcare workers present the patients with a view of the care situation.

In care practice, reflecting on invisible health conditions through the monitoring of a visible physical value can often stimulate patients to review how they care for themselves and push them to rethink the meaning of health. A visible blood sugar value is often considered the most useful data for evaluating care outcomes (I-DB-01, 49–51; I-NN-06, 177–181). Mary Wilde and Suzanne Garvin (2007) described conscious awareness as the phenomenon in which increased awareness transforms embodied knowledge, gained mostly through unaware, everyday living, into a more cognitively known dimension, providing individuals with an opportunity to think about their needs and plans for the self-management of body-work. This conscious awareness enhances reflection and the mental connections that form between experiences and symptoms. Turning invisible values into visible activities, focusing on understanding the values of all care actors, and balancing them might reveal feasible care services that can be applied in the real world.

Motivating patients to place value on care activities is never easy. In care practice, healthcare professionals sometimes use a type of force to push their patients to perform care (BD-DS2-02, p. 2; I-NN-06, 164–167). For example, a diabetes consultant told her patient, "Of course, you have wishes. But as a diabetes patient, you need to know your limitations. When you eat cakes, you have to do more exercise. You must be active because diabetes control means self-management" (BD-DS2-02, p. 2). However, manipulating patients may increase their cognitive and emotional suffering. Focusing on exchanging experiences and shared caring, as the second theme identified within the application of the logic of care in this research, may offer the possibility of improvement.

In the interviews, many patients and healthcare professionals mentioned that sharing their experiences with others can help patients address emotional pressure. Knowing someone else in the same situation can offer powerful support for patients who feel abnormal (BE-B1-01, pp. 4–6; I-DB-01, 326–330; I-DB-02, 36–40, 50–52; I-NN-06, 243–252; I-PP-08, 359–360; I-PP-11, 199–200). Contact with other patients helps patients realize that they are not alone in their situations, which makes them feel better (Dwarswaard et al., 2016). Comparing their situations against others who are in worse situations can help patients recognize the relative severity of their situation, reinforcing their identities and strengths (Dwarswaard et al., 2016). As one patient said, "There are still many other diabetics rather than me" (I-PP-08, 359–360).

In the context of diabetes care, patients rely closely on their healthcare professionals. Marian Verkerk (2001) named this form of care compassionate interference. Letting patients know that their healthcare professionals will accompany them during disease management was identified as important in this research (I–DB–02, 36–40; I–NN–06, 243–252). Patients and healthcare professionals work together as a team, and shared caring are described as a possible method for achieving successful diabetes care.

Within the logic of care, shared caring starts with patients and healthcare professionals being active participants in all types of caring activities and taking responsibility for their bodies (Mol, 2008, pp. 13–14). With this view, care responsibility refers not only to the responsibility of patients to care for their bodies but also to the legal and moral responsibilities of healthcare professionals to care for the bodies they serve.

In this research, shared caring was identified as something beyond the interactions between patients and any particular professional group. Shared caring involves the entire collective, the whole of society. When caring for chronic disease, care activities occur in the context of the patient's home and their interactions with society rather than merely in healthcare settings. A diabetes care team involves a network that can include different types of care institutions[14] (BE–B2–01, p. 3; I–FA–01, 44–49, 333–342; I–FA–02, 218–222) and various types of healthcare professionals[15] (BD–DS2–02, p. 2; I–FA–01, 333–342; I–FA–02, 38–45). Creating a close and efficient network among these institutions and professional groups was identified as important.

In care practice, many healthcare professionals realize the importance of collaboration in caring for and with patients with diabetes (I–FA–01, 44–49, 139–148; I–FA–02, 38–45; I–DB–02, 104–107, 283–288; I–DA–01, 366–369). When multiple professionals work together, healthcare professionals experience reassurance regarding improvements in the quality of care (BD–DS2–02, p. 2; BE–B2–01, p. 3; I–FA–01, 139–148; I–DB–02, 104–107). For example, providing patients with consultations with diabetologists and psychologists has been reported to be essential for identifying care problems (I–DB–02, 104–107). Offering diabetes training courses taught by diabetes consultants, physicians, and nutrition consultants is also considered useful for diabetes management (BD–DS2–02, p. 2). Transferring patients to psychiatric care when the patients reported problems within the mental sphere was mentioned by healthcare professionals as an important strategy (BE–B2–01, p.

---

14 A network involving multiple care institutions may include university hospitals, local clinics, discharge care centres, nursing care centres, and wound care centres.

15 The different types of healthcare professionals comprise diabetes specialists, general physicians, family physicians, psychiatrists, nurses, diabetes consultants, and nutrition consultants.

3; I–FA–01, 139–148). This type of care process involves a team, and tasks are divided between the members of that team in ever-changing ways (Mol, 2008, p. 21).

Based on the logic of care, people with diabetes learn that the amount of energy in the food they absorb should balance the amount of energy they expend, and their insulin dose should be adapted to both. However, so many variables are not accounted for that, often, the sums simply do not add up (Mol, 2009). Therefore, identifying a practical method in care practice is more important than insisting on the best method of applying care principles. The following two examples describe how nurses found practical methods to balance the desires of their patients with the principle of disease control: "Some family members brought chocolate for diabetes patients. They can bring chocolate for patients but in smaller quantities. Or they deposit the chocolate with us, and we give it to the patient, piece by piece" (I–NN–06, 223–227). "I have already gone to the store and bought a special chocolate for my patient" (I–NN–05, 64–66).

Care seeks moderation, and healthcare professionals seek to cultivate patients' minds (Mol, 2008, p. 29). Within the logic of care, offering support means neither fulfilling what patients want nor achieving what healthcare professionals need. Instead, identifying a counterbalance involves responding to patients by respecting their thoughts and exchanging experiences and values (Mol, 2008, p. 28). To be able to cultivate the patients' minds, empathy and consoling are strategies often employed by healthcare professionals in their care practice, based on the findings of this research. A nurse told me about her experience:

> I tried to keep them within a frame of care principles. But I would first go back a little bit and think about whether I was too rash. Or I said to them that I could understand them, and I do not want to have the disease either. I tried to empathize with the situation of the patients so that they feel that I understood them. This made the care situation became a little bit more harmonious. And most of the time, I console the patients. (I–NN–06, 153–160)

Finding a counterbalance does not include the idea that anything is forbidden. Based on the logic of care, caring is a matter of being attuned, respectful, and adaptable instead of controlling (Mol, 2008, p. 36). Abstinence is replaced with balance, and adaptive calculations replace relentless restrictions for diabetes care (Mol, 2008, p. 55). In this research, both patients and healthcare professionals highlighted the importance of maintaining a life that is diabetes-friendly (BG–DB1–01, p. 2) and enjoyable (BG–DA2–05, p. 4) during the process of caring for and with patients with diabetes.

Mistakes are allowed during the care process, and patients are not always required to have good blood sugar values (BG–DB1–01, p. 2; BG–DB1–01, p. 4; BE–B1–03, p. 2). As one diabetes consultant told her patient, "The blood sugar values don't have to be perfect. To fulfill some of your exceptions and desires are already allowed" (BE–B1–03, p. 2). In the words of Mol, "To enjoy yourself is not a sin" (Mol, 2008, p. 42). According to Mol, if a patient tells their healthcare professionals that they have sinned when things go wrong, good healthcare professionals should reply to their patients calmly and without self-moralizing (Mol, 2008, p. 41).

Mol (2008, p.101) further suggested that asking "What is it difficult to do?" can help both patients and healthcare professionals in practice more than instilling feelings of guilt when something goes wrong. This research data identified similar findings, that asking questions reflecting care values can offer support for both patients and healthcare professionals to reflect their values and to overcome care difficulties in diabetes management (BG–DS2–02, p. 3; BG–DA2–05, pp. 3–4). The questions often asked in care practice include "Are you satisfied with your care outcome?", "If not, why not?", "How can I change it?", "What is important for me?", "What is my goal?" and "What has been changed?" (BG–DS2–02, p. 3; BG–DA2–05, pp. 3–4).

Summarising the narrative experiences of the patients, their families, and their healthcare professionals, efficient diabetes care can be realized by turning invisible values into visible activities, focusing on differing values and balancing them, and providing feasible care services that can be implemented in the real world. However, diabetes care is a dynamic learning process, which focuses on the patient's problems and resolves them by leaving space for trying alternatives. As a diabetes consultant said: "Diabetes is a disease you must always try to adapt to until you have learned how to better deal with it" (BG–DB1–01, p. 2). The third theme identified in the logic of care was that of learning and ongoing.

According to the logic of care, care is an interactive, open-ended process that may be shaped and reshaped depending on the results (Mol, 2008, p. 23). To find appropriate care for an individual, continued attempts may be necessary. In practice, many healthcare professionals engage themselves in motivating their patients to keep trying during disease management to achieve a desirable care outcome (BG–DA2–01, p. 3; BG–DA2–05, pp. 2–3; BG–DS2–02; BE–B1–03, p. 2; I–DA–01, 280–282; I–NN–06, 170–176). They viewed attempting different approaches as their task when caring for and with a patient who has an undesirable care outcome (I–DB–01, 98–102).

In care practice, healthcare professionals described that it is impossible to "change the patient's direction in 180 degrees" (BG–DS2–07). Instead, educating their patients to "try to see what you still taste within the frame of what you are allowed to eat and with consideration of what is not only tasty but also acceptable for you" (BG–DS2–07) and "offering care services in a way that can be implemented in the patient's life" (I–FA–01, 397–401) are the better approaches. In the words of Mol (2008, p. 53), "gathering knowledge is not a matter of providing better maps of reality, but more of crafting bearable ways of living with reality or living in reality." Mol (2009) refers to this approach as tinkering.

Tinkering can be viewed as a dynamic learning process. According to the logic of care, when caring for chronic disease, self-care is a form of physical competence that patients must gain through learning (Mol, 2008, p. 45). In this process, both patients and healthcare professionals participate in learning about the patients' bodies, their disease, their personalities, and their living surroundings, making continued attempts until they have learned how to better deal with the disease (BG–DB1–01, p. 2; I–NN–06, 170–176; I–PP–11, 162–167). As one nurse told her patient: "I advise you to keep trying. One learns things only through collecting experiences. This is like when you learn to ride a bicycle, and you may fall at the beginning. But it will work eventually" (I–NN–06, 170–176).

To live well with diabetes, patients have to collect experience with caring, and healthcare professionals have to provide support tailored to the patient's individual needs and care situations. Therefore, care performance should be diverse and flexible. Even when the experience results in failure, patients can still learn from these experiences to avoid certain things that hurt them (Mol, 2008, p. 65).

Rather than merely transferring care knowledge, identifying a practical exercise that can be implemented in the patient's daily life is considered more useful during the learning process. For example, offering a cooking course rather than giving patients information on a paper form (I–NN–05, 735–743; I–NN–06, 512–516). In addition, focusing on positive experiences, whether these positive experiences are relayed by others or learned by the patients themselves, was reported by patients as helpful for dealing with their disease in daily life (BG–DA2–05, p. 4; I–PP–08, 232). Patients with exposure to positive experiences display enhanced motivation and increased effort toward self-management activities, resulting in more successful efforts to control their diabetes (Hinder & Greenhalgh, 2012).

Tinkering, according to the research data, involves leaving time and space for the patients to try things (I–FA–01, 390–397; I–NN–05, 72–80; I–PP–09, 62–69). A physician described his experience as follows:

> When a patient needs intensive insulin therapy with four injections a day, but the patient does not want it at all, then we will discuss and negotiate with him. I may try one injection a day as the first step. Until he recognizes, "Well, to inject insulin is not so bad"; maybe he can inject more frequently later. (I–FA–01, 390–397)

Within the logic of care, time is an indispensable element of diabetes care. Time is not a moment-by-moment concept when living with diabetes; therefore, continuing to try new approaches makes more sense than trying to offer optimal care services (Mol, 2008, p. 22). For healthcare professionals, allowing patients the time to try things while guiding the patients, accompanying the patients, providing some concrete goals, and focusing on the normativity of the patients' lives may lead to improved diabetes care (I–FA–01, 390–397; I–FA–02, 309–330; I–NN–01, 421–429; I–NN–06, 215–217).

In the literature, giving space to the disease in daily life is viewed as a type of coping strategy that allows for the integration of treatments, cures, or disease control into daily life (Hörnsten et al., 2004). Giving space in care practice does not mean leaving the patients to perform care alone. Healthcare professionals must accompany them, and the patients must be willing to share their feelings and experiences (GB–DB1–01, p. 7). By exchanging experience, as described by Lucy Leykum et al. (2011), the conceptualization of learning moves beyond the idea of one person to another. In the learning process, people learn together and build upon each other's understandings.

Based on the research data, healthcare professionals cannot decide what elements are good or bad for patients during the learning process, and telling a patient that he made a mistake is not likely to lead to success in diabetes management (I–DB–01, 55–58). Making judgments about patients' lives should be avoided. Instead of creating a sense of sin, the logic of care proposed that being sensitive, flexible, able to address each event as it occurs, and able to respond promptly is important in diabetes care (Mol, 2008, p. 37, 65). As one diabetes consultant commented: "Whether things are working or not, they are always in life. In life, it is natural that things may go up and down.... Even if it does not work, you can recognize it and seek help from someone else (I–DB–01, 55–58)".

Learning and tinkering are interdependent processes that occur within a care team, with a focus on the patient's living conditions, and considering what is achievable for the patients (I–DB–01, 98–102; I–DB–02, 47–57, 435–446). Attainable care, according to the research data, involves minimizing the limitations associated with disease management (BG–DB1–01, p. 4), being able to implement step-by-step changes towards a reachable goal (I–DB–02, 47–57), being flexible (BG–DB1–01, p. 4; BG–DS2–03, p. 3), conveying the plan clearly to patients (I–FA–01, 177–184; I–FA–02, 438–448), giving explanations and concrete goals, and keeping in touch with the patients (I–FA–01, 177–184; I–FA–02, 438–448).

Care outcomes will not always be desirable, but the caring process has to be continued. When the patients do not visit their healthcare professionals, the healthcare professionals will not see their patients anymore. Attempting to maintain contact with patients becomes a task and a challenge in caring for patients with diabetes (I–FA–01, 397–401; I–FA–02, 309–330; I–DB–01, 384–390). To stay in touch with patients, healthcare professionals emphasized the importance of standing on their patients' side, empathizing with them, and giving advice while avoiding coercion (I–FA–01, 397–401; I–DB–01, 384–390).

In diabetes care practice, however, patients argue that physical limitations might frustrate diabetes management. A low level of motivation among patients to participate in their diabetes management is commonly observed in care practice.

Unfortunately, healthcare professionals are sometimes unable to offer support for their patients due to a lack of time and limited care abilities. The families of patients and the patients' surroundings often prevent patients from engaging effectively in their care processes. In many cases, the medical care system and healthcare insurance must pay more attention to these situations. In the next section, these limitations will be explored, as revealed in care practice.

Limitations in Practice

If someone is well-trained and well-informed, it does not mean that he can deal with his diabetes optimally. It is because there is often a big difference between the knowledge of diabetes treatment and the implementation of what is necessary for daily life. And this is the problem of implementation. (I–DB–01, 124–128)

By analyzing practical cases, examining how patients integrate diabetes management into their daily lives, and how healthcare professionals accompany their patients in taming their disease, some concepts of the logic of care can be expressed and employed in diabetes care practice. Simultaneously, situations that might prevent the implementation of the logic of care can be observed in care practice. First, the physical conditions of patients often limit their care activities. Second, the level of interest that both patients and healthcare professionals have in diabetes care can determine how deeply they engage themselves in caring. Third, how well a healthcare team communicates amongst itself and how well the patient communicates with the healthcare team can influence whether care is delivered efficiently. Fourth, a lack of ability to perform diabetes care by patients, nurses, or family physicians can be a major disadvantage in the context of diabetes care practice. Finally, diabetes care has been reported as incomplete and inefficient due to limitations associated with working within a medical care society that is guided by the principles of patient sovereignty and economic expenditures.

The first difficulty that emerged in the analysis of diabetes care practice was the physical limitations of patients. In practice, many patients with diabetes viewed the limitation of their physical conditions as factors that restrained their diabetes management behaviors (BG–DS2–03, p. 3; BG–DS2–07, p. 2; I–PP–02, 267–269; I–PP–03, 454–457; I–PP–04, 111–113; I–PP–06, 69–71). Often, the patient's physical conditions, such as age, memory, concentration, visual and motor capacity, and the presence of other serious diseases, can prohibit the performance of daily activities necessary for diabetes control (I–PP–02, 267–269; I–PP–03, 454–457; I–PP–06, 69–71; I–PP–09, 590–594; I–NN–04, 143–147).

Patients felt less stressed and reported fewer limitations in their daily lives during the beginning phase of diabetes, particularly patients who only required oral medication to control their diabetes or who were able to maintain stable blood sugar values (BG–DA2–05, p. 5; I–NN–03, 553–558). In these cases, the patients are less conscious of having diabetes and exerted less effort to control their diabetes. When patients have another disease that may lead to worse consequences for their health, they pay more attention to the other disease and spend less effort on the activities associated with diabetes management (I–PP–04, 111–113).

Comparable findings were described in the literature. Patients refer particularly to physical restrictions associated with disease and pain as important factors that influence their abilities to perform daily activities (Hasseler et al., 2010). Patients who are diagnosed with diabetes but are symptom-free and do not experience adverse consequences do not need support aimed at addressing these consequences (Dwarswaard et al., 2016). Instead, these patients may view other problems or diseases that are more serious as being more important (Hörnsten et al., 2004).

The second difficulty revealed was the relative interests of both patients and healthcare professionals in participating in diabetes management. Not everyone is interested in diabetes care, which includes both patients and healthcare professionals. The research data shows that low motivation among patients in participating in care activities increases the difficulty of care delivery (I–DB–02, 28–30, 91–94,155–156; I–NN–02, 241–257; I–NN–03, 231–234, 278–293; I–NN–06, 111–120), especially for chronic diseases because most care takes place outside of healthcare institutions (I–FA–02, 228–239; I–DB–02, 599–602).

Typically, healthcare professionals have to spend more time dealing with their patients' problems if their patients are inactive (BE–S1–01, p. 1). For example, a diabetes consultant spent one hour to identify and print out the blood sugar values from a patient's old insulin pump to allow for discussion with the patient about diabetes control because the patient did not want to participate in their disease management (BE–S1–01, p. 1). In addition, a conversation between a patient and a healthcare professional may run in different directions without intersecting if each party is focused on different goals (BE–B2–01, p. 4).

In care practice, motivating patients to be active is an important issue. One diabetes consultant emphasized, "I used to do everything for my patients, but now I don't do it anymore because I think the patients should do something for their illness by themselves. They have to be active" (BE–S1–01, p. 2). The literature also identified that patients with higher levels of autonomous motivation are more likely to maintain a healthy diet and test their blood glucose levels (Heisler et al., 2003; Shigaki et al., 2010).

However, when caring for patients with diabetes, healthcare professionals constantly encounter stubborn patients (I–NN–06, 111–114) or non-compliant patients (I–NN–03, 278–293) with low motivation for participating in disease control. Caring for this type of diabetes patient was described by healthcare professionals as like "one tread on a rubber ball and is always on the outside" (I–DB–02, 155–156) Patients with low motivation may not yet be ready to accept their diabetes diagnosis

(I-NN-02, 241-257) or may not be ready to change their care behaviors (I-NN-06, 319-323). During this period, nurses experience difficulty helping their patients move from 'to know' to 'to do' in care practice.

The results of this research showed that patients prioritized life and lifestyle, which they identified as reasons for low motivation in disease management. The priority of life noted by patients was influenced by concerns about body image[16] (BE-B2-01, p. 4; I-PP-08, 12-14) or the values of the patients' life (I-NN-06, 116-120, 319-323; BE-B2-01, p. 2; I-PP-01, 378-381). As one patient repeatedly mentioned during her diabetes consultation: "I have no time. I must care for my partner. He has dementia. I cannot leave him alone. For example, he is now sitting outside and waiting for me" (BE-B2-01, p. 2).

Diabetes care is often based on a strict medical viewpoint of diabetes as a metabolic disturbance, whereas the patients' experience of disease is more commonly viewed as a medical errand and having to navigate new social and psychological problems that diabetes introduces into their daily lives (Kälvemark et al., 2004). Healthcare prioritization represents situations in which individuals are required to take a stand between divergent or conflicting needs and concerns (Nordhaug & Nortvedt, 2011). Merely promoting the positive physical value of diabetes care is often insufficient for patients, particularly when the patients' social conditions result in health having a low priority on their scale of survival values (Thompson et al., 2006, p. 187).

For diabetes management, encouraging patients to increase their movement and adjust their nutrition are common issues. Patients' caring activities are deeply influenced by their original life patterns. When the original diet pattern of a patient is similar to the diet required by diabetes management, the patient finds following the care principles to be much easier because they already had a healthier lifestyle (I-NN-03, 231-234; I-PP-05, 41-44; I-PP-08, 197). Conversely, when the patients' original lifestyle differs from the principles of diabetes management, they have a harder time adjusting their lifestyles (I-DB-02, 129-137; I-NN-05, 99-100; I-PP-08, 92, 411-415). As one nurse highlighted, "I can't replant a very big tree. It is difficult, difficult, and difficult" (I-NN-05, 99-100).

Healthcare professionals and patients both realize that changing their living patterns is necessary but difficult. As one patient said, "I am a kind of comfortable person. I have never gone hiking in my life" (I-PP-08, 92, 411-415). Another patient said, "I am too lazy to move" (I-PP-02, 116). Compared with this finding, older patients with type 2 diabetes were reported in the literature as having less enthusiasm for changing their lifelong habits (Pill et al., 1999). According to Tol et al. (2015), adults are considered less likely to make and sustain significant changes in their

---

16 The body image the patients mentioned include the loss of hair (BE–B2–01, p. 4) or the fear of becoming overweight (I–PP–08, 12–14).

lives unless they feel a strong need to change. If the patient does not experience strong feelings about the current situation, the likelihood of sustained behavioral change is small (Tol et al., 2015).

The research data shows that similar to patients, some healthcare professionals, particularly physicians, expressed limited interest in diabetes care. Some nurses complained that this low interest could make diabetes care difficult because they could not receive an immediate response when they reported the patients' bad blood sugar values to their physicians (I–NN–04, 160–170; I–NN–06, 394–401). Diabetes consultants also complained about physicians having limited interest in participating in diabetes training courses (I–DA–01, 447–452; I–DB–01, 477–482, 533–537). This research suggested that physicians may have less interest in diabetes care due to the organization of healthcare institutions and the payment structure of healthcare insurance, which typically undervalues diabetes care. In many care institutions, diabetes is often treated as merely a side diagnosis for patients (I–DB–02, 348–354; I–NN–03, 146–153; I–NN–04, 571–579). Compared with other diseases, diabetes requires more time and effort from healthcare professionals. As one physician described:

> If I have not seen a patient and get his medical record with HbA1c 10 [percent], honestly, I would first think, "Oh no". Because it means that you have to be elaborately active, and it costs time. So, in the first moment, I have to say, quite honestly, I don't have much interest in treating a patient with HbA1c 10 [percent] or even more because you know it costs more effort, often more persuasion, and more explanations. (I–FA–02, 410–415)

The diabetes consultants indicated the importance of physicians participating in the diabetes training courses due to their better knowledge regarding the pathology of the disease, and patients expressed increased trust in physicians relative to other healthcare workers (I–DB–01, 477–482; I–DA–01, 447–452). The presence of physicians suggests to patients that the issue should be taken seriously because the doctors spent their time on it (I–DA–01, 447–452). This availability can be viewed as a type of commitment to patients. The reduced interest in the healthcare system can result in reduced care services received by patients, precipitating care tensions around the themes of trust and power in care practice.

Efficient communication that allows for constructive negotiations with others is considered to be a determinant element for creating a collaborative healthcare team (Clark, 2005; Manski–Nankervis et al., 2014; Martin–Rodriguez et al., 2005; Mol, 2008). In the context of diabetes care, patients and healthcare professionals often differ in their beliefs and attitudes regarding diabetes care. Communication and negotiation are important for bridging the gaps among the various care actors and forming alliances among the care team. Open communication with patients fosters discussion and patient autonomy and improves care outcomes (Clark, 2005; Manski-Nankervis et al., 2014).

Unfortunately, communications in care practice are often reported as inefficient both within and between healthcare institutions. Various types of communication failures were identified, including the failure to record or transmit information (I–DA–01, 410–419; I–NN–01, 258–272; I–NN–02, 45–54; I–NN–03, 461–469; I–NN–04, 422–431), the lack of transparency (I–DB–02, 121–131; I–NN–02, 45–54; I–NN–04, 401–404, 436–439; I–NN–06, 328–333), differences in opinions (I–NN–01, 246–253; I–NN–02, 378–386), the reluctance of healthcare actors (I–DB–01, 681–683; I–NN–03, 100–103; I–NN–04, 415–417), and the lack of time and money (I–DA–01, 366–376, 424–428; I–DB–02, 291–311; I–NN–01, 246–253).

In Germany, the communication flow between different healthcare professionals is structured by two different systems: the consultation system and admission notes. Interprofessional communication within a care institution commonly occurs through the consultation system[17], whereas external teamwork that involves multiple healthcare institutions (such as between hospital physicians and family physicians or rehabilitation hospitals) is arranged through the transmission of an admission note[18]. Theoretically, these two communication systems should be able to support the exchange of information regarding a patient's condition among different care providers.

However, according to this research, the information flow can be interrupted, deleted, misunderstood, insufficient, and untransparent (I–DA–01, 410–419; I–FA–02, 228–239; I–NN–01, 258–272; I–NN–02, 45–54; I–NN–04, 401–404, 422–431, 436–439; I–NN–06, 328–333). Many healthcare professionals have experienced the loss of information during their daily work through the use of admission notes, particularly when patient care occurs at an external care institution, such in a home-care setting (I–NN–01, 258–272; I–NN–02, 45–54; I–NN–03, 461–469; I–NN–04, 436–439). Similar findings have been reported in the literature. According to Jody Gittell (2009), medical records are bulky and inconvenient to move from provider to provider (Gittell, 2009, p. 172). Primary care physicians experienced problems with delayed information transition (Schlette et al., 2009). Direct communications, such as the telephone, are preferred over referral letters or feedback reports, which may result in better information transfer in care practice based on

---

18 An admission note (Arztbrief in German) is a part of the medical record that documents the patient's status (including the disease history and the findings of physical examinations), the reasons why the patient is being admitted for inpatient care to a hospital or other facility, and the initial instructions for that patient's care. In Germany, when patients are discharged, the hospital physicians will write an admission note to the patients' family physicians. If patients are transferred to other medical institutions, their admission notes will typically also be transferred. However, nursing care institutions, such as home-care centres, are often excluded from this communication system.

the research data and the literature (J. McDonald et al., 2012; I-NN-01, 532–536; I-NN-04, 204–209).

In this research, communications between nurses and physicians are often reported as inefficient. Nurses are sometimes excluded from the communication flow between patients and physicians, especially in the context of home-care settings (I-NN-04, 401–404; I-NN-06, 328–333). The lack of communication makes caring work difficult. Nurses complained that they could not perform the correct work without a clear indication from the physicians (I-NN-01, 258–272; I-NN-03, 461–469; I-NN-05, 644–650; I-NN-06, 341–344). The diabetes consultants claimed that it was difficult to offer appropriate care if they receive a transfer note with insufficient information about patients (I-DB-02, 121–131).

Without communication within interprofessional collaborations, care conflicts may occur due to different judgments regarding medical care. As a home-care nurse observed: "The patient's medical plan was made differently by the hospital physicians and by the family physicians (I-NN-02, 378–386)". Or as another nurse claimed: "The medical plan is prescribed at the hospital, but the medical decision is made at home. The clinician would say, "Yes, we've done everything for the patient, but his family physician did not follow it" (I-NN-01, 258–272). When dealing with the distinct care opinions of the physicians in different care settings, nurses typically preferred to keep their distance from a conflict situation (I-NN-02, 378–386). Nurses may also attempt to find a resolution by pushing for increased communication among the care team and drawing attention to the conflict (I-NN-03, 132–135). When differences in opinion or care conflicts were revealed between two different types of care professionals (e.g. between nurses and family physicians), cooperation with a third healthcare professional (e.g. a diabetologist) was often used to help nurses avoid confrontations with family physicians in practice (I-NN-02, 83–91).

Conflicts among multiple professionals are not always bad. According to Gittell (2006), efforts to resolve conflicts provide opportunities to build a shared understanding of the work process and strengthen the relationships within which coordination occurs. The findings of this research reinforce this argument. Some clinical physicians in this research viewed conflicts as opportunities to improve because their care interventions can be evaluated and reconsidered through discussion with other physicians (I-FA-02, 292–303). In addition, exchanging experiences in caring can help them to build a network with other care institutions (I-FA-01, 69–78). However, a low level of willingness to collaborate has been identified as a problem in diabetes care practice.

According to the research data, some family physicians are reported as neither listing to clinical physicians nor desiring to collaborate with them (I-NN-04, 415–417), or being unwilling to transfer their patients to specialists, such as diabetologists or diabetes consultants (I-NN-03, 100–10; I-DB-01, 681–682). Margaret Miers (2003a, pp. 116–117) noted a primary point of resistance against shared professional surveillance through effective teamwork could be the discursive practices of different professional groups, which serve to perpetuate differences rather than to foster agreement between care workers. The study by Gittell et al. (2003) reported that communication and relationship patterns are deeply embedded in professional identities and organizational cultures and are not easily changed. A high workload, a lack of skills and interest, and limited time in communicating could contribute to reducing the willingness of physicians to cooperate with other professionals (Gittell, 2009, p. 187; Nortvedt et al., 2008).

Care performance by a care team is not only influenced by the culture and the values of the outside society but is also influenced by the personal values and professional identities of the healthcare providers (Martin–Rodriguez et al., 2005; Matziou et al., 2014). Within the scope of the ethics of care, the development of trust and respect between different healthcare professions and disciplines can facilitate cooperation. However, trust only develops over time with good communication (J. McDonald et al., 2012; Rørtveit et al., 2015). The lack of problem-solving communication can result in a lack of trust between different healthcare professions (Manski–Nankervis et al., 2014).

Offering good care requires competence (Callaghan & Williams, 1994; Vanlaere & Gastmans, 2011). The question is whether all care actors, including the patients, have sufficient competence to implement good care into daily practice. A limited competence for diabetes care was identified in this research as a factor that prohibits the effective implementation of the logic of care in care practice. Care competence, as discussed in this section, involves two dimensions. The first dimension refers to the patient's abilities, including their knowledge, care skills, and confidence in their abilities to care for their bodies and disease. The second dimension draws on the competencies of healthcare professionals, which involve professional competencies and personal competencies when offering individualized diabetes care.

In the literature, those patients who have high trust in their care competence can live well with diabetes (Hasseler et al., 2010; Hibbard & Greene, 2013; Robinson, 2016). However, clinicians sometimes lack trust in their patients' ability to care for themselves, follow treatment plans, and make appropriate lifestyle choices (Robb & Greenhalgh, 2006). This research identified evidence that the failure to implement appropriate care activities among patients was often due to physical disabilities (BG–DS2–07, p. 2; BG–DS2–07, p. 5), low motivation (I–PP–02, 116; I–PP–08, 92, 411–415), psychological pressure associated with their disease and their living conditions (See Understanding the Disease), and an insufficient understanding of their responsibilities due to a lack of information (BG–DS2–04, p. 4) or a misunderstanding of the information provided (BG–FA2–06, p. 3).

The second dimension of care ability refers to the professional and personal care competencies of healthcare professionals. This research finding suggests that the professional competence of family physicians in diabetes care is often doubted by patients, nurses, and diabetes consultants (I-PP-03,72-78; I-PP-05, 127-133; I-PP-08, 102-106; I-NN-01, 59-60; I-NN-03, 87-89; I-DB-01, 17-29). For example, one nurse questioned, "The patient's family doctor holds the opinion that as long as the blood sugar is lower than 500 mg/dl, it is okay. In this situation, you have to rethink if he is the right doctor for dealing with diabetes" (I-NN-03, 87-89).

Most diabetes care in the German healthcare system is organized and delivered by family physicians; therefore, if family physicians do not recognize their lack of care competence or choose not to transfer their patients to diabetes specialists, the patient's health could be endangered. As one patient complained, "I have already told my family doctor about getting hyperglycemia frequently. But he did not react to it. He should send me to a diabetologist. He was so reluctant to do it. It is terrible. Terrible!" (I-PP-08, 158-160).

Limited professional competence in diabetes care was also reported by many nurses, particularly home-care nurses (I-NN-03, 600-604; I-NN-06, 384-388, 407-413). Due to a lack of professional knowledge and care skills, in addition to the limited time available for caring, nurses are aware of their inability to provide diabetes consultations and discuss the patient's medical plans with physicians (I-NN-02, 584-594; I-NN-03, 52-55; I-NN-04, 265-271, 350-352). This can also cause the development of a mistrusting relationship within a care team (I-FA-02, 550-555).

In the literature, the lack of competence has been described as impacting trust relationships (Martin-Rodriguez et al., 2005; J. McDonald et al., 2012). In this research, patients were more likely to complain about the perceived lack of competence among their family doctors than among their home-care nurses. However, even when patients questioned the professional competence of their family physicians, they continued to trust their family physicians, and most care conflicts appeared to occur among healthcare professionals. This phenomenon is discussed in the literature and indicates that the physicians' authority has a greater impact on the care relationships between physicians and patients than on the relationships between physicians and nurses.[19]

The development of trust is strongly related to the interpersonal caring attributes of healthcare professionals (Dinc & Gastmans, 2013; Laugharne et al., 2011). Recently, an increasing amount of literature has focused on the importance of personal competence in caring and nursing (Kleppe et al., 2016; Rørtveit et al., 2015). The research data reinforces the importance of personal competence in care

---

19 Within German medical society, authority plays an important role within care relationships. In the German healthcare system, medicine is considered to be powerful, and medical care is viewed as a professional endeavour in care practice. The centralisation of medical care in society results in uneven power distributions in professional relationships. In the next section, The Logic of Power, this issue will be further explored.

practice. A healthcare professional who has sympathy for patients and can listen to them is reported by patients as someone they trust (BG–FA2–06, p. 3).

Efficient diabetes care should include all of society when attempting to care with patients. The places that patients live in and visit should also represent resources where support can be obtained. Families and society, unfortunately, were reported in this research as prohibitive factors that made the implementation of the logic of care difficult. Often, the patient's families and society have little interest in diabetes care. The limitations to care implementation can occur in some situations. First, the opinions of family members can differ from those of healthcare workers or patients. When all of the family members do not agree with a decision, it becomes difficult for decision-making about the ways of caring (I–NN–06, 258–262). Second, families with a migration background often prioritize a different pattern of nutrition that differs from that recommended by German healthcare professionals (I–NN–03, 377–380). Third, family members can have difficulty understanding diabetes and struggle to provide sympathy for patients during their diabetes management (I–PP–11, 226–233).

The partners of patients played variable roles in diabetes management. However, when the partners of patients view self-management in moral terms, or when the family's general concept of good life contrasts with the principles of diabetes management, conflicts can arise within the family. Carole Robinson (2016) warned that family members learned that their priorities for living well were often pre-empted by disease management or competing healthcare professional concerns. Over time, expectations were unmet, and it became clear that compliance and passive waiting were unproductive, resulting in mounting frustration and eroding trust in the patient's care situation and family dynamics. Both patients and family members were perceived as experiencing frustration and loss of trust in patients and the healthcare team (Robinson, 2016).

In addition to families, the social environment in which the patients live can also impact their diabetes management. Living with diabetes within a society that misunderstands their disease can be challenging for patients with diabetes. The lack of knowledge about the disease and stereotypes of diabetes patients held by the general public may restrict patients' confidence in diabetes management. One patient told me: "There is no one who can understand me, and no one has sympathy with me. If someone knows I have diabetes, I would immediately be considered as the one who takes too many candies" (BE–B1–01, p. 4).

In this research, the patients complained that they were not understood by their friends and colleagues (BE–B1–01, p. 4; GB–DB1–01, p. 5; I–PP–11, 324–327). Discussing their diabetes management with others is difficult for patients because others have little interest in the issue or know too little about the disease (I–PP–01, 157–163; I–PP–09, 579–582). To be able to discuss their diabetes management with others, the patients usually have to spend time and effort describing their disease story and explaining everything about diabetes management (BE–B1–01, p. 4; GB–DB1–01, p. 5). An uncomfortable situation for the patients may develop if their friends or colleagues do not have sympathy for them. In care practice, patients often seek support from healthcare professionals who have professional competencies and can understand them. As one patient said: "I want to get a professional answer. And I need help from someone professional, like doctors" (I–PP–11, 324–327).

Disease management at home does not resemble disease management at the hospital. Both patients and healthcare professionals recognized the difficulty of maintaining care principles in the patients' everyday lives (BG–DS2–02, p. 4; I–NN–05, 44–47; I–PP–09, 374–382). The environment in which patients live is full of temptations contrary to good diabetes management. As one patient said, "The sausage stalls are everywhere. There is a bakery every 300 meters! Everyone has their specialty. Whenever I stand in front of a counter, I don't know anymore what I should take" (BG–DS2–07, p. 4). Susan Hinder and Trisha Greenhalgh (2012) elaborated that it is more difficult to control diabetes on weekends because life is less predictable. Therefore, the patients led restricted social lives and were reticent to go out to places that they were unfamiliar with (Hinder & Greenhalgh, 2012).

The healthcare system and healthcare insurance were identified in this research as prohibitive factors for the implementation of the logic of care. In care practice, both patients and healthcare professionals complained about the insufficient financial support received from healthcare insurance, which steers the delivery of healthcare. Without sufficient financial support, care activities offered by many healthcare professionals are limited. Due to financial limitations, diabetes consultants have been forced to discontinue a diabetes care program in collaboration with a sports medicine department that was shown to be efficient for diabetes care (BG–DS2–03, p. 2). Diabetes consultants complained of working in small consultation rooms where there is no separate enclosed room with a door with which privacy can be established, and their conversations with the patients might be interrupted by others (BE–B2–01, p. 1). Diabetes specialists complained of being underpaid (I–DB–02, 368–378), and occupational positions for diabetes consultants are rarely available (I–DB–02, 368–378). Family doctors cannot prescribe more expensive drugs that can be helpful in patient care[20] (I–DB–01, 17–18). The ability to offer diabetes training courses is limited because of limited manpower and limits on expenditures (BD–DA–01, p. 3, I–DB–02, 348–354). A diabetes consultant claimed: "I must say, what we do and where we will go are guided by the economic aspect. We are only a small department in the hospital, so what we can do is limited" (I–DB–02, 348–354).

---

20   In practice, the types of medicine that can be prescribed vary between clinics and office-based physicians' practices. Typically, family physicians are limited by the budget of the healthcare insurance.

Time was identified in the literature as particularly significant when caring for patients with chronic illness (Clark & Hampson, 2003; Dinc & Gastmans, 2013; Fox & Chesla, 2008; Nortvedt et al., 2008; Paterson, 2001; Young, 2016). The medical model that addresses time efficiency with a focus on pathology may not offer good care for patients with chronic diseases. The lack of time for caring has been reported in this research as a major problem due to restrictions established by healthcare organizations and healthcare insurance (I–DA–01, 23–28; I–DB–01, 471–473; I–FA–01, 450–470; I–NN–03, 600–604; I–NN–04, 265–271).

Almost all of the healthcare professionals in this research described suffering from time pressure. Healthcare workers were commonly instructed to work quickly because they have so many patients to care for. However, offering diabetes care requires time. Without time, individual care is difficult to implement (I–DA–01, 228–234; I–DB–02, 428–432; I–NN–04, 571–579), the quality of care suffers (I–DB–01, 557–570; I–FA–01, 450–470), patient education is difficult to provide (I–DA–01, 23–28; I–DB–01, 471–473; I–FA–01, 450–470; I–NN–03, 185–194, 600–604; I–NN–04, 265–271), the continual evaluation of interventions cannot be performed (I–DB–01, 471–473, 557–570), communications with the care team are restricted (I–DB–01, 557–570), and interventions for care improvement cannot be implemented (I–DA–01, 112–118).

These problems correspond closely with the structure of the German healthcare system, which is organized through the use of a third-payer system.[21] Unfortunately, German healthcare insurance providers are often criticized for insufficient financial support to healthcare professionals who want to offer good care, especially in the context of diabetes care, which is viewed as a "talking" medical treatment (BD–DA–01, p. 3; BE–B2–01, p. 1; BG–DS2–03, p. 2; I–FA–01, 454–457; I–NN–04, 233–240). A physician argued: "When I talk with a patient for half an hour, then I get seven euros. So, the "talking" medicine is not adequately paid in Germany. And diabetes care is a talking medicine" (I–FA–01, 454–457).

Comparable findings were described in the literature. Clark and Hampson (2003) reported that nurses felt they did not have adequate time and resources to treat their patients with diabetes effectively. Per Nortvedt et al. (2008) identified that both doctors and nurses appear to be worried about their lack of time for more comprehensive approaches to patient care. Twigg et al. (2011) noted that care tasks in the private home sector might be rushed due to the timetable determined by the minutes allotted to each visit. Sylvia Fox and Catherine Chesla (2008) criticized the context of the modern healthcare system, which often pushes nurses to provide

---

21 A third-party payer system means that patients do not pay healthcare providers directly for their medical treatment within this healthcare system. The healthcare providers calculate the costs of medical services and then receive payments from healthcare insurance (Tscheulin & Dietrich, 2010).

care more attuned to medical issues and leaves little time for the development of connected relationships. Leyla Dinc and Chris Gastmans (2013) highlighted the difficulty of developing a trust-based nurse-patient relationship without sufficient time. Jacqui Young's study (2016) illustrated how patients experience feeling uncomfortable due to the limited time available for physicians in consultation.

According to the research data, many patients and healthcare professionals complained of difficulty contacting physicians or making appointments for consultation or diabetes training courses (I–NN–03, 392–398; I–NN–04, 521–525; I–PP–02, 475–484; I–PP–09, 36–37), which may be due to a lack of manpower among nurses and diabetes consultants (I–DA–01, 23–28; I–FA–01, 450–470) and the goals of healthcare institutions (I–FA–01, 301–316). As a result, healthcare professionals are overwhelmed with caring for too many patients and the patients have long waiting times in some cases. Connie Ulrich (2010) claimed that nurses appeared to be doing more and more with these limited resources; however, even when nurses do the best they can, they may not feel good enough, and moral tensions may emerge.

In Germany, healthcare insurance steers healthcare delivery. Patients complained that they have often been treated differently depending on which type of healthcare insurance they have (I–PP–02, 475–484). Because of the third-party payer system, German healthcare insurance decides which types of care services they will pay for. Cost consciousness and prices determine the healthcare market. In the words of John Spiers (2003, p.125), "Money talks, preference walks. Cash compels. Conversation with consumers in a real market concern what they want. Cash provides security and opportunity." This style of care prioritization makes diabetes care more difficult because it affects how people are heard, whose voices matter, how they try to address matters and the words that they use.

Summary

Care is a dynamic activity. Exploring the theories that underlie the practice of care is not meant to provide maps for real practice but to craft bearable ways to adjust to reality. In diabetes care practice, care needs must not focus on what might be best to do but should focus on what can be done and what can be achieved while working within the framework of the logic of care. The logic of care theory represents a suitable guideline for diabetes care and must be applied broadly to common phenomena in some cases, whereas in other cases, it must be applied using a narrow but specific explanation. By recognizing the common concepts underlying the theory, shaping the concepts according to care experience, and inserting the modified concepts into reality, the logic of care theory could be expanded and transformed into a form that is feasible and acceptable in the real world. Regrettably, care limitations and care ambivalence have been noticed in the context of diabetes care. The physical conditions of patients often limit their care activities. The level of interest that both patients and healthcare professionals have in diabetes care can determine how deeply they engage themselves in caring. How well a healthcare team communicates amongst itself and how well the patient communicates with the healthcare team can influence whether care is delivered efficiently. A lack of ability to perform diabetes care by patients, nurses, or family physicians can be a major disadvantage in the context of diabetes care practice. Finally, diabetes care has been reported as incomplete and inefficient due to limitations associated with working within a medical care society that is guided by the principles of patient sovereignty and economic expenditures. The care environment represents an inseparable part of caring, which has an intensive impact on how healthcare professionals act, how they reflect their profession, and how care relationships are established and developed. Due to limited care resources, healthcare institutional regulations, and medical policy, care implementation can encounter practical difficulties.

In the word of Mol (2008), the logic of care is not a single configuration in health care. Other types of care logic are co-existence, moved, interdependent, and incorporated with the logic of care depending on the practical care situations (Mol, 2008, pp. 104–106). The other forms of care logic that emerged in the context of diabetes care are continually discussed in the next section.

Other Care Logics in Practice

If utilizing the logic of care makes sense in diabetes care practice, good care should be delivered. Regrettably, care limitations and care ambivalences were identified in this research. Summarising the research data, three other types of care logic were identified in German diabetes care practice: the logic of choice, which is associated with sovereignty and autonomy; the logic of efficiency, which refers to regulations and statistics; and the logic of power, which is concerned about legislation and authority.

The Logic of Choice

> Yes, with this patient, I don't have any chance to achieve the desired care outcome. If she does not want to do it, I cannot do anything at all. I mean, that's her body, her blood sugar. I cannot do anything for her. I cannot force her to do things.... I have to accept it resignedly. (I–NN–04, 340–345)

The logic of choice in German diabetes care is often guided by the concept of consumer sovereignty,[22] which is given high priority in the healthcare market. Care is sometimes dismissed in the name of autonomy. Patients, thus, are often treated as customers, and choices are made according to the patient's wishes. In current German healthcare practice, diabetes care services are delivered as products waiting to be chosen by healthcare users, who represent the customers. Care decisions are made by customers because customers have purchasing power in making their own choices on the market (I–DB–02, 423–427; I–NN–04, 340–345). Additionally, patient satisfaction has often been used in care practice as the main indicator for determining whether good care is offered (I–NN–01, 510–512).

In effect, healthcare professionals experience great difficulty offering care services based on their professional judgment against their patients' will (I–DA–01, 119–127; I–DB–01, 65–69; I–DB–02, 423–427; I–NN–01, 105–111, 409–414; I–NN–04, 340–345). As a diabetes consultant said: "Most of the time, care decisions are made by the patients instead of the doctors. You realize the difficulty while you try to change something, but the patients said, "No, I cannot do it"" (I–DB–02, 423–427).

According to the literature, respecting patient sovereignty and autonomy should be valued in caring because patients are asked to be responsible for care. If they are unable to be active in decision-making or experience being unattended to, they might express frustration, leave the physician's care practice and do what they think is best (Rogers et al., 2005). When patient sovereignty and autonomy are overvalued, unfortunately, the professionals' position in healthcare society depends on their ability to serve the interests of society or those of their customers, and the values of professional activities are determined by their customers rather than by the health outcomes (Parker, 1999; Robinson, 2016).

In care practice, care follows the logic of choice rather than the logic of care. Analyzing the literature and the research data, some problems were apparent in diabetes care. When the logic of choice is applied, the patient's vulnerability may be ignored and the patient's dependency is overlooked. Addressing patients as healthcare customers may ignore patients' fear and distress (Van Heijst, 2011). An emphasis on individual autonomy might result in too easily assuming vulnerability and diminished capacity, which can blind healthcare professionals to alternative methods of assessing and supporting decision-making for their patients (Cole et al., 2014; Kukla, 2005).

Working within the framework of the logic of choice may also produce confusion when attempting to distinguish between the wants and needs of patients. To

---

22 Consumer sovereignty is a phrase that emphasises the rights of consumers. In terms of citizen- and patient-centred care, sovereignty is usually presented in healthcare as a mechanism to improve the quality of care (Ryl & Horch, 2013).

care about something and merely to want something are two different concepts. According to Spiers (2003, p. 121), not all healthcare professionals understand the expectations of their patients and their families or introduce their perspectives within the framework of scientific practice and evidence-based care. Placing too much focus on the capacity for choice may ignore the features of patients' social lives (Spiers, 2003, p. 121). When healthcare professionals begin to talk in terms of commodification, they can quickly begin to prioritize the time and costs of a service rather than the needs of those being cared for (Olshansky et al., 2008; Tronto, 2010).

When the logic of choice is applied, patients' willingness can act in opposition to their health, resulting in the emergence of a contradiction between security and autonomy. Based on the literature, ensuring patients' security is viewed as a responsibility of healthcare professionals (Kunyk & Austin, 2011; Tronto, 1993). However, because the current healthcare system prioritizes consumer sovereignty and patients' autonomy, the willingness of patients becomes the priority of care, and patients are treated as customers and citizens whose choices are honored, even if the patient's wishes result in further harm to their bodies (Bostan et al., 2007; Ryl & Horch, 2013; Torpie, 2014).

According to the research findings, what healthcare professionals can do for their patients becomes limited when they are working within the framework of the logic of choice. Even in situations in which they recognize emerging harm to their patient's health, in care practice, many healthcare professionals experience care limitations and care frustrations (I-DB-01, 65–69; I-NN-01, 105–111, 409–414, 412–414; I-NN-04, 340–345). Healthcare professionals refer to patients as noncompliant when patients make decisions that do not fulfill their care expectations (I-NN-01, 105–111, 409–414, 412–414; I-NN-04, 340–345).

In such cases, patient-centredness is misunderstood as "always keeping patient needs and desires first ahead of standards or policies" and "putting patient's best interests first" (K. V. Smith & Godfrey, 2002). In addition, patients are forced to take care responsibility, regardless of whether they desire this responsibility (Weaver et al., 2008). When healthcare professionals cannot see a situation in its entirety, they are legitimately unsure about what is right or best to do, recognizing that they may make a mistake and lose any guarantee of desirable outcomes. Consequently, any customary sense of certainty may be disturbed, and care responsibility may be transferred to the patients (Weaver et al., 2008).

The care relationship between patients and healthcare professionals, from this perspective, becomes a consumerist type of relationship. Within a consumerist type of relationship, patients can receive desired care because the patients are placed at the center of care, and care services appear to be offered that are tailored to the needs of the patients (Robinson, 2016). Due to the changes in how healthcare professionals interact with patients within a consumerist type of relationship, this type of relationship is also embedded with ethical tension because the patients may not have sufficient care competence for decision-making, and mistrust relationships may form (Robinson, 2016).

Creating a non-consumerist type of relationship is important but difficult to implement in practice. When the logic of choice is being applied, healthcare professionals suffer from the ambiguity of respecting patients' autonomy and ensuring patients' safety. Although they might feel pity when their patients reject their care services (I–NN–04, 111–112), healthcare professionals recognized that they could not force their patients to do things (I–DA–01, 268–271, 299–304; I–DB–01, 65–69; I–NN–01, 59–60, 105–111, 309–317; I–NN–04, 340–345). They said, "We force no one here" (I–DA–01, 299–304), "We come here not because of controlling" (I–NN–01, 59–60, 309–317), and "It is your free choice" (I–DA–01, 309–315).

A hazy boundary exists between freedom and control because illness always implies a certain ignorance (Gastmans et al., 1998; Varelius, 2006). Control, in the context of diabetes practice, is sometimes necessary (Thompson et al., 2006, p. 182; Varelius, 2006). Healthcare professionals should cooperate with the desires of their patients but convince them to rely on the expertise and authority of trusted healthcare professionals to guide, mediate, and manage their healthcare as a method to empower their patients in a transformative form of autonomy that also results in optimal health outcomes (Cole et al., 2014; Duttweiler, 2007)

Working within a medical society guided by the logic of choice causes healthcare professionals to experience tension and ethical dilemmas. On the one hand, the healthcare professional is asked to provide a satisfying experience to patients that respect customer sovereignty and patient autonomy. On the other hand, they are tasked with ensuring the patient's safety and security and providing good care through their professional echo. Consequently, concerns regarding the best interests of the patient may become ethical considerations for healthcare professionals.

The Logic of Efficiency

> Everyone should work well, as efficiently as possible, quickly, and cheaply. Yes, it is always the concern about money, exactly. You are requested to achieve this goal whether you can achieve it or not. But sometimes, it is not attainable. (I–DA–01, 14–19)

Care acts in modern care situations must also consider economic concerns. Along with the larger phenomenon of the commodification of health, the economic incentives of care practices should not be ignored. Often, healthcare workers are expected to demonstrate their capacity to deliver high-quality care cost-effectively. This duality, care as an ethical concept involving concern for others, and care based on economic necessities and the exchange of goods, can pose significant challenges for both healthcare workers and care receivers. Institutional regulations and rules designed to support the implementation of practical care delivered in an economically efficient manner may be misunderstood as a form of professionalism that fragments care into pieces.

The logic of efficiency, which was identified in this research, is based on a healthcare society organized according to economic expenditures and the misconduct of legitimate regulations. Regulations and norms have been described as useful tools and reflections of professionalism in healthcare society, especially in support of organizations that utilize these tools to achieve coordination, monitor standards, and ensure the delivery of quality care and the prevention of public harm (de Casterle et al., 2008; Gilson, 2003; Gittell, 2009, pp. 149–150; Gunnarsdóttir & Rafferty, 2006).

In institutional care, care procedures are often standardized to ensure the efficient completion of patient care tasks and legitimacy provides the foundation for coordination among relatively autonomous healthcare providers. In the German diabetes care system, DMPs are offered as a legitimate foundation for healthcare professionals to offer standard care services and for the receipt of payment from healthcare insurance. The family doctor model protects the patient by guaranteeing that doctors participate in regular home visits from the family doctor so that the doctor can receive financial benefits from healthcare insurance. Working within these legitimate models, patients appear able to receive collaborative care based on the funding arrangements and both patients and healthcare professionals have a legal duty to participate in various caring activities (I–PP–11, 406–410).

When dealing with a complex chronic disease, however, whether a legitimate norm or regulation is capable of fulfilling the needs of patients remains an open question. The legitimacy and regulations associated with care practice have been reported in the literature as problematic due to poor performance in high-profile cases, misconduct among healthcare professionals, the lack of regulatory authority, and the lack of procedures for reforming these regulatory mechanisms among healthcare professionals (Gunnarsdóttir & Rafferty, 2006). Consequently, the level of involvement that professionals have with the regulatory system and the roles played by external actors (such as state institutions) can vary (Gunnarsdóttir & Rafferty, 2006). Patients who are imposed on by these standardized procedures may fear challenging those on whose care they depend. Clinically imposed behavioral norms may also become oppressive (Entwistle et al., 2010).

According to the current research, some care problems can be revealed in care practice when the logic of efficiency is practiced. First, when care is determined by a regulated model, patients may become passive in caring, preferring to wait for a visit from their physicians instead of being more active in their disease management. For healthcare professionals, regulation may allow for the implementation of only those care services that are regulated instead of considering the individualized care needs of their patients. Regulation, in this case, may inhibit innovation and demotivate both healthcare professionals and their patients.

Some practical cases reinforce the rigidity of regulations. Frequently in care practice, a patient will have no medical reason for a longer hospitalization, based solely on clinical regulations and medical indications; however, they may require a longer hospitalization due to psychological or social grounds. For example, patients must be discharged even when they are unable to perform care for themselves at home (I–NN–02, 99–105). In care practice, institutional regulations appear to frame perfect procedures for guiding patients and healthcare professionals during the discharge process. How the procedure is implemented in practice and whether it provides the patients with a sufficient level of continual care outside of the care institution can be uncertain (I–NN–01, 557–578).

These cases highlight the other problem identified when the logic of efficiency is applied, referred to as the clinical gaze, in which patients are treated as objects within standardized institutional regulations. Patients become objectified, and healthcare professionals encounter patients as essentially a collection of signs and symptoms rather than as individual people (Benner, 2001; Fox & Chesla, 2008). This view can be common in the context of long-term care. Rees et al. (2009) observed that nurses sometimes exercised power over their patients when routines took preference over individual needs, resulting in care delivery being determined by schedules rather than by patients' needs. However, nurses experienced feelings of failure in these situations because they had not acted in their patient's best interests (Rees et al., 2009).

The biggest problem identified in the logic of efficiency was the monopoly exerted by care efficiency statistics in healthcare. Due to regulations, which often originate from supplier interest groups that are concentrated and well-organized, healthcare institutions can lobby effectively to influence the level and contents of regulation to their benefit. This monopoly may influence the supply of health workers, control wages and prices, establish levels of services, and harmonize qualifications and requirements. or set and enforce common standards of practice (Gunnarsdóttir & Rafferty, 2006). Healthcare regulations tend to rely on hierarchy and a variety of centralized state-run and professional agencies for their implementation (Gunnarsdóttir & Rafferty, 2006). When nurses tend to align explicitly with the system and speak with the system's voice rather than speaking with their lifeworld voice, the profession's field of discretion has become narrower (Robb & Greenhalgh, 2006).

Healthcare monopolies can be easily observed in care practice when healthcare is calculated in terms of time and money. Daily tasks noted on the calendar must be finished (I–DB–01, 627–634), and care services that require additional time may instead be performed haphazardly (I–NN–02, 126–133; I–PP–02, 514–520). A patient's daughter complained:

> Nurses have ten minutes to care for a patient. If they stay for twelve minutes, then they have only eight minutes for the next patient.... But, you know, if a patient has a serious problem, nurses need a longer time to care for such patients. Then, nurses have to care for other patients faster and faster.... Unfortunately, this is a big problem for the current healthcare, that patients wouldn't be seen as human anymore, only as statistics. (I–PP–02, 514–520, 532–534)

This case presents vividly how care can be treated as a statistic within the framework of the logic of efficiency and how patients can become objects labeled with prices instead of as people. Corresponding to this research finding, Jolanda Dwarswaard et al. (2016) addressed patients' relationships with their healthcare professionals and proposed that patients wish to be treated as people, which can help patients focus on their own needs. Treating patients as people and using the term patient instead of the term customer was deemed important in care practice. As one physician elaborated:

> If one understands medicine as a pure service enterprise, one would say, "That is my customer who wants my services". This concern nowadays surely exists in many levels of care institutes. But for me, the expression in terms of patients is more appropriate. Because behind the term patient is something quite different than a customer. It is much more human. (I–FA–01, 206–219)

Unfortunately, the research data also indicated that under economic pressure, healthcare professionals are often overwhelmed by offering holistic care, which can take both time and money. Even when healthcare professionals view offering care without concern for humanity as inappropriate, the care services they can offer can be limited (I–DB–01, 181–184; I–DB–02, 626–630). Generally, healthcare professionals viewed this type of healthcare as short-sighted and unsatisfied with care environments tailored by expenditures (I–DB–02, 368–378). Referring to this finding, Helen Kohlen (2009, pp. 142–143) claimed that when nurses constantly talked about the lack of time and resources required to fulfill their work, the talk was characterized by acceptance due to the discourse of costs and cost containments that was used to enable control over patients and the patient care practice.

Within the logic of efficiency, the quality of care is often calculated based on the quantity of achievement from an economic perspective. Alan Maynard (2006) explained that most transactions in the healthcare market involve not only doctors and patients but also the purchasers and providers of healthcare, both public and private. Doctors owe a duty not only to their patients but also to their healthcare systems, which involves the agencies they work for and their funders (Maynard, 2006). Nursing, like other professions in healthcare, must also be concerned with the quality of care under pressure to produce value for money (Thompson et al., 2006, p. 9). In care practice, the research data shows that care is calculated economically in many cases. A patient who requires a high cost in medical resources and time would be identified as unwelcome:

> It's again something about money. This can be responded to by reducing the duration of hospitalization at the station. The patients are not allowed to stay so long in the hospital. They must be discharged because it is financially bad. People always said that the only thing that bothers hospitals is the patients. It's quite sarcastic! (I–DA–01, 529–541)

When healthcare professionals are working within the logic of efficiency, the research findings demonstrated that a focus on numeric values often results in many invisible messages connected with the psychological and social aspects of care that can be ignored (I–DB–01, 173–181). As described in the literature, healthcare professionals who take a narrow approach to problem-solve in response to the broader interests of the patient's ability to live with diabetes can create a conflict between the professionals and the patients (Robb & Greenhalgh, 2006; Zoffmann & Kirkevold, 2005).

A focus on numeric values by professionals can cause patients to feel unwelcome and viewed as a subject within care relationships (Kleppe et al., 2016; Vanlaere & Gastmans, 2011). As one patient in this research described, "When I went to a doctor, the doctor viewed my blood sugar data and said 'good'. Then, he lets me go. My problem would not be solved" (BE–B1-01, p. 5). In this case, the patient experienced ignorance, felt unwelcome, and her care problems were not discussed, which could lead to a mistrust care relationship.

Without a holistic approach to caring, patients may develop a deep distrust of the care system and avoid receiving care (Dinc & Gastmans, 2013; Ells, 2001; Reach, 2014; Rowe & Calnan, 2006). As one patient said:

> I do not talk about diabetes with my family doctor at all. It does not make sense. He controls my heart disease. But it bothers me that he wanted to give me this medicine for decreasing my blood lipids. I have already argued about it with him because there was a side effect. I do not know if he does not know it, or he thinks that "I don't care about if the patient gets muscle pain or not. She has just to swallow it". But I do not swallow everything he prescribes. (I–PP–08, 296–302)

Care practice is often presented as a big business-based institution. Working within such business-like care institutions, diabetes care can become a fragmentary, low priority, and characterized by ineffective collaborations, conflicts, and moral distress (I–DB–02, 74–79; Kohlen, 2009). In this research, patients acknowledged that nurses were often more concerned with tasks regulated by the care institutions than with the patient's needs, which cost time and money; however, this was viewed by patients as normal nursing practice (I–PP–02, 501–510). A similar finding was reported by McCabe (2004), who observed that patients attributed nurses' poor communication skills to them being too busy rather than blaming the nurses. Mol (2010) elaborated delicately that if care practices are only talked about in terms that are not appropriate to their specificities, they will be submitted to rules and regulations that are alien to them. This threatens to take the heart out of care, removing kindness, effectiveness, tenacity, and strength (Mol et al., 2010, p. 7).

Care should encompass more than the care provided with consideration for the logic of efficiency. Regulation cannot be viewed as the sole responsibility of a professional group or the fundamental professionalism that underpins the performance of medicine; regulation should be designed to be integral and flexible as the basic conditions for legal norms that connect patients' needs around their lives (Robb & Greenhalgh, 2006). In the words of Rebecca Kukla (2005), "We can be conscientious about living up to norms that we have chosen freely, after extended reflection and deliberation, or to norms that we find ourselves bound by because of the authority of experts or the influence of culture." Living within a caring society that is based on the ideas of medical authority and hierarchy, a single care choice may be conscientious, but conscientiousness cannot occur in isolation. In addition to the logic of choice and the logic of efficiency, the logic of power was identified, in which legislation and medical authority construct healthcare relationships and impact care performance.

The Logic of Power

> There is a young doctor in a station who has no experience in caring for diabetes patients. He always rotates and makes a treatment, which makes the nurses tear out their hair. But the nurses can do nothing. He throws everything around, but he is not so experienced. However, he is a doctor, and we are bound by the rules that we must do what he said. (I–DA–01, 510–514)

Care invariably occurs in a politically charged and legally complex environment. In this research, a clear division of responsibilities has been described among patients, nurses, and physicians in various care encounters, illustrating the unequal power distributions across these groups. Within a society in which care is constructed according to the logic of power, legislation is viewed as the foundation of care. Legislation can clarify and regulate care responsibilities but also greatly restrains the variety of care activities. Institutional hierarchies may also limit healthcare workers' responses to care appeals, especially in diabetes care. Non-cooperation and mistrust in care relationships within a care team can develop.

The first problem associated with the logic of power is that legislation is often overused as the care foundation of professionalism. In German healthcare, medical issues, such as pharmacological treatment or other specific treatments, are regarded as being solely the physicians' responsibility (Rosemann et al., 2006; Salloch, 2016). Physicians have the regulatory power of professional jurisdiction over other healthcare professionals in their respective federal territories within the medical professional system in Germany (Salloch, 2016). In addition, physicians have been situated in an elitist and powerful position for centuries due to their exclusive knowledge and their monopoly on services, which are of utmost importance to all members of society (MacDonald, 2002b; Salloch, 2016).

This power imbalance could easily be observed in care practice when a nurse said that patients would accept what the doctors say without knowing whether it works or not (I–NN–01, 296–300). A diabetes assistant said, "I'm not a doctor, so I am not allowed to say that we have to take another kind of insulin." (I–DA–01, 220–226, 289–293). In care practice, all healthcare professionals, except for physicians, mentioned their powerlessness in making medical decisions (I–DA–01, 220–226; I–DB–01, 394–407; I–NN–01, 296–300; I–NN–02, 24–29; I–NN–04, 386–394; I–NN–05, 644–650).

Without legitimate power, patients' wishes regarding medical treatments cannot be adjusted by non-physician professionals. Nurses, in contrast to physicians, are often considered to have less autonomy in their professions due to their lack of control over the contents of their practice, the context of their practice, and their competence (MacDonald, 2002b; Manojilovich, 2007). Nursing professional roles, then, may depend upon the laws, ethical guidelines, and fiscal constraints that govern healthcare (Paulsen, 2011). In effect, physicians become the most powerful professionals in a healthcare team. The responsibility of arranging healthcare for patients and coordinating healthcare among the healthcare team must be assumed by powerful physicians (Nugus et al., 2010).

In care practice, the power of physicians and legitimate regulations force non-physician healthcare professionals to accept physicians' decisions in caring, even when they disagree with these decisions, which greatly restricts the professional autonomy of non-physicians. They said, "Sometimes we do not always agree with these instructions given by the physicians, but we have to do what the doctors said" (I–DA–01, 253–254); "Even if I have another opinion, I am not allowed to decide everything" (I–DB–01, 418–425); and "I have to accept physicians' decision even though I sometimes do not like to do it. But I try to think, "Okay, let's try it". Perhaps the doctor has just found the right way" (I–DB–01, 394–407).

Many healthcare workers do not have the option to go against regulations because this would require them to act illegally. Martin McKee and his colleagues (2006) illustrated that the division of tasks among various healthcare professionals reflects their considerations but does not indicate who would be best positioned to perform these tasks. As the research data presented, healthcare professionals attempted to see other opinions as alternative options, revealed by different perspectives and tasks performed by other healthcare professionals.

Mary Corley's study (2001) noted that many nurses described compromising their values due to hospital policies or standards, a physician's request, or nursing administration requirements. Nurses were also sometimes forced to act against their principles and ethical guidelines, and in some cases, legal requirements were impossible to accomplish because of organizational constraints, such as a lack of resources or a lack of power (Corley et al., 2001). Sofia Kälvemark and her colleagues (2004) viewed these contradictions as a form of pressure for nurses. An ethical dilemma can develop for non-physicians when their legal obligations conflict with their moral responsibilities (Holm & Severinsson, 2014).

The second problem caused by the logic of power, which was identified in this research, was that authority is often misunderstood as trust in care relationships. In a traditional caring context, the development of trust depends on the healthcare workers' behaviors and is related to situations, roles, competence, and the organizational structure (De Raeve, 2002a; Rørtveit et al., 2015). In this research, patient's trust in physicians was closely connected with the physicians' social status and their medical authority, sometimes regardless of the actual knowledge and competence of the physicians (I–DA–01, 319–327, 495–499, 507–509; I–DB–01, 525–528; I–NN–02, 220–223, 227–235). Often, the words spoken by physicians have legitimate meanings for patients. As a nurse described: "What the doctor said is right. What the doctor said is already something legitimate" (I–NN–02, 199–214).

This trust relationship allows patients to stay loyal to their physicians during their disease control process, even though the patients are sometimes unsatisfied with their medical therapy or with the care services offered by their physicians (I–NN–02, 220–223; I–NN–06, 444–448). Based on the research data, patients trust their family physicians the most (I–PP–09, 651–654; I–DB–02, 172–181; I–NN–05, 585–601). When differences in care opinions emerged at different healthcare institutions or among different healthcare professionals, the patients would choose to trust their family doctors in many cases (I–PP–09, 651–654; I–DB–02, 172–181). Both patients and healthcare professionals described this trust as having been established within a long-term care relationship between the patients and their family physicians (I–PP–09, 651–654; I–DB–01, 412–416; I–DB–02, 172–181; I–NN–03, 668–680).

Even though nurses have less power to make a medical decision, they are reported as the group that is most able to influence patients because nurses are close to their patients and understand their needs, particularly in the context of homecare practice (BG–FA2–06; I–DB–01, 412–416; I–NN–01, 71–79; I–NN–03, 668–680; I–NN–05, 429–430). Patients often talk with their doctors about specific medical questions but share their emotional feelings with non-physician professionals

(BG–FA2–06; I–DB–01, 412–416; I–NN–01, 71–79; I–NN–03, 668–680; I–NN–05, 429–430). Corresponding to this research finding, the nurses' strength is reported as their popularity, reflecting the embodiment of their service ethic, which can be viewed as at the heart of professionalism (Wilkinson & Miers, 2003, pp. 34–35). By understanding the patient's needs and suffering, trust can be created within a patient-nurse relationship (Callaghan & Williams, 1994; Rørtveit et al., 2015).

Medical authority in care practice is an important factor that influences how a trusting relationship between patients and their healthcare professionals is built. Often, a person who has a higher administrative level and a higher academic position has a higher degree of authority and earns a stronger degree of trust from the patients. For example, a young physician told me that her chief, a medical professor, has fewer conflicts with his patients than she does due to his higher degree of authority (I–FA–02, 330–334).

In practice, authority is granted not only by the occupational title but also by the perception of professional authority. Making authority visible in some cases can help healthcare professionals earn the trust of their patients. A diabetes assistant described:

> Authority plays a role in the trust relationship with the patients. Well, I do not want to take myself as an example, but I'm already a little bit older, have rimless glasses, and the patients have often thought they are talking to a doctor when they come to me. Then I said, "One moment, I'm not a doctor". But I noticed something different between me and a young student when we explain things to our patients, such as how to use a blood sugar measuring machine. The patients take what I said more seriously because they think that Mrs. Schmidt is older, she has professional experience. (I–DA–01, 319–327)

In care practice, authority is sometimes used as a tool to foster appropriate practices. A comparable finding was reported by Kukla (2005), who illustrated that physicians use the weight of their medical authority and their ability to demand accountability as tools to foster appropriate practices and instill ethics and self-management techniques in their patients.

However, the overuse of authority can lead to care frustration and ethical tensions in some care circumstances. First, patients' needs can be disregarded. Maynard (2006) stated that the practical care relationship between physicians and patients is imperfect because physicians often pursue not only their patients' interests but also their preferences for income, leisure, and professional satisfaction. Second, the blind trust of patients in their physician's opinions, which can be viewed as an abuse of power, can put the patient's health in danger (Calnan & Rowe, 2006). Physicians have a comparative advantage due to their knowledge of diagnoses and treatment options in medicine. This asymmetry causes patients to delegate part or all of the decision-making process to the doctor, who becomes an agent of the patient (Maynard, 2006). If the competence of the physicians is insufficient for the care needs of the patient, the patients' blind trust in their physicians can be harmful to their health, which was observed in this research (I-DB-02, 172–181; I-NN-1, 59–60).

Laura Nimmon and Terese Stenfors-Hayes (2016) warned that power is inherently relational and cannot be owned by physicians. Patients must recognize the hierarchal position and legitimate authority of physicians who wield power and be complicit in physicians' strategies for handling power (Nimmon & Stenfors-Hayes, 2016). However, changing the patients' beliefs and attitudes regarding their interactions with authoritative physicians is difficult within a stereotypical patient-physician relationship. The notion of hierarchy in German medical society is prioritized when healthcare is practiced under the logic of power.

The notion of hierarchical medical care can be found in the research data, such as when a home-care nurse is reluctant to contact a diabetologist because of her low hierarchical status as a nurse within the healthcare system (I-NN-06, 362–368). In a hierarchical organization, doctors have traditionally defended their professional autonomy, independence, and professional status within their relationships with other healthcare workers to maintain the hierarchy of health professions (J. McDonald et al., 2012). Nurses, then, are expected to accept this authority and not participate in the decision-making process of patient care.

The traditional hierarchical structure of the healthcare system may work against the development of a partnership between patients and healthcare professionals, resulting in moral distress for nurses (Austin et al., 2005; Gittell, 2009, p. 206; Martin-Rodriguez et al., 2005; J. McDonald et al., 2012). Nurses are considered to be the people who have the most contact with patients and the group in whom patients place the most trust, but focusing on the imbalances of power within nurse-patient relationships may increase the vulnerability and dependency of patients (Dinc & Gastmans, 2013; Robinson, 2016).

The third problem caused by the logic of power is the unequal power distribution among various healthcare professionals. According to the research data, the unequal power distribution within a care team greatly restricts the professional autonomy of non-physician professionals, especially nursing professionals (I-DB-01, 399–413; I-NN-01, 71–79; I-NN-06, 370–383). Nurses are the largest occupational group in healthcare; however, numerical strength does not appear to generate occupational power. The superior educational qualifications of physicians make physicians more valuable in the healthcare system and allow physicians to remain in dominant roles, whereas the replaceability of nursing work subordinates the professional roles of nurses (Miers, 2003b, p. 83; Porter, 2003, p. 102; Thompson et al., 2006, p. 81). Consequently, nurses must follow the orders of their superiors, sometimes against their convictions (Kälvemark et al., 2004; Udlis, 2011).

If power and care decisions are made by physicians, and nurses are expected to be submissive, dutiful, and obedient, then care responsibility should rest with the doctors. However, responsibility for care implementation is an inseparable component of nursing professionalism. As one nurse emphasized, "I am not an order recipient. I have to be responsible for what I do. I have responsibility for the implementation." (I–NN–06, 370–375). Care tensions emerge because nurses are responsible for delivering care but have no corresponding authority for decision-making according to their professional judgments of what represents good care.

The fourth problem that accompanies the logic of power is that patient empowerment is rarely implemented in diabetes management due to the medical hierarchy. Modern healthcare is increasingly characterized by patient-centered rhetoric, in which physicians share power equally in their interactions with patients. The notion of empowerment is then introduced to help patients become more confident in their ability to manage their illness and motivate them to do the hard work of disease management during times of crisis (Fox & Chesla, 2008; Meetoo & Gopaul, 2005; Nimmon & Stenfors-Hayes, 2016).

Empowerment can be applied using diverse approaches and could be viewed as a ploy to shift responsibility for care onto patients or clients, regardless of their situations (Callaghan & Williams, 1994; Meetoo & Gopaul, 2005). This research found that patients are often asked to make the final decisions in caring from the perspective of customer autonomy in the healthcare market, which can make the patients feel empowered to participate in their care procedures and bear responsibility for care outcomes. However, a type of false empowerment may be offered within a hierarchical relationship in which patients are vulnerable, nurses are powerless and lack care competence, and physicians carry authority (Joseph-Williams et al., 2014; Kukla, 2005).

Improving professional autonomy and creating a successful collaboration with a healthcare team requires a change in the current medical society, which operates within the framework of the logic of power. According to the literature, a shift from traditional hierarchical structures towards more horizontal structures is necessary (Martin–Rodriguez et al., 2005). Securing professional positions and balancing responsibilities to improve accountability, regulation, and the management of professional activities has been suggested (Gunnarsdóttir & Rafferty, 2006, p. 188). Understanding and communicating one's contributions to the work performed by other professionals can be helpful (Martin–Rodriguez et al., 2005), and engaging oneself in political decision-making is also recommended (Thompson et al., 2006, p. 187).

Although the concept of shared power represents an overarching goal of modern patient-centered healthcare, this concept does not fully capture the complex situations in which healthcare workers experience, perceive, invoke, and equalize power during encounters in diabetes care when operating under the logic of care. These situations represent future challenges that healthcare professionals must learn to navigate and address.

Summary

Caring for patients with a chronic disease, such as diabetes, embodies an extraordinary range of distinctive meanings and activities, depending on the individual care situation in which humanity and society intertwine. The logic of care is not implemented alone but is often accompanied by other care logic in practice. The logic of choice is focused on the concepts of sovereignty and autonomy; the logic of efficiency is focused on the concepts of regulations and statistics, and the logic of power is focused on legislation and authority; these types of logic work in parallel with the logic of care. Sometimes, these care logics may intensify the implementation of care activities and lead to success. Other times, care frustrations can develop due to the diverse viewpoints of these various care logics, their different understandings of what good care represents, and their dissimilar evaluations of care performance. When different types of care logic are active, care conflicts and ethical dilemmas can develop in response to the misunderstanding of autonomy, hyperfocus on what is normal, disregard for humanity, overemphasis on legislation, and blind trust in authority.

When the logic of care is not properly implemented in care practice, healthcare professionals are likely to encounter various contradictions at multiple levels. When a situation is guided by the logic of choice, healthcare professionals suffer from the combined pressures of ensuring care security, on the one hand, and respecting patient autonomy, on the other hand. Patient sovereignty can become the priority of care. Regulations and standardization are viewed as beneficial for professional care, but humanity can be lost behind statistics when guided by the logic of efficiency. The logic of power emphasizes the legislation used to frame care responsibilities, and medical authority promotes patients' trust in the patient-physician relationships but can erode trust in a patient's relationships with other healthcare professionals. The implementation of empowerment and shared caring could be prohibited within a hierarchical medical society. The blurred boundaries between moral responsibility and legitimate obligation can generate care tensions and conflicts.

Living in a society that is guided by the logic of choice, how should healthcare professionals approach the best interests of the patient when these interests run contrary to the healthcare workers' vision of good care? If healthcare professionals have to provide patients with the opportunity to make decisions, how can healthcare professionals ensure that the patient has sufficient information and the capacity to make decisions freely regarding the treatment of their vulnerable bodies? Working within healthcare institutions that are organized according to the logic of efficiency, how should healthcare professionals implement legitimate regulations designed to fulfill the economic goals of the institution while continuing to respect the needs of humanity? If the regulations standardize care responsibility, how should nurses process their professional awareness of responsibility within healthcare systems guided by the logic of power, in which nurses have neither the legal right nor the authority to make decisions? These questions are worth continued investigation.

Chapter 5: Care Tensions and Ethical Dilemmas

The questions of care are fraught with ethical quandaries. Care activities should be flexibly guided by individual care circumstances, accounting for the needs of both the person receiving care and the person providing care and the time and settings where care occurs. Ambivalence and tensions regarding the notion of care can arise when care occurs within hierarchical and commercial healthcare settings. In this chapter, the three emergent themes identified relative to ethical care dilemmas are illustrated, including autonomy in a vulnerable body, care responsibility without authority, and professionalism around care boundaries.[1]

Autonomy in a Vulnerable Body

Autonomy emphasizes the patients' rights in decision-making processes and their willingness to participate in care activities. An ongoing debate considers whether healthcare professionals should treat their care receivers as customers or as patients and who should make care decisions and take responsibility for those decisions. On the one hand, healthcare workers see themselves as being limited by the business of serving their customers, and on the other hand, they feel obligated by their care ethos to offer therapeutic care to their patients. However, overemphasizing the autonomy of patients who have vulnerable bodies may impede the patients' safety in some cases. A therapeutic relationship with patients appears to be necessary for diabetes care. Patient's autonomy could be limited by health priorities, and coercion can sometimes represent a type of care. Institutional regulations often form a type of judgment in care practice, and care is frequently performed passively when guided by the logic of choice and the logic of efficiency. Tinkering with bodies instead of taming the disease represents an alternative option for rethinking the dilemma of autonomy within a vulnerable body.

---

1   Partial quotes and contents referring to care tensions and ethical dilemmas have previously been published in the book *Care in Healthcare: Reflects on Theory and Practice*. Please see Liu and Kohlen (2018).

Freedom or Control

> Yes, we have a few customers. We have them, and that is probably true. Just like when someone came to me. I would ask him, "How can I help you?" and "What do you need?" (I–DB–01, 703–714)

Whether to treat care receivers as patients or as customers have long been discussed in the context of diabetes care. Within Western society, individuals typically participate in free and self-regulating markets, in which consumers' choices are the dominant values. Care, then, is viewed as the product, and patients are treated as customers. Mol et al. (2010, pp. 9–10) referred to this type of care as "framing care", which refers to care as a product for sale on the market.

Respect for human beings and their dignity and rights are important values in nursing care. Working within the context of a free and self-regulating market can result in these values being ignored, and the focus of nursing care may be transferred instead to the patient's autonomy to make free choices. This transformation, however, can greatly limit the care activities of healthcare professionals in their daily practice. "He [a patient] wants it" (I–NN–06, 100) has become the basis for care decisions, and "I can force nobody to do things" (I–FA–02, 190–193; I–NN–05, 104–105) is often the excuse used by healthcare professionals distance themselves from care circumstances when a diversity of views compete during the decision-making process.

However, patients are people characterized by the vulnerability. The question is, therefore, whether vulnerable patients are capable of making appropriate decisions regarding their disease management and whether healthcare professionals can separate their professional identities from the decision-making process, particularly when the decisions made by patients may result in negative consequences for the patient's health. If care is a matter of respecting patients' choices, are healthcare professionals no longer responsible for the care provided based on decisions made by patients? How should healthcare professionals understand patient autonomy and address the tensions that may develop between freedom and control in their daily practice?

The underlying problem of autonomy in a vulnerable body is the idea that the patients' vulnerability makes them unlikely to make correct decisions for their health. The term patient suggests a person who is a passive recipient of active care or treatment given by another person or agent. The term patient also suggests that the person being cared for is in a dependent state due to their pain or suffering (Kendall et al., 2011; Rogers et al., 2005). Therefore, the patient's right to choose is somewhat paradoxical because the patient is regarded as relatively helpless, and physicians or nurses are presumed to know what is good for them (Paulsen, 2011; Schei, 2006; Thompson et al., 2006, p. 178). Patients have roles to play when addressing their diseases by following the prescribed regimens, and clinicians must acknowledge the patients' roles as patients, not customers.

According to the logic of care, patients are not citizens who have rights and are able to make free choices (Mol et al., 2010, p. 10). Restricted by the sick body, the decisions that diabetes patients can make are limited (Entwistle et al., 2010; Mol, 2008; Spiers, 2003; Stein–Parbury, 2009, p. 247). Based on the literature, patients' vulnerability comes not only from their sick bodies, which limit the options available to them but also from access to fewer resources and less experience (Mol et al., 2010, p. 9). Within the scope of the ethics of care, respect for autonomy offers little guidance to healthcare professionals and merely respecting patient autonomy in decision-making can place a patient in danger (Schei, 2006).

Analyzing the literature and the research findings, the first danger identified associated with autonomy in a vulnerable body is the passivity of care performance. When the right to choose is delegated to the patient, healthcare professionals are left in the passive position of waiting for patients to make decisions and hoping that patients will choose to utilize their care services and products. If patients refuse their care services, a caring relationship may end. The patients' safety may be impeded because the care needs of patients' vulnerable bodies may be ignored. Among healthcare professionals, respect for patient autonomy may stop them from attempting to dissuade patients from making self-defeating decisions when those decisions do not align with the professional echo of advocating for patient safety. When healthcare professionals begin to act passively, they can experience a type of moral distress due to acting against their beliefs regarding what constitutes doing good for their patients.

Viewing healthcare receivers as consumers have resulted in the proliferation of paradoxical and excessively challenging situations in healthcare, undermining the roles of health professionals as patient advocates (Barlow et al., 2018; Gastmans, 2013; B. Pope et al., 2016). Unfortunately, although some healthcare professionals attempt to advise their patients during the decision-making process, advice without power, suggested by either physicians or nurses, rarely leads to successful outcomes (I–FA–02, 190–193; I–NN–05, 104–105).

A certain degree of coercion and control can be necessary in some cases, especially in cases where the patients are too vulnerable to make decisions. Entwistle et al. (2010) noted that patients might feel abandoned rather than autonomous when their clinicians refuse to do more than inform them of their options and insist that they have to choose. A similar finding can be found in this research, as the patient said: "I do not have the strength to decide by myself. I need help" (I–PP–11, 244–246).

Susan Chase (2004) suggested that healthcare professionals that offer a decision that negates the patients' choices can be viewed as beneficial for the patients. The concepts of coercion and control do not mean that patients should be forced to act against their will. Instead, these concepts indicate the need for an open space in which to conduct a dialogue to express a variety of caring interpretations. Even though patients are vulnerable and dependent, they still desire the option of making choices. Without the possibility of making decisions, patients may feel even more vulnerable, which can lead to increased noncompliance (Stein–Parbury, 2009). Consequently, threats to freedom will make patients feel more attracted to doing what they have been forbidden to do (Anderson & Funnell, 2005; Zoffmann & Kirkevold, 2005). Coercion and control among healthcare professionals do not require them to force or forbid their patients to make choices. Instead, coercion and control place the focus on identifying alternative actions and compromises among diverse viewpoints. A nurse described:

> Working with forbidden does not work. So, it only works through the way of enlightenment of the patients. It often works quite well with the help of presenting their blood sugar values. I think it works better this way than when I say to the patients directly that "this and that you are not allowed to eat". And to work with alternatives! We also know through our own experience that prohibitions are connected with something negative. (I–NN–03, 241–250)

The second danger identified in association with autonomy in a vulnerable body is the precarious nature of care responsibility. Understanding the broader concepts of how the principles of autonomy balance the principles of responsibility may equip nurses to better engage in community practice (B. Pope et al., 2016). A care contract[2] designates the roles of care actors, defines the duties of patients and healthcare professionals within a caring relationship, and is often deemed to be the legal foundation of caring in real-world practice situations (I–FA–01, 219–227; I–NN–01, 203–208, 213–226). A well-regulated contract can be described as a commitment in which both the patients and the healthcare professionals agree to participate in caring activities and are prepared to take responsibility for their actions (I–FA–01, 368–379; I–NN–05, 366–381). A physician explained:

> We would not say to patients, "You must now inject insulin". That makes no sense if a patient does not want it. Instead, we have to agree with the patient through communication to convince him, to explain to him clearly why we recommend him something so that he also supports the decision. He has to do it by himself. We give recommendations but do not deal with treatment. Diabetes is a disease that the

---

2 A care contract is a legally binding document that exists within the German healthcare system. A care contract is a written agreement that must be in place before patients can visit a care institute or receive care services. The care contract will outline types of service patients can expect to receive, the fees they will be charged, and other important terms, such as notice periods, cancellation policies, and the complaints procedure.

patients have to take responsibility for the decision and the treatment they made. (I–FA–01, 368–379)

Patients often require expert instruction regarding specific practices, which they must learn and impose upon themselves to be viewed as responsible citizens. Care could, therefore, be performed by forcing patients to fulfill the duties regulated within their care contract. This research finding reinforces the argument in the literature that a choice can only be viewed as a single moment within a given set of practices when the parties involved take responsibility for their commitments. When patients commit to a relationship with healthcare professionals, patients can engage in self-exploration and be able to take responsibility for caring (Kukla, 2005; Ogden et al., 2003).

However, unclear duties and roles for both patients and healthcare professionals can be regulated within a care contract (I–NN–05, 366–381). Care responsibility, in this case, may be transferred from one party to another. Similar to others described in the literature, presents a tense and uncomfortable situation due to contradictions between care and protecting patients' rights. The transfer of responsibility is one method that nurses use to resolve or cope with ethical dilemmas; however, seeking to answer the call of a vulnerable patient who is asking for care represents an essential duty of being a good healthcare professional (Austin et al., 2005; Gastmans, 2013; Hörnsten et al., 2004; Jaworska, 2009; Jormsri et al., 2005; Thompson et al., 2006; Van der Hoff & Buijsen, 2014).

Respect for freedom and the delegation of responsibilities is not only implemented at the level of individual autonomy and self-determination but also at the level of respect for individuals as members of a human community in which everyone is interdependent and interconnected (Kukla, 2005; Jormsri et al., 2005; Thompson et al., 2006, p. 182). When the logic of choice, the logic of efficiency, or the logic of power are driving care, rules and judgment are often embedded into the process of decision-making and can interfere with patient autonomy.

Hidden Rules and Judgement

It's a difficult care situation to care for patients in their own homes. In the clinic, they sign a contract. Therefore, they have to do everything we offer them. But it is different at home. They are the king of the house, and I have to take what they say into account while I am offering care. (I–NN–05, 371–374)

When caring for diabetes patients, respect for patient autonomy may overshadow the potential understanding of patient vulnerability, whereas the overuse of expertise to control a relationship may create an uneven distribution of power. According to the literature, true autonomy does not exist, and a choice does not have to be ideally and perfectly autonomous unless a specific problem with the agent's capacity for autonomy or the adequate conditions of its exercise is identified (Jaworska, 2009; B. Pope et al., 2016). However, identifying specific problems or adequate conditions in care practice can be difficult, particularly when rational rules and moral judgment are embedded within a decision-making process. Analyzing the research data, three hidden rules about patient autonomy were identified, which can be viewed as both prohibiting and promoting patient autonomy.

The first hidden rule refers to the surroundings in which the patients live. Based on the literature, a patient's personal life and their home environment can affect a nurse's state of mind and potentially influence their ability to effectively communicate (Dinc & Gastmans, 2013; Robinson, 2016). This is specific to nurses who provide home care. When caring for patients with diabetes, most patients control their disease outside of healthcare institutions. The research data shows that patient autonomy in the context of home-based care is often intensified because patients are considered the kings of their households. This type of awareness may reinforce patients' power and confidence in decision-making but reduce professional autonomy (I–NN–05, 371–374).

The second hidden rule refers to institutional rules, which highlight how the dominance of discourses fuelled by ideologies of choice can result in the unintended consequence of displacing alternate functions and service provisions that might be better able to meet consumer needs while remaining economically expedient (Kendall et al., 2011). In care practice, patients and healthcare professionals experience limitations due to institutional rules. Time pressure and rigid care rules established by institutions are defined as problematic. Autonomy is, therefore, not always available to care actors other than patients and physicians. As a diabetes assistant claimed:

> I often see diabetes patients who inject insulin who have black dots on their skin because they do not change the needles in their insulin pens regularly. If I do not suffer from time pressure, I will ask them how often they change the needle. Then, I can arrange a small consultation with them at the same time. But I do not have this time. (I–DA–01, 246–254)

The third hidden rule is related to the emphasis on a therapeutic relationship between patients and healthcare professionals. According to the research data, within a therapeutic relationship in which the duties and responsibilities of each party have been established, patients are often requested to change something to achieve a medical good instead of following their desires. Healthcare professionals have to prevent their patients from making self-defeating decisions and guide their patients toward correct behaviors during disease management (BG–DB1–01, p. 3). Patient autonomy becomes a less important issue for a practical care agenda.

The literature indicated that clinician-patient relationships require more than customer service oriented by the customers' decisions, and patient autonomy in decision-making may be transferred away from the patients and into the hands of healthcare professionals and institutions (Thompson et al., 2006, p. 187; Torpie, 2014). Within clinician-patient relationships, this transfer of power is often the result of both the patient giving the decision-making power to healthcare professionals willingly and the decision-making power being taken from patients by powerful healthcare professionals. Caring for diabetes patients is much more than merely treating disease, often involving individual emotions and the impacts of society. Rather than focusing on restricting patient autonomy, the meaning of autonomy and its effects within a therapeutic relationship should be addressed more broadly when caring for patients with a chronic disease.

When discussing autonomy in a vulnerable body, the hidden judgment of good or bad decisions made by either patients or healthcare professionals can be revealed. Analyzing the research data, a focus on decision-making can create judgment embedded with blame for both patients and healthcare professionals. A patient that makes a wrong choice can be identified as problematic (Kendall et al., 2011). According to Agnieszka Jaworska (2009), choices based on a miscalculation may represent a failed attempt to express one's authentic self in one's actions or reflect conflicting wayward desires or emotions, and judgment of these choices can result in blame. As the research finding presented, a doctor may blame a patient who cannot comply with medical regimens; a nurse may blame a doctor who fails to respond to her, a patient who is noncompliant, or herself for a failure to do more for her patient; a patient may blame a doctor who cannot handle the disease properly, lack confidence in their decision-making abilities due to conflicting priorities, or anticipate self-blame if outcomes are poor (I–DB–02, 155–156; I–NN–01, 110–111; I–NN–03; 112–116; I–PP–03, 72–78; I–PP–05, 127–133; I–PP–08, 110–113).

Making choices associated with judgment often leads to moral tensions. The greatest difficulty in nursing work occurs when an ethical choice is clear, but the implementation of the morally acceptable action is thwarted. Sometimes nurses have to do things for the patient's benefit even though they are not aligned with their moral viewpoint or the institutional rules (Austin et al., 2005; Kälvemark et al., 2004). Both the literature and the research data suggested that nursing care in such situations is not a matter of determining what is the right thing to do but instead is a matter of determining what is the possible thing to do. As one nurse illustrated:

> It is not my job to motivate my patients now and say, "Oh, come on, you will still have a good health condition in ten years". I do not give patients any euthanasia, but I can make them feel comfortable so that the patients in their last living years still can do what they like to do and can still enjoy life. (I–NN–05, 358–361)

Care, according to Kukla (2005), could be properly established by healthcare professionals responding to the needs of their patients rather than attempting to force patients to perform care activities or pressing freedom on them. In this case, ensuring the quality of the patient's life is more valuable to the nurse than prolonging the patient's life. She reinforced the importance of humanity by describing "the patients in their last living years still can do what they like to do and enjoy life". However, this nurse can also be viewed as pushing care responsibility away, as she said, "It is not my job to motivate my patients".

Healthcare professionals are never totally free from making decisions during their caring work, nor are they prevented from passing judgments about what is good or bad or what is right or wrong, based on the literature and the research data. Investigating a person's capacity for critical reflection be more useful in a care situation than offering rational criticism because care practice is changeable and unpredictable. As Mol (2009) illustrated, care activities cannot always unfold according to plan because contingencies and surprises always occur, and a wise choice made at a single, crucial moment might not be suitable at another time when trying to control a body suffering from a disease. In healthcare, care should be approached as a matter of tinkering bodies rather than taming disease. Celebrating patient autonomy or focusing on their obligations in care situations are inappropriate responses when caring for patients with diabetes. Instead, concern for relationships, a focus on situations, and cooperation among individuals and collectives may offer opportunities for care improvement.

Taming Disease Versus Tinkering Bodies

> I never rebuke my patients because I often feel that they are forced to come here and are pushed to show their blood glucose values. When a patient said to me that "Oh, this is my HbA1c", this is for me like we got a lecture earlier at the school. I did not like to lecture my patients, and neither wanted them to feel that they got a lecture when they came to me. Instead, I would like to try one more time with the patients in another way, such as asking them, "Why did it not work out?" and "Do you want it to get better?" It's not my disease management. Therefore, the patients themselves must want to do it, and then we can take a look at where is the difficulty and why is it difficult. (I–DB–02, 41–47)

Care practice is full of conflicts between rationality and emotion, contradictions between theory and practice, and diversity between individuals and the collective. Similarly, freedom and control over medical decisions alone do not constitute patient autonomy within the framework of hidden rules and judgment. Patients do not benefit when the uneven potential and power are disguised in discourses about patients' rights and autonomy or those that portray the patients as consumers of care who appear to have the freedom to choose.

Care should not focus merely on taming and controlling the disease but should also integrate the values of the individual and the collective, which allows all parties to critically assess their own values, determine desirable outcomes upon reflection, and initiate actions to realize their desires by compromising values and integrating with society depending on the care situation. This process is referred to as tinkering. In the words of Mol et al. (2010, p. 13), "seeking a compromise between different 'goods' can be a matter of practical tinkering, of attentive experimentation."

Tinkering bodies is rooted in concern for care relationships. The relationship with patients usually has a value beyond that of caring instrumentally for medical needs in medical settings (Gastmans, 2013; Schei, 2006; Van Heijst, 2011). Tinkering bodies places a focus on situations. Rather than focusing on the decision-making process, Mol (2009) established that it might help to look at what happened in practice. From the perspective of patients, patients' suffering and vulnerability are associated with situational, developmental, and illness-related events and connote universal needs (Weaver et al., 2008). According to the logic of care, the good is not something to pass judgment on, in general terms and from the outside, but something to do in practice as care continues (Mol et al., 2010, p. 13).

Analyzing the literature and adding the contributions collected during this research indicates that tinkering bodies occur differently depending on situations, the values of individuals (involving personal feelings and exceptions), and the common good within a collective. Tinkering bodies presents a dynamic movement that is mediated not only by patients but also by healthcare professionals. Inserting personal experience into a care situation can offer support for healthcare professionals to empathize with their patients during the process of tinkering. Concern for the needs of both the individual and the collective is expected during tinkering. Sometimes, the general concept of good care must be abandoned to treat patients individually in response to each circumstance that occurs.

Dealing with feelings was identified in this research as an important element for tinkering bodies. The psychological loads experienced during day-to-day disease management may reduce the motivation of patients to engage themselves in caring activities. Healthcare professionals often have to care for and care with patients who are non-compliant, which can generate care frustrations and care fatigue (See Understanding the Disease). However, noncompliance and carelessness are different problems, and non-compliant patients may be those who are the most vulnerable and experience the most anxiety regarding the management of their disease. Addressing the emotional suffering of patients instead of blaming them is important in a caring relationship.

To be able to tinker with bodies, various strategies can be applied in care practice. For example, placing focus on patients' quality of life, attempting to empathize with patients, motivating patients to engage in care, motivating patients to reflect on their health values, and identifying resolutions together with patients can be viewed as strategies for tinkering bodies in care practice (I-DB-01, 721–733; I-DB-02, 41–47).

The literature suggests that healthcare professionals should act as curious listeners who can invite patients to reflect on their concerns or as compassionate stranger who can touch the patient's experience but remain distant enough to maintain professional objectivity (Kohlen, 2009; Robinson, 2016). Whether healthcare professionals can play roles as curious listeners within the framework of the logic of efficiency and whether healthcare professionals can distance themselves appropriately and serve as compassionate strangers without disrupting their trust relationships with patients within the framework of the logic of power remain unclear. In addition, society and the healthcare system often restrict patients and their healthcare professionals from performing emotional work (Liaschenko, 2001).[3]

The process of tinkering in real practice is strongly influenced by legislation and the construction of the medical society. Tinkering bodies is not just a task for patients but is a mission that healthcare professionals have to learn. Healthcare professionals have to tinker with their care activities by continuing to try new approaches, being flexible, empathizing, and responding to the needs of patients by tailoring to the individual and society. However, working within a medical society in which medical power and patient autonomy take precedence can make tinkering bodies challenging for both patients and healthcare professionals in care practice (I-DA-01, 268–282).

Collectives cannot be eliminated from the process of tinkering bodies because caring activities are always entangled with others, and care for patients with diabetes requires social resources and support. As Joseph Selling (1999) claimed, the needs and desires of the individual can be confronted with the needs and desires of others. When dealing with the collective, tinkering bodies allows healthcare professionals to identify compromises within the framework of rigid institutional and medical rules. As one physician said, "I have to think of the business-like station and its customer orientation, but I am trying to do things as much as possible at the medical level" (I-FA-01, 241–243). A more flexible organizational space in which decision-making depends on situational circumstances and is based on a broader set of relationships is necessary (Bachmann, 2003; Tronto, 2009).

Care requires viewing each situation individually rather than following institutional regulations or the normative concept of good espoused by care and ethical theories. Moving from individualism to care based on relationality, from passive care to

---

3   Joan Liaschenko (2001) noticed that emotional work is invisible in a product-driven society, and nurses may view emotional work as extra, outside of their official work responsibilities, which are shaped by institutionalised medicine.

mutual concern, and from control to respect for vulnerability and values is becoming increasingly vital in the context of diabetes care. Rather than taming the disease, tinkering bodies is caring for humanity by concentrating on care situations and connections with the collective to better support healthcare professionals in addressing care tensions caused by autonomy in a vulnerable body, particularly when the frameworks of the logic of choice, the logic of efficiency, and the logic of power are used to orient medical society.

Summary

The first care tension and ethical dilemma revealed in this research is autonomy in vulnerable bodies. It refers to the ambivalence when healthcare workers see themselves as limited by the business of serving their customers but feel obliged by their care ethos to offer therapeutic care to patients.

When the logic of choice is prioritized, the value of freedom and control is embedded in care activities. Often, care performance can become passive because healthcare workers are waiting for their patients to make decisions and hoping their patients choose their care services. If their patients refuse their care services, the care relationship may end. The hidden rules may additionally influence the implantation of caring. Patients' safety may be impeded because the care needs for patients' vulnerable bodies may be ignored, resulting in a struggle for the healthcare workers who are weighing patients' health against patient autonomy in this situation.

The judgment of good or bad may be embedded within the contradiction of performing care according to the patient's wishes, which may be humanitarian but may not be in their best interests. Finally, care responsibility may be avoided in an evasive way. Whether patients are capable of making care decisions due to their vulnerability and whether healthcare workers can avoid care responsibility must be considered.

Approaching a chronic disease by attempting to control or forbid actions is unlikely to result in success. Rather than taming the disease, attempting to tinker bodies is recommended for diabetes management, which focuses on care situations, is concerned about care relationships, seeks compromises between different ideas of good, and provides institutional space to make exceptions.

Care activities cannot always unfold according to plan, and a wise choice made at a single, crucial moment might not be suitable to control a body suffering from disease throughout the entire disease process. From the perspective of tinkering, patients' autonomy can sometimes be limited by health priorities, and coercion can sometimes be viewed as a type of care.

Care Responsibility Without Authority

Both care decisions and care activities are associated with responsibility and authority. Although care responsibility is a worthy value in healthcare, an uneven distribution of power associated with medical authority in healthcare can have an invisible impact on the representation of responsibility within a care team. Ethical dilemmas associated with responsibility without authority were described by some healthcare workers in this research, especially nurses.

Nurses regularly have responsibility for care implementation and the well-being of patients but have only slight authority in administering care therapies. The caring work performed by nurses runs the risk of being reduced to the execution of orders. A nurse might see a patient's needs and might feel responsible for them, but ultimately, the nurse is required to execute a physician's decisions or follow strict quality manuals. Moral competence is, consequently, restricted by a lack of legal competence.

Within an authority-based and hierarchical medical relationship, trust and power within a care team are closely related but care responsibility can become poorly defined. The overruled duties and responsibilities may sometimes result in the allocation of blame, and the restricted capacity of professional autonomy can generate moral distress. By sharing care responsibilities instead of placing blame, healthcare professionals in practice have the opportunity to change these relationships.

Trust or Power

> Doctors have a very high value in their position. I have recently found a sentence quite funny. It is, "The cheapest, the best, and side-effect-free medicine are doctors themselves". And that is why it is so important for a diabetes training course that a doctor takes part in it. Dr. Mayer from our department is not great, but he is a doctor. Then, he has a different authority over the patients. (I–DA–01, 495–499)

Power and trust are intertwined. Trust is a foundational component of every relationship and can be characterized as an attitude of confidence in someone and refers to imbalances of power in relationships (De Raeve, 2002a; Dinc & Gastmans, 2013; Maynard, 2006; Rørtveit et al., 2015). An uneven power distribution, associated with mistrust and hierarchy in German diabetes care practice, was noticed within both patient-physician relationships and physician-nurse relationships.

In German hierarchical medical care, trust and authority are customarily intertwined, based on both the literature and the current research findings. In care practice, the invisibility and authority of physicians also influence the patient-nurse relationship subtly but powerfully. Patients' blind trust in physicians can often be observed in care practice. The visible nurse is less trusted and less powerful than physicians but is held responsible for the implementation of care (See The Logic of Power). The research data suggest that this can result in the development of mistrust within the patient-nurse relationship, the patient-physician relationship, or the nurse-physician relationship due to a perceived lack of competence, the uneven power distribution associated with hierarchy and authority, and the lack of response and personal attachment (I-NN-03, 685-691; I-NN-04, 350-352).

In the literature, patients' powerlessness does not appear only within the patient-physician relationships but can also present within a nurse-patient relationship. Within these power-based relationships, the most vulnerable one has the potential to be neglected or abused, particularly within an ethical relationship in which care is provided by a paid caretaker (Barlow et al., 2018). In this research, nursing power was rarely discussed within the patient-nurse relationship. Instead, trust-based relationships appeared to play a more central role, which may be due to both patients and nurses having less power overall within the framework of German medical care, as both are at lower positions within the hierarchy compared with other healthcare workers.

According to Rogers et al. (2005), many decisions within a care team are decided by physicians who believe that decision-making is their role and responsibility alone. This view of physicians allows patients to abandon their care responsibilities when patients prefer paternalistic relationships with their doctors (Rogers et al., 2005). However, many patients desire a more open and equal relationship with their medical staff (Rogers et al., 2005), which represents a contradiction. This ambivalence was also presented in this research. Although patients desired their voices to be heard, they have less confidence in making decisions or talking with their doctors, especially when the decisions concern medical treatment. The patients are afraid of making the wrong decisions, and consequently, the patients often choose to obey what their doctors say and push care responsibilities away from themselves.[4]

This care model can introduce problems when caring for patients with diabetes. First, the illusion of controlling diabetes care by professionals is often based on the use of an acute-care paradigm to measure diabetes disease. This type of disease control, however, is a testimony to the power of paradigms and is often not appropriate for chronic illness (Anderson & Funnell, 2005). Second, this model may attempt to control patients rather than relate to them as individuals (Thompson et al., 2006, p. 190). Third, the use of power and control was often observed in healthcare professionals' behavior, whereas collaboration and support were either not present or inadequate (Fox & Chesla, 2008). Patients who encounter this type of relationship may

---

4   The related discussion and quotes from the current research associated with this issue are presented in The Logic of Power and Freedom or Control.

experience alienation, helplessness, hopelessness, oppression, paternalism, dependency, and a loss of control over their lives (Fox & Chesla, 2008).

Doctors read the patient, the story, and the body, so patients always engage in reverse to read and interpret the physicians, judging whether they appear interested in caring for the patient as a unique person (Schei, 2006). This argument reflects the importance of responding within a trusting relationship and places emphasis on personal attachments. Responding to patients has deep personal significance and can bond patients to their healthcare professionals when a trust relationship is built. As one nurse illustrated in this research, patients' trust can be earned by paying more attention to the patients and taking their demands seriously (I–NN–03, 515–517). By responding to patients, nurses can insert their influence on patient care.

In nursing care, offering an intensive bond with the patients can support the building of a trusting relationship between nurses and patients within a rigid medical society (I–DB–01, 417–422; I–PP–07, 394–397). A patient reasoned it as "because they come to me every day and ask me how I am and what I need" (I–PP–07, 397). Nurses appear to have some power within the trust relationship when nursing care intensively bonds nurses and patients together. In the words of Ian Thompson, the culture of trust or distrust within a ward team may have a great deal to do with how much or how little power or scope nurses have, both individually and collectively, to negotiate care provision (Thompson et al., 2006, p. 86). The question is then, are nurses aware of their power within the trust relationships they form with their patients? Is this type of trust relationship between nurses and patients powerful enough to support nurses in acting according to their professional goals? If not, how do nurses address the care dilemmas that arise when they are powerless to act according to their own beliefs and professional echoes regarding what is best for patients?

Unfortunately, the current healthcare environment for nurses is almost always a sense of responsibility without authority, and nurses' moral competence is strongly restricted by their legal rights. Although nurses are asked to take responsibility, their power in decision-making is limited. Nurses described this tension in terms of "doctors have the last words", "nurses are dealt a bad hand", and "your hands are tied" when diversity in decision-making opinions occurs between physicians and nurses (I–NN–03, 687; I–NN–06, 418–429). Nurses feel obligated to advocate for their patients when they observe something inappropriate to their sense of good care. However, nurses have neither the legal right to make medical decisions nor the professional power to negotiate with physicians. A nurse described a care difficulty in her care practice as follows:

> There are always the same doctors, arrogant snobs, who think they know everything, and I am the stupid one. With them, I can only suggest my patients change their family doctors. You have to call some family doctors more than ten times be-

> fore they do something for their patients, even when the patients' conditions are bad. It is the same circumstance at nursing homes. One time, I called a doctor four times on the same day and requested him to take a look at a patient in a station where he was in charge. The fifth time I called him, I told him that I did not take responsibility anymore. Then, he came. This seems the way to let him be aware of his duty. (I–NN–06, 431–439)

This quote reveals a distrusting relationship between the nurse, the physician, and the patient; although the nurse advised her patient to change physicians when the nurse could not respond to her patient's problem and ensure her patient's safety, she relegated the responsibility to the physician. Although the nurse said that she would no longer accept responsibility, a conflict may have developed with her professional echoes because the nurse believed that both she and the physician are required to do something good for the patient. Wendy Austin and her colleagues (2005) noted that when nurses experience moral distress, they frequently find themselves in the middle of conflicts caused by the tension between the powerful institutions and administrators that employ them and the patients with whom they engage. From the nurses' perspective, this ethical dilemma arises because nurses lack the authority to act on their own, exercise their judgment, take initiative, and go against doctors (Malloy et al., 2009).

Improving nursing power in care practice is essential. Milisa Manojilovich (2007) stated that nurses' power might arise from three components: a workplace that has the requisite structures to promote empowerment; a psychological belief in one's ability to be empowered; and the acknowledgment that power exists in the relationships and care that nurses provide. Questions arise regarding how the nursing profession acts within a workplace framed by legal rules and institutional regulations, how nurses identify their duties and responsibilities, how responsibilities are determined within the framework of medical duties, how healthcare professionals recognize the pervasiveness of moral dilemmas and understand the inherent effects of these dilemmas on care practice, and how they address the impacts of bearing responsibility without authority.

Invisible Duties and Responsibilities

> There are many frustrations for the patient as well as for the doctors during diabetes management. A lot of blame often accompanies frustration. The doctor blames the patient who does not want to lose his body weight. The patient blames the doctor that the doctor cannot handle his disease properly. These are conflicting situations in which one must always be careful and prevent oneself from going into the situations. (I–DB–01, 167–175)

Overruled duties and responsibilities that are not clearly assigned may sometimes result in the assignment of blame, and the restricted capacity of professional autonomy can cause moral distress among healthcare professionals. Analyzing the research data, clear distinctions between duties and responsibilities within care relationships between patients and healthcare professionals can be difficult to determine. Within the scope of broader economic and rational thought, Elizabeth Kendall and her colleagues (2011) noticed that individuals are responsible for both their successes and failures, and healthcare decisions are assumed by customers to be voluntary, desirable, and effective. The individual who chooses poor health is then labeled irresponsible (Kendall et al., 2011). The assignment of blame may be revealed by debates regarding care responsibilities. As the patients said, "You cannot blame anyone if you reject to do what your doctor suggested" (I–PP–03, 364–372), or "I will blame myself if I eat and drink [against the care principles]" (I–PP–11, 118–121).

According to the literature, patients often feel judged and blamed for not following the advice provided by healthcare professionals, even when that advice involves lifestyle changes that are very difficult to implement and sustain (Anderson, 1995; Anderson & Funnell, 2005; Tronto, 2009). When patients are asked to take responsibility for their bodies, do they have to assume all responsibility for care outcomes, even when those outcomes are negative? How should a patient respond to situations in which the patient follows all of the prescribed care principles but the care outcome remains undesirable? Is the patient still responsible for an undesired care outcome, or is the patient free from blame because the patient did nothing wrong? An excessive focus on responsibilities and the assignment of blame remains problematic in caring for and with patients with diabetes.

The current problems in healthcare and nursing care, according to the literature, are partly due to an organizational system that appears to ascribe too many duties and too much responsibility to both team members and patients (Jormsri et al., 2005; Redman, 2005). However, overruled duties and responsibilities may greatly restrict nursing professional autonomy. Bearing too much responsibility may be exhausting for healthcare professionals and can lead to the development of shame and mistrust (Allen et al., 2016; Holm & Severinsson, 2014). A sense of failure to assume moral responsibility and moral distress may arise when nurses believe that something is wrong but are limited by their work capacity (Holm & Severinsson, 2014; Lindh et al., 2007; Peter & Liaschenko, 2013; Pill et al., 1999).

Nurses rarely make decisions about patients' treatment modalities on their own and constantly require advice or authorization for clinical decisions or are required to obey clinical protocols and nursing paradigms. Consequently, nursing work often becomes routine work (Anderson & Funnell, 2005; Barlow et al., 2018; Kangasniemi et al., 2015; Miers, 2003b, p. 94; Varcoe et al., 2012). The research data reinforces this assumption. Nurses admitted that they are often performing routine work tailored merely to biomedical therapy because alternative definitions exist for the roles and responsibilities of nursing (I–NN–02, 569–584).

However, working according to routine can produce problems in healthcare. First, constrained indicators, such as reduced contact time and physician discretion, may impinge negatively on care relationships with patients (Allen et al., 2016). Working by routine may also threaten the primary roles of nurses, which are often focused on a holistic approach to care and involve weighing several occasionally conflicting motivators within care relationships (Butts & Rich, 2008, p. 56). The focus on biomedical discourse, consequently, can prevent the consideration of other important values in healthcare (Nortvedt et al., 2008; Trapani & Cassar, 2016; Weaver, 2007), and patients may, therefore, be treated as cases (Kohlen, 2009, p. 144). Even when nurses attempt to act in a position of dual agency with patients and doctors, their interdependency makes their actions difficult because of different levels of authority within relationships (Robb & Greenhalgh, 2006; Trapani & Cassar, 2016).

In nursing care practice, nurses can have difficulty making clear distinctions between legal duties and moral responsibilities during their caring work and clarifying who has responsibility for what, whom, and why. Instead of arranging duties and responsibilities, shared care may be better arranged through team cooperation. As one nurse described, "I know where the limitation of my competence is and where I am not allowed to do things. Then, it is the point where the doctor has to hand over the caring work" (I–NN–06, 440–444).

Recognizing their limitations does not mean that nurses can separate themselves from taking responsibility. Care responsibilities and care activities can shift dynamically depending on the situation. At any given moment, nurses may act as care-doers and be responsible for care implementation, and at other moments, they may turn to act as mediators for their patients, responsible for coordinating care activities with other healthcare professionals.

When caring for chronic disease, arguing about the arrangement of care responsibilities or assigning blame does not contribute to success. However, accountability may empower healthcare professionals to ensure patients' values and protect patients' rights. Providing the best care has practical limitations, and diabetes care should be approached as patient-centered care, in which healthcare professionals and patients work collaboratively and share care responsibilities. Within this type of care model, according to Robert Anderson and Martha Funnell (2005), "no single one of us can bring about a paradigm shift, but we can accept responsibility for working toward that end." Instead of allocating blame or arranging duties during caring work, shared care and responsibilities should be applied, especially in the context of caring for and with patients with diabetes.

Blame Allocation Versus Shared Responsibility

> What is most important for a good collaboration is that everyone accepts the decision of others. And what is the most difficult for achieving a good collaboration is that all three parties, including patients, doctors, and nurses, have a consensus....Surely, everyone has his interest. But we work together. Therefore, we have to find out a compromise while conflicts with others are arising. (I–NN–01, 96–104)

Many of the tensions and sources of conflicts within a healthcare team may be due to a lack of clarity regarding the scope of responsibilities associated with the roles being performed by various members or a lack of clarity regarding which rules apply and who is responsible to whom for what. The overruled roles and duties may adversely restrict the performance of care activities by nurses in many care situations. Care practice is full of restrictions, such that responsibilities, duties, and rights become intertwined, and individuals become unable to separate them into single objects in reality. Deciding what actions are good or bad for patients is not something that healthcare professionals can do for their patients. Arguing about who is responsible for whom cannot lead to success in diabetes care.

Clarifying care responsibility and allocating blame is less useful to care work than shared caring and shared responsibility. In the literature, patients can be encouraged to be active participants by sharing doctoring and care responsibilities with their healthcare professionals, which is recommended for diabetes care (Duttweiler, 2007; Mol, 2008, p. 65). Within relationships in which caring and responsibility are shared, the literature highlighted partnerships and collaborative relationships (Fox & Chesla, 2008; Ponte et al., 2007; Dwarswaard et al., 2016), dynamic processes (Mol, 2008), committed consent (Tronto, 2009), and the interdisciplinary shifting of clinical, political, and organizational power (Hakesley-Brown & Malone, 2007).

Analyzing the literature and the current research findings, shared caring and responsibility in the context of diabetes care can be expanded and identified in terms of addressing failures and learning from mistakes, establishing an interdisciplinary and communicated collaboration, building a transparent commitment involving ethical considerations, sharing experiences for humanity, and being aware of the power and shared power.

Care situations are always changing and unpredictable. Within the logic of care, judging one's life should be avoided, and failures are allowed (Mol, 2008, p. 87). Shared care, from this perspective, involves attending to suffering and pain and addressing unfolding tensions and shifting problems. Finding someone to blame and determining who is responsible is unnecessary in a shared care practice. Instead, addressing failure is a more important task that healthcare professionals must learn to practice. Rather than punishment, Mol suggested allowing people to feel safe enough to examine what is going wrong and why it is important (Mol, 2008, p. 60). Asking "What is it difficult to do?" can help both patients and healthcare professionals more than instilling feelings of guilt when something goes wrong (Mol, 2008, p. 101).

Moving away from a vertical hierarchy is necessary to facilitate a collaborative and multidisciplinary care practice. Establishing an intensive collaboration with the healthcare team can be viewed as the foundation for the process of shared care and responsibilities. To create an efficient collaboration, the focus must be shifted away from historical and gendered roles and professional silos, in which each healthcare professional acts as an independent practitioner, to instead foster contributions to the work of the team. Each member of the team must honor a common commitment, share goals, cooperate with communities, and focus on performance, positive intent, and mutual respect and the settings in which each individual works.[5]

To achieve this goal, patients must also actively participate in the process of their disease management. Diabetes control depends on the patients, and the responsibility for making self-management decisions and living with their consequences also rests with patients. Patients are, therefore, viewed as the primary actors in managing their health, and they must be willing to create a partnership with their healthcare professionals (Anderson & Funnell, 2005). Being an active patient also means realizing their limitations in professional care, trusting their care professionals, openly discussing their daily efforts related to diabetes care, expressing their disagreements with healthcare professionals, asserting their own needs or values related to the treatment, and accepting help from their care professionals (Duttweiler, 2007; Mol, 2008; B. Pope et al., 2016; Shirley, 2007).

For healthcare professionals, this type of relationship means that they must be certain of what should be done and what is worth doing, regardless of who should do it (Barlow et al., 2018; Mol, 2008). Healthcare professionals must be willing to provide support until patients attain a full understanding of their disease management responsibilities and can integrate disease management techniques into their daily lives (Anderson & Funnell, 2005; Maio, 2009; Raspe, 1999). Healthcare professionals must shift from feeling responsible for patients to feeling accountable to patients (Anderson & Funnell, 2005). Healthcare professionals should act as collaborators and support patients in making the best possible care decisions based on the patients' health priorities and goals (Mol, 2008).

Working within a cooperative team is often described as an action that can create safety and offer support for many healthcare professionals (Butts & Rich, 2008, p. 58;

---

5   References can be found in the literature by Barlow et al. (2018), Kangasniemi et al. (2015), Manski-Nankervis et al. (2014), McKee et al. (2006), Mol (2008), B. Pope et al. (2016), Shirley (2007), and Tol et al. (2015). The current research findings are presented in Patients' Needs in Diabetes Care and The Logic of Care.

McKee et al., 2006; Palviainen et al., 2003). When healthcare professionals recognize their limitations and boundaries in caring, finding support from their collaborative team can provide them with a level of reassurance during patient care (I–NN–05, 474–477, 494–495).

To establish effective cooperation, good communication within a care team cannot be ignored. Without good communication, a mistrustful relationship or misunderstandings in caring can develop. As an example, one patient told me that she tried to explain to her family doctor that she was fine not because of the medication the doctor prescribed but because she refused to take the medications prescribed by him (I–PP–08, 307–309). Without communication, the doctor would never understand how his patient controlled her disease. He might never recognize his mistakes in providing her with prescriptions and think that everything is fine. The patient may lose her trust in her doctor because she does not use the medication her doctor prescribes. Poor outcomes may lead the patient to blame her doctor because he gave her the wrong medication, and the doctor may blame his patient because she failed to take the medication he prescribed. Care conflicts and the assignment of the blame can occur.

Corresponding to this research finding, many studies in the literature highlighted the importance of an open and direct dialogue that occurs frequently and timely and is accurate and problem-solving rather than blaming to effectively balance competing responsibilities and enhance self-awareness of the conflicts related to ongoing and distressing professional vulnerabilities (Havens et al., 2010; Holm & Severinsson, 2014; Matziou et al., 2014; Ramvi, 2015; Robinson, 2016). Unfortunately, the research findings also indicated that this type of dialogue in care practice is often lacking due to time pressures and the authoritarian nature of modern medical care. Even though all healthcare professionals realized the importance of communication and sometimes attempted to address conflicts between different professionals, arranging efficient communication was difficult in many cases.[6] Many conflicts, especially those associated with issues of moral distress, as reported by Kälvemark et al. (2004), can only be discussed during coffee breaks in a very informal manner at care institutions.

Building a transparent commitment involving ethical considerations was identified as an important element during the process of shared caring and responsibilities. Both the literature and the current research demonstrated that many clinical professionals agreed that contracts formed between healthcare workers and patients should become explicit rather than implicit in their roles.[7] Making a contract

---

6   The care problems caused by a lack of communication are presented in Limitations in Practice.

7   The related references can be found in the literature by Barlow et al. (2018), Callaghan & Williams (1994), Holm & Severinsson (2014), McKee et al. (2013, pp. 98–99), Rogers et al.

that is concrete and transparent, takes people's experiences in diabetes seriously, and incorporates these experiences into care plans can be useful for building a partnership that features shared responsibility.

Committing oneself and accepting responsibility involves not only doing what one is responsible for doing but also a willingness to stand by that commitment (Kukla, 2005). By committing, the one who is committed is not only empowered to do things but is ready to take responsibility for the outcomes. When mistakes occur, the act of assigning blame places focus on identifying the failures of others. However, someone who has committed themselves to a regulated contract with a concrete purpose may rethink and reflect on a situation with a committed responsibility.

During the process of shared care and responsibilities, sharing experiences while respecting humanity is essential. All healthcare actors have to discover the values or norms that define good care and share their condition of vulnerability (Van Heijst, 2011). Therefore, healthcare professionals, whose attitudes impact patient care, must be supported in extending their shared expertise when working with those who have chronic illnesses, viewing the patient as part of the healthcare team, and treating the patient's condition-specific biomedical knowledge as a valuable resource, not a threat (Snow et al., 2013).

In the context of diabetes care, the shared experience can enhance the trust relationships that form between healthcare professionals and patients by providing patients with emotional support and building their confidence in living with their chronic condition (Dinc & Gastmans, 2013; Dwarswaard et al., 2016). To share experiences with patients, healthcare professionals should be aware of patients' unvoiced needs, including the emotional aspects of living with a chronic condition; listen to patients with sympathy to understand the patient's suffering; demonstrate care and tolerance; display a genuine and respectful attitude; accept patients' cultures, lifestyles, and decisions without pre-judgment; provide good advice, reassurance, and encouragement; and build a relationship based on partnership (Dinc & Gastmans, 2013; Dwarswaard et al., 2016; Robinson, 2016; Walker, 2003, p. 182).

In care practice, being aware of the power and shared power is advocated because professionals with less power are not always able to offer good care within a medical society in which uneven power distribution is embedded. The exercise of collaborative power[8] in the negotiated order of healthcare services between physicians and nurses could sometimes be observed. Although nurses recognized their

---

    (2005), and Shaw (2006), and relevant examples from the current research are described in Patients' Needs in Diabetes Care and The Logic of Care.

8   Instead of controlling agendas and hierarchies, collaborative power is concerned with broadening access to the network and adapting one's own preferences to better communicate with the network and move towards the centre of the network (Slaughter, 2011).

powerlessness in making medical decisions, pressuring physicians by urging team communication and collaboration provide nurses with an avenue for improving care outcomes (I-NN-04, 386-394). When nurses attempt to use collaborative power by informing physicians of their patient's conditions, the nurses may maintain the credibility and legitimacy of nursing care. According to Nadia Robb and Trisha Greenhalgh (2006), the nursing role in these types of cases is to serve as a link, mediator, and negotiator between physicians and patients. These nursing roles are important in healthcare because nurses are the only group who knows both languages and belongs to both the healthcare system and the lifeworld of patients (Robb & Greenhalgh, 2006).

Sharing power is an overarching goal that many healthcare workers appropriately seek to achieve in modern patient-centered healthcare; unfortunately, both the literature and the research data highlighted that physicians often fail to modify their identities to accommodate the nursing profession and continue to wield their power through the cultural and symbolic capital legitimized by the institution of medicine.

Medical authority continues to impact the care relationships that develop within the German healthcare society, and many healthcare professionals lack any training or experience with sharing power, which can make implementing shared care and responsibilities within a care team difficult. To implement change, Kohlen (2009) examined the micro-policy sphere and proposed that care is practiced well when the expertise and competencies of healthcare professionals are provided and require permissive institutional conditions that are associated with the responsibilities of healthcare politics (Kohlen, 2009, p. 134).

Although changing the historical stereotypes and hierarchies that currently guide the authoritarian German healthcare system can be difficult, being aware of the power and understanding how power affects care relationships and practice can be considered the first step towards improvement. According to Nimmon and Stenfors–Hayes (2016), those who are aware of this power strategically share, exert, moderate, and relinquish power in response to situational contexts to best meet the needs of the patients. Based on the recommendations in the literature and the concepts learned from the current research, healthcare actors, including physicians, nurses, and patients, must be able to recognize that power is inescapable, understand how power affects their relationships and care practices, and make professional power more explicit and visible, especially for the nursing profession.[9]

---

9   The related references can be found in the literature by Broer et al. (2012), Kohlen (2009), Manojilovich (2007), and Nimmon & Stenfors-Hayes (2016). The current research findings are presented in Other Care Logics in Practice.

Summary

The second tension and ethical dilemma discussed in this section is care responsibility without authority. It refers to the contradictions which exist within a healthcare environment when individuals experience care responsibility without authority, and moral competence is strongly restricted by legal rights. This ethical dilemma is especially experienced by nurses.

When the logic of power is prioritized, unequal power and mistrust relationships can often be observed, resulting in the assigning of blame and feelings of guilt for all healthcare actors and the development of care frustrations. Distrusting relationships among a care team can develop, and nurses' roles are commonly framed by a biomedical discourse and the medical needs of patients.

Nurses are responsible for care implementation and the well-being of patients but only have slight authority when administering care therapies. The caring work by nurses risks being reduced to the execution of orders or the following of strict quality manuals. These overruled rights and duties may lead to confusion regarding what rights they have and what practical and legislative boundaries exist between professions. A grey area exists between legal duties and moral responsibilities in care practice.

Care responsibility can shift dynamically depending on the situation. Healthcare workers often face great difficulties distinguishing between their duties and responsibilities during caring work and clarifying who is responsible for what and why. Rather than assigning blame, all care actors must learn effective ways to address failures and share care responsibility.

Shared responsibility involves establishing an intensive collaboration, and building a partnership in which all actors share a common commitment, everyone communicates and respects each other, and everyone shares experience and power. Although it can be difficult to disrupt historical stereotypes and hierarchy in authoritarian German healthcare, being aware of the power and how power affects care relationships and care practice represents the first step towards improvement.

Professionalism Around Care Boundaries

Care is viewed as a professional performance of the healthcare agenda. Healthcare workers often wish that a care activity could be fulfilled according to their professional identities, tailored to the holistic view of individual care, which requires a great deal of time and money. However, care activities are often guided by institutional standards, focusing on the efficiency of care and the reduction of expenditures. These diverse care interests frequently result in the development of ethical tensions that can confront the professionals' awareness and identification when healthcare workers are caring for patients. Often, attempting to achieve a professional care goal or accepting an undesired care result becomes a challenge. The struggle between preserving one's professional identity and respecting humanity can result in the development of ethical dilemmas, accompanied by care frustration and compassion fatigue among healthcare actors. Nourishing courage that motivates healthcare actors to reflect on their moral responsibilities and encourages them to be willing to try alternative approaches is more valuable than asking healthcare workers to act with obscured bravery that forces them to deal with ethical dilemmas.

Keep Trying or Acceptance

> During my medical education, I grew up with the professional identification that the care receivers are not customers but patients. Unfortunately, I also have to be concerned about the business dimension, especially for the hospitalized patients who are often cared for in a bit of a customer-oriented and service-oriented way at the hospital. Surely, we have more and more limitations due to business-economic expenditures. In my opinion, it is not enough to care for the patients adequately, in some cases, because the healthcare situations are often far away from the organizational rules. (I–FA–01, 231–243)

Caring has boundaries and limitations. The development of models for estimating costs and expenditures became a prerequisite for the development of internal healthcare markets. Healthcare professionals often encounter conflicts between fulfilling economic requirements established by business-oriented healthcare institutions when attempting to offer individual patient care according to their professional judgment (Freidson, 2001; Miers, 2003b; Paulsen, 2011; Robb & Greenhalgh, 2006; Salloch, 2016). Care tensions and ethical dilemmas may occur.

A common care dilemma mentioned by healthcare professionals, especially nurses, is the struggle between continuing to try new approaches, defined as keeping trying until a desirable care outcome has been achieved or accepting an unsatisfying compromise due to care limitations and boundaries. According to the literature, the need to "keep trying and not give up" is viewed as additional work for healthcare professionals in the collaborative, and for many healthcare professionals, letting go can lead to ethical distress when they are caring for or with patients (Lemay, 2010). Professional moral identities became evident when they observed improvements in the health of patients or communities or when they can maintain the identity of their patients, despite the disruptive forces of illness and hospitalization (Peter et al., 2016). Unfortunately, healthcare professionals often have to let go in many practical cases due to care limitations and institutional boundaries. When the logic of choice, the logic of efficiency and the logic of power drive healthcare, nursing professional autonomy is restricted, and the space for trying alternatives is limited.

In the literature, the patient's best interests and what will result in the best outcomes are among the most important aspects for nurses to consider when they make decisions regarding patient care and when they are confronted with ethical dilemmas (Barlow et al., 2018). Considering patients' interests in some practical cases is often misunderstood as a matter of respecting patient autonomy. When a patient's autonomy to make free choices is prioritized, nurses have less space to act in their professional roles. In effect, nurses are often too weak to challenge the resistance of patients in many care circumstances. However, nurses may question whether patients have the right to remain passive in caring and may struggle with whether they should accept this decision from their patients, which can lead to feelings of frustration and fatigue. As one diabetes consultant told me:

> Some days, I'll have no patience anymore and say to [the patient], "It is silly for me. You came to me. I considered something good for you, but it seems to have no possibility for you to change it. Then you do not need to come to me anymore."
> (I–DB–02, 182–192)

Care occurs in a dynamic lived practice, in which people choose to engage rather than be treated as a static, commoditized, and homogenized package. Without taking time to understand the patients within the broader health ecologies and social networks that stretch across and beyond the formal healthcare system, an appropriate care decision for a care situation cannot be made. In care practice, nurses trying to decide whether they can go further with their patients are often influenced by how much time they are allowed to spend engaging in care activities and how much background they have regarding the disease and their patients. For example, one nurse said that she did not know exactly how her patients cared for their bodies because it was hard to analyze the daily lives of patients during her short visit (I–NN–04, 82–89).

Healthcare workers need time to get to know patients and to try things, especially when dealing with a chronic disease like diabetes (I–DB–01, 160–164). When the logic of efficiency is driving healthcare, many healthcare professionals experienced a lack of time that prohibited their activities in caring and prevented collaboration within a care team (I–DA–01, 477–487; I–DB–01, 86–89, 160–164; I–NN–04, 528–532, 543–549). Corresponding to this research finding, the literature also indicated that multiple and time-consuming actions are reported as extra workloads for many nurses, and time pressure was indicated as a factor that affected the abilities of healthcare professionals to practice care (Anderson & Funnell, 2005; Rogers et al., 2005; Varcoe et al., 2012). Consequently, understanding patients can become less prioritized by care institutions, and caring work can become a matter of fulfilling institutional routines formulated by institutional standards. Nursing work often becomes executing physicians' orders or strict institutional manuals.

According to the research data, time-pressed nurses have less latitude to adapt their routines to patients' wishes and needs. Nursing work becomes implementing daily routines. However, this situation is not a comfortable care situation for nurses. As one nurse described:

> Because we have so many patients to care for, I believe it has become normal work for many nurses [in caring for the patients with diabetes] that we stick, we inject [insulin] when everything works well. But we don't think about what it means. Is there something different that you can still do? And so on. We don't have much time for it. It is becoming the normal practice that we stick, inject, and finish a visit for a patient within 3 minutes. But I would like to have more time to do my work differently. (I–NN–02, 569–584)

Working within a healthcare society guided by the logic of efficiency, based on both the literature and the research data, calculations of the bottom line become determinants of what healthcare professionals can do during their everyday work. This transformation, according to Twigg et al. (2011), occurs when care is provided directly by public bodies or is funded by them, and therefore must conform to strict budgeting criteria. Kohlen (2009, p. 146) criticized that care services become the organization's business. Healthcare professionals often experience moral distresses when they are required to accept an undesired outcome that goes against their professional judgment of what constitutes good care (Kangasniemi et al., 2015; Varcoe et al., 2012).

This tension is caused by nurses' vulnerability and the lack of opportunity to exercise care. Care tensions can be viewed as a resource of burden that can obstruct the nurses' ethical formation and is associated with feelings of shame and the development of mistrusting relationships (Holm & Severinsson, 2014; Thorup et al., 2012). Real caring work is embedded with emotional labor, which may impact caring activities implemented by human beings, including both patients and healthcare professionals. Healthcare workers must constantly fight to improve their professional autonomy against hierarchical power, achieve a balance between good medical care and economic expenditures, and preserve their moral position in caring, which can cause care fatigue due to feelings of uncertainty, disappointment, helplessness, hopelessness, fear, and guilty.

Initial Distress Around Profession and Humanity

> The patient was exasperated one day and told me, "Stop now, I don't want to hear about it [diabetes care] anymore". Then I said, "Okay, let's let it go". Then I said

nothing about it anymore. I had argued with him because of his diabetes. But there is nothing changed, and he still eats chocolate. Then, he has to inject more and more insulin, and he is getting fatter. He wants that. One day you have to give up....I have already annoyed him by always saying, "Please come here, and we take a small walk". Then, you have to accept it. Although it is a difficult decision, what should I do? I cannot beat him and push him on the way? He is an adult, and he must know what he wants. (I–NN–06, 93–105)

Care practice is often full of conflicts, contradictions, and uncertainties due to decreasing professional autonomy and job satisfaction; increasing workforce shortages and the associated burden of overtime; unacceptable rates of assault and injury; and emotionally draining experiences, including moral distress and initial distress associated with feelings of frustration, fatigue, powerless, anger, and anxiety (Austin et al., 2009; Kunyk & Austin, 2011; Ulrich et al., 2010; Varcoe et al., 2004). Analyzing the research data[10], the moral distress and initial distress that healthcare professionals suffered from often occur during circumstances in which they are constantly trying to provide professionally good care for unwilling patients, ensure the duties and humanity of all parties, preserve their values in daily care practice, and fight for their professional autonomy against institutional hierarchy.

According to the literature, nurses are reported to be uninclined to let go and leave patients to sort out their own lives based on their professional ethos (Dwarswaard & Van der Bovenkamp, 2015; Pill et al., 1999). However, having to always keep trying is not easy for healthcare professionals, especially when a care situation is connected to the emotional agency of either the healthcare professionals or their patients (I–DB–01, 193–201; I–NN–06, 93–105). Although the healthcare professionals in this research did not emphasize their care fatigue when talking about difficulties encountered in caring, many care situations are full of emotional tension (I–DB–01, 193–201; I–NN–03, 344–346; I–NN–06, 93–105). The statement often illustrated by healthcare professionals is something like, "I always try it again and say to the patient again and again....But I don't always have the feeling that I have to do this every day again" (I–NN–03, 344-346), "He wants that. One day you have to give up" (I–NN–06, 93–105), or "Even though I know now how to deal with this situation, it's sometimes already toilsome for me." (I–DB–01, 193–201)

In care practice, many healthcare professionals complained that they could not go further with patients who are unwilling to take part in caring. Although healthcare professionals realize that the character of diabetes requires strict day-to-day control tailored to the patient's life experience, over time, diabetes management becomes increasingly difficult. Caring for this type of patient often means that healthcare professionals have to address not only the emotion of their patients but also

---

10 The current research findings are presented in Other Care Logics in Practice.

their compassion. Consequently, they begin to treat their patients as statistics rather than as people (I–DB–02, 94–99). Initial distress can occur, associated with feelings of helplessness, hopelessness, and fatigue (I–DB–01, 331–335; I–NN–03, 255–262, 344–346; I–NN–06, 93–105). Corresponding to the research findings, patient resistance is reported in the literature as a factor that impacts nurses' care attitudes and emotions (Thorup et al., 2012; Zoffmann & Kirkevold, 2005).

The research findings demonstrated that care work performed by nurses in this care situation often becomes passive, treated as a routine job instead of creating a connected relationship[11] with patients. As one diabetes consultant said, "I still have to do my job. However, there is no humanity basis when I do it" (I–DB–02, 94–99). Sometimes, healthcare professionals excused this situation as being due to a personality mismatch. A diabetes consultant explained: "You surely have the patients. With them, you realize, "It does not work" because he does not like me personally, and I cannot fulfill his or her needs" (I–DB–02, 94–99).

Balancing institutional standards and personal humanity can be difficult. Limited by everyday routine work, nurses are often compelled to perform an identity that lacks authenticity to ensure that patients will value and treat them appropriately (Peter et al., 2016). The patient-nurse relationship, however, can feel duplicitous for nurses because they are inauthentic and, thus, irredeemable from the perspective of integrity and trustworthiness (De Raeve, 2002a; Kleppe et al., 2016). Within the intimate emotional relationship that develops between a healthcare professional and a patient, a mismatch between nursing ideals and nursing practice can lead to dissatisfaction among nurses.

Based on the literature, when nurses are unable to act on their beliefs because they are not in positions of power and cannot make the final decisions concerning patient care, they may change their attitudes to embrace reluctance, giving up, and withdrawing from patients (Kälvemark et al., 2004; Kangasniemi et al., 2013; Nortvedt et al., 2011; Peter et al., 2016; Zoffmann & Kirkevold, 2005). A similar finding was identified in this research as follows:

> In a nursing home, I have experienced that the patients' families sometimes have no interest in caring at all. Then, I did not talk to the patient and his family anymore. I explained it to them, documented it, and passed this information on to his family doctor. (I–NN–06, 258–262)

---

11 A connected relationship is characterised as being genuine and honest; increased reciprocal respect and trust present the possibility for healthcare professionals to believe in the patient and know that requests for care, attention, or time are based on the patients' legitimate needs and concerns (Fox & Chesla, 2008).

In this case, the exchange of different values was lacking, and a sense of tension developed. Caring was converted to passivity, and the nurse withdrew herself from caring activities because of her emotional judgment of the patient. When caring for patients who are identified as non-compliant and who are less willing to participate in caring, nurses may ask themselves, "What are you still expected to do? (I–NN–03, 255–262)" and "What is the extent of my responsibility (I–DB–01, 259–269)?". Vibeka Zoffmann and Marit Kirkevold (2005) noted that perceptions of undervalued experience and knowledge caused resistance by professionals to the ideals and practice of professionalism and their professions in the form of anger and distress, which could be concealed from professionals.

When the power lies with the professionals, according to Zoffmann and Kirkevold (2005), patients seldom allow those who cause their resistance to becoming aware of it. Usually, they behave as if nothing is wrong when they meet with these professionals and discuss their dissatisfaction only with other patients or perhaps with other professionals (Zoffmann & Kirkevold, 2005). Consequently, nurses may distance themselves from their professional identities and withdraw from the care relationship with patients after suffering from initial distress (I–NN–06, 93–105). These actions can jeopardize a trusting relationship between a patient and the healthcare professional, resulting in a transfer of care responsibilities. As a result, blame can occur, the trust relationship is damaged, and care responsibilities are silently transferred.

Constantly fighting against hierarchy can also cause healthcare professionals to experience care frustration and compassion fatigue, especially for non-physician professionals. In a hierarchical care practice, the power of physicians results in non-physician professionals experiencing the expectation of acting in a submissive, dutiful, obedient, and petitioner role, according to the research data. This role can damage team cooperation and create a top-down communication structure within a care team. This type of communication is often intrinsic to healthcare organizations, despite being characterized by a lack of psychological well-being among those lower in the hierarchy (Kangasniemi et al., 2013). As a diabetes consultant complained: "I often go into the role of a petitioner. I had to stand in front of the consultation room and wait until a doctor came out. I noticed that I was unwelcome because the next patient was already waiting there" (I–DB–02, 291–311).

In the literature, creating dialogues for mutual situational reflection can lead to problem-solving and help healthcare professionals address compassion fatigue (Murray, 2010; Peter et al., 2016; Zoffmann & Kirkevold, 2005). Compassion fatigue among nurses represents a sense of hopelessness regarding the possibility of positive change, based on the literature (Austin et al., 2009) and the research data. In care practice, an open dialogue can, unfortunately, be difficult to arrange. Nurses rarely have opportunities for formal discussions or to share their care frustrations and compassion fatigue in their work settings. Increased concern regarding the emotional agenda of healthcare professionals and offering them a platform for exchanging experiences or expressing their emotions is important.

The nature of caring focuses on caring for ill and weak people, with a traditional reliance on an ethos of selfless care and dedication. However, healthcare workers are also people who have their own needs, rights, and emotions that should be respected and cared for. Dealing with the emotional pressure and suffering of healthcare actors represents another task that healthcare professionals must learn to address. Healthcare policy also has a responsibility to place more concern on the needs and rights of healthcare workers. In care practice, healthcare workers often hide their humanity behind their professionalism. The next section addresses how to support healthcare professionals when they encounter care tensions and ethical dilemmas.

Obscured Bravery Versus Nourished Courage

> If I recognized that "okay, the patient is not able to do everything", I have to try things with smaller steps over a longer period than usual. But there is also a situation in that patients do not want to do things. Then, I have to accept it too. When I was a young consultant in this profession, I always thought that I had to save the whole world. But I've learned over the years that I cannot achieve this goal. I can only offer my help and say to the patients, "I will accompany you", and ask them, "What do you want? What do you expect? And how can I help you?" These questions I will frequently ask myself, too. (I–DB–01, 259–269)

Working within a healthcare environment full of care boundaries and ethical dilemmas, nurses are often expected to develop and maintain effective relationships with patients and other healthcare professionals while constructing relationships in which moral agency, professional identity, trust, and responsibilities are embraced. Nurses are overwhelmed, and care frustrations and compassion fatigue are increasing.

In the literature, many scholars encourage nurses to act as courageous nurses when dealing with the ethical dilemmas they encounter when personal or organizational hindrances prevent them from fulfilling their moral duties towards their patients (Lindh et al., 2009; Numminen et al., 2017; Rahman &Myers, 2019; Thorup et al., 2012). Nurses who exhibit moral reasoning and act with moral courage demonstrate a willingness to speak out and do what is right when they meet resistance (Butts, 2015; Curtis, 2014; Lachman, 2007; LaSala & Bjarnason, 2010; Weaver et al., 2008). Courage, thus, appears to play a significant role in nurses' ability to engage in care.

However, the relationship between moral courage and moral distress is not straightforward, and learning from one's failures rather than blaming oneself is often difficult in a real care environment (Gallagher, 2011). Courage encompasses taking responsibility for another person's vulnerability and well-being in a trusting relationship and preserving another person's dignity (Numminen et al., 2018). This type of courage can add to compassion fatigue felt by nurses and reduce their willingness to act, particularly when faced with the possibility of standing alone against hierarchical and authoritarian decisions.

The questions raised in care practice include how can moral courage be inserted into nursing care, and how can nurses achieve the space to act out their moral courage under pressure from the logic of choice, the logic of efficiency or the logic of power. Rather than elaborating on the hidden bravery of nurses and forcing them to deal with ethical dilemmas, nourishing courage and inviting and supporting nurses to reflect on their moral responsibilities is encouraged in the context of German healthcare. According to the literature and the research data, nourishing courage involves enhancing ethical sensibilities, making the nursing profession valuable, improving the competencies of caring, helping nurses become aware of their vulnerability, leaving space for caring, being able to let go, and establishing supported care surrounding.

To nourish courage, nurses have to enhance their ethical sensibilities, which are considered necessary for all truly sensitive and morally competent clinicians. Without ethical sensitivity, nurses may demonstrate their strength rather than recognize their patients' vulnerability. Without ethical sensitivity, nurses' responses to patients can be either inaction or routine-oriented actions (Gjengedal et al., 2013; Milliken, 2016; Nortvedt, 2008). However, the presence of ethical sensitivity is not sufficient to ensure ethical actions, particularly when a context is prohibitive, which can result in blocked moral agency and subsequent moral distress (Milliken, 2016). Based on the research data, ethical sensitivity can be expanded to include reflecting and responding, which means that nurses have to be able to review each care situation and ethical dilemma, listen to their inner voices, prioritize the values of the nursing profession, and address their vulnerability in the practical agenda.

Awareness of care situations and ethical dilemmas represents the first step of reflection. When caring for patients with diabetes, Anderson and Funnell (2005) encouraged nurses to reflect on their experiences outside of the acute-care paradigm and to see the existing acute-care paradigm as a psychological mirror. Such reflection can create the psychological space necessary to adopt a new paradigm that is truly appropriate for the reality of diabetes care (Anderson & Funnell, 2005). This type of reflection can sometimes be observed in practical cases when nurses rethink what they are doing, what they expect, what they need, and what a trained nurse should represent when caring for patients (I–NN–02, 569–582; I–NN–03, 721–725).

In the literature, listening to one's inner voice and continually asking questions have been proposed (Anderson & Funnell, 2005; Lachman, 2007; K. V. Smith & Godfrey, 2002). Trying to soothe one's inner feelings with relaxation techniques, using self-talk and moral reasoning to process information, considering a variety of options, and pushing out negative thoughts can help nurses to remain calm in the face of confrontations (Lachman, 2007; K. V. Smith & Godfrey, 2002). Unfortunately, nurses' willingness and moral bravery to fight for their virtue and professional good is often obscured in care practice. Most of the time, nurses are overloaded and have a limited capacity to consider improvement (I-NN-02, 569-582). In many cases, nurses ignore their ethical sensibilities and focus on performing their medical duties when faced with ethical conflicts (I-DB-02, 94-99; I-NN-06, 93-105).

By recognizing the importance of the nursing profession within society, nurses may be encouraged to maintain their moral identities (Mol, 2010; De Casterle et al., 2008; Peter et al., 2016; Van den Hooff & Goossensen, 2014). Nursing needs to be understood as a real profession rather than being criticized as being in pursuit of power (Mol et al., 2010, p. 9). Nurses require a certain degree of self-trust to act autonomously and place intrinsic value on the acts of caring and nursing (McLeod & Sherwin, 2000; Mol et al., 2010, p. 9). Nurses are encouraged to apply a perceiving eye[12] instead of a recording eye[13] when performing their caring work (de Casterle et al., 2008; Van den Hooff & Goossensen, 2014; Rahman & Myers, 2019). Taking carefully calculated risks, changing the ways of relating, having difficult conversations, and developing appropriate inquiry skills are recommended for nurses when they perform nursing work.

In this research, enhancing competencies was also viewed as a necessary step for improving the nursing profession (I-NN-03, 721-725; I-NN-04, 259-261; I-NN-06, 474-476). According to the literature, a necessary precursor for both autonomy and power is competence, which has its foundation in educational preparation (Manojilovich, 2007). Care competency refers to more than just the knowledge and skills necessary to care for a special disease. In summarising the literature and the practical cases, competencies can be identified as the ability to respect patients' needs (Thompson et al., 2006, p. 182; I-NN-03, 333-339; I-DB-01, 65-73), examine relationships with authority (Butts & Rich, 2008, p. 290; Rahman & Myers, 2019, p. 151; I-NN-03, 333-339; I-DB-01, 65-73), continuing professional growth (American Nurses Association, 2001; I-NN-03, 721-725; I-NN-04, 259-261; I-NN-06, 474-476), identifying the self-understanding necessary for professional development (Ramvi, 2015; I-NN-02, 569-582), and developing personal attributes, such as attentiveness, responsiveness, and courage, which may influence a nurse's ethical formation (Thorup et al., 2012; I-NN-02, 569-582; I-DB-01, 65-73).

---

12 A perceiving eye is characterised by openness towards the world and other persons, allowing sensation and emotion to work together (de Casterle et al., 2008; Van den Hooff & Goossensen, 2014).

13 A recording eye involves placing oneself outside of a situation, classifying, systematising, and differentiating within the framework of an already existing conceptual system (de Casterle et al., 2008; Van den Hooff & Goossensen, 2014).

Creating nourished courage requires that nurses be aware of their vulnerability and manage their anxiety. When performing caring in a realistic world, nurses have to know their professional boundaries and have the strength to reject demands from others when they experience moral distress consisting of a sense of moral burden, moral responsibility, vulnerability, and heroic deeds (Numminen et al., 2017; Rahman & Myers, 2019). Leaving care space and being able to let go is sometimes necessary for diabetes care. The research data shows that maintaining flexibility in caring and leaving space to act are necessary for nurses (See The Logic of Care). Accepting an undesired outcome is also a task that nurses have to learn (I–DB–01, 65–73; I–NN–03, 333–339). As a nurse said: "You cannot do more and go any further at some point. Then you have to think, what is still meaningful that I can do and where is the limitation?" (I–NN–03, 333–339). Mol (2008, p. 95) explained, "Healthcare professionals need to actively take their care into hands and to let go whatever it is they cannot tame".

Without a supportive care environment, nurses can have difficulty developing moral courage. A supported care environment within a courageous organization provides nurses with the necessary support to be able to fulfill their obligations as professional care workers without compromising integrity. Based on the literature, a supportive care environment can be identified as one in which a care team shares collaborative decision-making and care responsibility (LaSala & Bjarnason, 2010), in addition to creating a caring culture that supports openness and ethical discussions (Hemberg et al., 2017; Rahman & Myers, 2019).

Supporting nurses in the development of ethical competence is the duty and responsibility of healthcare organizations (Rahman &Myers, 2019). Organizational systems must be able to embrace the virtues of moral courage, wisdom, and integrity by providing better support resources and structures to decrease moral distress. For example, offering additional education in ethics and a forum for discussing any ethically troubling situations experienced in daily care practice (Kälvemark et al., 2004), recruiting individuals for the right values, and supporting effective responses to external threats (Gastmans, 2002; Gittell, 2009, p. 229; Rahman & Myers, 2019; Weaver et al., 2008), and engineering and revising formal structures and processes to provide a safe, trustworthy, effective, and efficient service delivery setting in which healthcare workers are able to enjoy their work (Allen et al., 2016; Rahman & Myers, 2019).

Caring for chronic diseases, such as diabetes, requires interprofessional support from within a care team (I–DB–01, 78–85, 226–231; I–DB–02, 205–211; I–NN–03, 41–46) or the support of the community in which the different healthcare organizations work (I–DB–02, 319–330). Caring for a complex chronic disease requires different types of cooperative caregiving rather than focusing on the distinctions between healthcare professions. In care practice, discussion and cooperation among a care team can offer support for nurses and diabetes consultants who encounter care difficulties.

Current medical care society is deeply impacted by the logic of choice, the logic of power, and the logic of efficiency, resulting in many care activities being restricted. Recognizing these social forces and reflecting these forces in their daily work become difficult tasks nurses are expected to perform (B. Pope et al., 2016; Rahman & Myers, 2019). In nursing, having the political intelligence to facilitate courage is essential. Therefore, nurses require the skills not only to develop and maintain professional relationships when addressing ethical dilemmas but also to understand and navigate organizational politics constructively by aligning their behaviors with the organizational purpose and engaging with political and organizational decision-making on macro and micro scales (Barlow et al., 2018; Rahman & Myers, 2019).

Individuals should not be the only responsible agents, and the healthcare system must be able to support both individual and communal professionalism and accountability. Nourished courage fosters a supported, safe space for reflecting and responding to care frustrations and compassion fatigue. Rather than necessitating hidden individual bravery, nourished courage emphasizes that no one has to work alone or assume care responsibility alone. Instead, every actor and organization is involved, intertwined, and tinkering. Each entity attempts to understand and respect each other, everyone is encouraged to act according to their profession and moral agency.

Summary

The tension identified as professionalism around care boundaries particularly arises when the logic of efficiency is prioritized. When abiding by institutional standards, with consideration for economic expenditures in practice, ethically incongruent care can be expected, which goes against the professional ethos to tailor care for a holistic view of the individual.

The commercial and economic healthcare society may result in healthcare workers experiencing a lack of professional autonomy, and grey areas can develop between moral good and institutional standards. The goals and rules of the institution often become the driving forces for actions and procedures, with healthcare workers acting as facilitators or negotiators instead of focusing on the patient's well-being. Consequently, healthcare professionals constantly have to fight against hierarchy to achieve good medical outcomes and motivate noncompliant patients. Care frustrations and compassion fatigue are associated with feelings of uncertainty, disappointment, helplessness, hopelessness, fear, and guilt.

The care environment is full of emotional tensions. Rather than celebrating the obscured bravery of healthcare workers when faced with ethical dilemmas, concerning the emotional agenda of healthcare professionals, focusing on nourishing courage, and inviting and supporting nurses to reflect on their moral responsibilities are suggested, particularly for nurses. Nourishing courage involves enhancing ethical sensibilities, leaving care space, valuing the nursing profession, improving the competencies of caring, and establishing nourished care surrounding in which dialogue and responsiveness can occur among a healthcare team, the healthcare system, and society.

By being open to one's vulnerabilities and sensitive to one's shortcomings and inadequacies through self-reflection, nourished courage can be established. Letting go represents an essential ability that all healthcare professionals must learn. In the words of Mol, "to try, to adjust, to retry, and to let it go at the right time" is the way to help healthcare professionals waver from righteousness when faced with the difficulties of translating care theory into reality.

Chapter 6: Conclusion

Brief Comment

Diabetes is a chronic disease that can lead to unrecoverable physical damage, extreme psychological burdens, and unexpected social life changes for patients. Diabetes management occurs not only inside an individual's sick body but involves collective actions in which various hands must work together. When dealing with such a complex and unpredictable chronic disease, caring can shift dynamically and cooperatively. Regrettably, care activities in the current healthcare society can be very restricted by the notions of respecting patient autonomy, medical authority, and economic expenditures. Consequently, care frustrations and care dilemmas can develop, greatly challenging the trust relationships between patients, nurses, and physicians. An alternative method for delivering care in the context of diabetes is crucial.

Intending to establish a logical care pattern involving ethical considerations for diabetes care and nursing, this research approached care from the perspective of the logic of care to explore patients' needs in diabetes care and examine the difficulties associated with practical care implementation. Analyzing the research data collected through an integrative review and a practical investigation, including field observations and in-depth interviews in the context of diabetes care settings in Germany, the research findings were generalized around three themes: understanding the disease, the care logic in diabetes care, and care tensions and ethical dilemmas.

Diabetes management is an endless and troublesome lifelong challenge. To be able to live well with diabetes, patients recognized the importance of being active participants in disease management. They are focused on integrating their knowledge of controlling their disease into their daily lives. However, the healthcare environment can narrow healthcare performance and caring situations are full of contradictions. Although patients are aware of their duties to care for their bodies, maintaining themselves day-to-day within the frame of care principles can be exhausting. Patients are told they should be able to enjoy their lives, but their lives are full of uncertainty and limitations. Although patients recognize their dependence on medicine and their need for a healthcare team, they still wish to have freedom and to be independent. Push patients moving from "To Know" care knowledge to "To Do" care activities becomes difficult.

To offer an alternative method for addressing this type of care situation, the logic of care described by Mol was introduced. This research conceptualizes the logic of care and adds expanded meaning derived from observations of practical cases. Patients' needs in diabetes care were explored and identified in terms of responding to and reflecting health values, exchanging experiences and shared caring, and learning and ongoing. Caring for and with patients with diabetes within the framework of the logic of care was elaborated in some cases to identify broad, common themes, whereas in other cases was associated with narrow but specific explanations. By stretching the concepts of the theory and inserting the practical care experience, the logic of care could be expanded and transformed until it was feasible and acceptable in real care practice.

Even so, care limitations and care ambivalences were noticed within the German healthcare society, particularly when other types of care logic were found to guide healthcare, including the logic of choice, associated with sovereignty and autonomy; the logic of power, concerned with legislation and authority; and the logic of efficiency, focused on regulation and statistic.

When the logic of choice governs healthcare, healthcare workers suffer from the pressure to ensure care security on the one hand and respect patient autonomy on the other hand. Patient sovereignty can be transformed into the priority of care, and care performance may become passive in response. When the logic of power emphasizes legislation in the framing of care responsibilities, medical authority builds patients' trust in patient-physician relationships but reduces trust towards other care relationships, and unequal power and mistrust relationships can develop within a hierarchical medical society. Although regulations and standardization are deemed beneficial for professional care, humanity can become hidden behind statistics within healthcare operating according to the logic of efficiency.

Ethically incongruent care that does not align with professionalism and is not tailored to a holistic view of individual care may be delivered. Consequently, patients' safety may be impeded, judgments of good or bad may be embedded, and the assignment of blame and the feeling of guilty can emerge for all healthcare actors. When frustrations occur, care responsibility may be evaded, and compassion fatigue may develop in response to feelings of uncertainty, disappointment, helplessness, hopelessness, fear, and guilt.

To support healthcare professionals who encounter care tensions and ethical dilemmas during daily practice, tinkering approaches are encouraged over attempts to tame disease, shared responsibility should be encouraged over blame allocation, and nourished courage should be promoted to replace hidden bravery. All healthcare actors are encouraged to consider the patients' humanity and to work together by sharing caring, performing caring activities, and acknowledging each worker's contributions. Failures should be assessed without blame, to modify care while continuing to improve and learn.

A Logical Care Pattern for Diabetes Care and Nursing

Caring for a patient with diabetes is associated with an extraordinary range of distinctive meanings and activities depending on the care situations and relationships in which humanity and society intertwine. Private actions inside the body, public interactions outside the body, and moral and ethical activities all contribute to diabetes care. Corresponding to the recapitulations summarised from the current research and responding to the research goal, a logical care pattern for diabetes care and nursing care can be formed with five dimensions: holistic individual care, collaborative shared care, visible and attainable care, reflected attentive care, and nourished professional care.

Holistic individual care, the first dimension of the logical care pattern, refers to the wholeness of caring for a subject from an insider's perspective. Healthcare is full of unpredictable variables, with high levels of specialization that are driven by the complexity of the human body, the human mind, and the social world in which humans live. Rather than treating and controlling the functions of organs, diabetes care must be expanded to include awareness of patients' unvoiced needs; concern for patients' emotional responses to living with a chronic disease; sympathy for patients' suffering; enlightenment and accompanying the patient through disease management; a genuine and respectful attitude; acceptance of patients' cultures, lifestyles, and decisions without pre-judgment; good advice; patient safety; and trust relationships.

Patient autonomy can sometimes be limited by health priorities, and coercion can sometimes be viewed as a type of care within the concept of holistic individual care. From this perspective, care is not merely the value of taming and controlling diseases but also tinkering with bodies, integrating the values of both the individual and the collective. Patients, healthcare professionals, and society must view patients as individuals in need of care and create opportunities to exchange understanding and empathy for suffering. In addition, time and money must be invested in attempting alternatives for care. Both parties should reflect upon and assess their values to determine whether these values are desirable. Depending on the care situation, patients and healthcare professionals have to initiate their activities in society through compromise and integration.

The second dimension that constructs the logical care pattern refers to collaborative shared care, which emphasizes creating a collaborative care practice in which healthcare professionals, patients, their families, care organizations, and society participate in caring activities and share care responsibilities. Care is not merely a task for patients to perform, it is the mission of healthcare professionals, and all of society must be able to learn and act in response to individuals who need care. Healthcare is strongly influenced by legislation within an authoritarian and hierarchical medical society; therefore, moving away from a vertical hierarchy to facilitate a collaborative and multidisciplinary care practice is essential. Rather than assigning responsibility by focusing on historical roles and professional silos in which each healthcare worker acts as an independent practitioner that contributes to the work of the team, each member of a care team should share a common commitment and common goals, cooperate with communities, focus on performance, and establish respect for each other.

Collaborative shared care focuses on sharing care responsibility among a care team instead of assigning blame. Care practice is full of restrictions, and responsibilities, duties, and rights are often intertwined. Once care responsibilities are assigned to one party, either healthcare professionals or patients, blame may occur, and an authoritarian attitude within care relationships may be revealed. Bearing too much responsibility may exhaust care actors during the provision of care, resulting in feelings of shame and mistrust. Instead of arranging duties and responsibilities, diabetes care should be delivered through team cooperation, in which the care responsibilities are shared. Collaborative shared care in the context of diabetes care can be explained as addressing failures, learning from mistakes, establishing an interdisciplinary and communicative collaboration, building a transparent commitment with ethical considerations, and sharing experiences with respect for the patient's humanity.

Visible and attainable care is the third dimension of the logical care pattern. Care is a dynamic process embedded with many visible and invisible interactions. Often, invisible trust and hierarchy in medical care are intertwined. The visible financial expenditures can narrow invisible health values and the invisible quality of care for patients. The invisibility and authority of physicians influence the patient-nurse relationship in a subtle but powerful manner. The nurse, who is visible, is less trusted and less powerful than the physician; yet the nurse is held responsible for care outcomes, which can induce a mistrustful relationship, passive care performance, and shifted care responsibilities.

To offer the possibility of change, visible and attainable care focuses on providing feasible care services that can be implemented in the real world, making care visible by motivating the involvement of healthcare workers, strengthening the effects of disease management, accompanying patients during their care through improved relationships, and seeking an acceptable care approach rather than a desirable care approach to facilitate a continual caring process. In addition, visible and attainable care encourages healthcare workers to be aware of their power and the importance of sharing power with the healthcare team. In particular, the contributions of nurses can be reformed, and the invisibility of the nursing profession can be reduced by recognizing power, understanding how power affects relationships and care practice, making professional power more explicit, exercising collaborative power, and raising public awareness about the nursing profession.

The fourth dimension of the logical care pattern focuses on reflected attentive care. Care is a matter of attentiveness to needs and the reflection of the circumstance that surround care relationships. Awareness, therefore, represents the beginning of a caring process. Often, a patient who is attentive, articulate, and able to express his complaints has a better chance of receiving appropriate treatment and care. Due to the restrictions associated with institutional regulations and expenditures within a hierarchical and commercial healthcare society, healthcare professionals often face difficulties responding to patients' needs. Reflected and attentive care allows space for both patients and their healthcare professionals to consider their values regarding disease management and caring. Practically, reflected attentive care could be performed by continually asking questions, increasing one's value of health, avoiding self-moralizing, leaving space for caring, moderating harmonious care situations, being sensitive to moral distress, and accepting letting go in certain care circumstances.

Care fatigue and emotional tensions can emerge in the context of diabetes care, particularly for powerless professions in circumstances in which they constantly have to fight the application of medical paradigms against humanity, maintain professional autonomy against hierarchy, preserve their values in caring against commercial society, and ensure their legitimate rights and duties against moral responsibility. The loss of passion for caring and increased emotional tension may cause healthcare professionals to become passive in their care activities and withdraw from care relationships with their patients. Nourished professional care, which is the last dimension of the logical care pattern, is important.

Nourished professional care underlines the ethical sensibilities of healthcare professionals, especially in the nursing profession. Encouraging nurses to identify care situations, listen to their voice, reflect on their values in caring and nursing, recognize the importance of nursing work within society, recognize their vulnerability, and know their professional boundaries are valuable in practical caring practice. Nurses should be encouraged to enhance their professional and personal competencies, consider the possibilities of what could be done in relationships, continue professional growth, and develop personal attributes that support their ethical formation. However, nurses are also allowed to reject demands from others when they experience moral distress, moral burden, moral responsibility, vulnerability, or the need to perform heroic deeds.

Creating nourished professional care requires a caring environment in which the moral courage of healthcare professionals can be established, encouraged, and developed. It also requires a safe space in which healthcare professionals can express and reflect on their care frustrations and the compassion fatigue they experience. Rather than advocating for hidden individual bravery, nourished professional care emphasizes that no one has to work alone or take on care responsibility alone. Instead, every actor and organization is involved, intertwined, and tinkering. They understand and respect each other and are encouraged to act according to their professional and moral agency. They share care and responsibilities.

Diabetes care, in summary, moves from caring for individualism to caring with and about collaboration and relationality, from taming the disease to tinkering bodies and emotions, from blame allocation to shared responsibilities and power, from advocating hidden bravery to creating nourished courage and professionalism. This logical care pattern, grounded on the logic of care theory, is shaped and transformed with broad practical meaning that can bridge the theoretical understanding of disease management to practical implementation in the context of diabetes care and nursing care settings. It may also offer support for healthcare professionals when they encounter care tensions and ethical dilemmas, particularly when healthcare delivery is excessively oriented by the logic of choice, the logic of power, or the logic of efficiency.

References

Abdul, M., Khan, B., Hashim, M. J., Govender, R. D., Mustafa, H., & Kaabi, J. A. (2020). Epidemiology of type 2 diabetes – Global burden of disease and forecasted trends. *Journal of Epidemiological Global Health, 10*(1), 107–111.

Albine, M., Harry, B., Guy, W., & Cor, S. (2008). Self-management of type 2 diabetes mellitus: a qualitative investigation from the perspective of participants in a nurse-led, shared-care program in the Netherlands. *BMC Public Health, 8*(91). https://doi.org/10.1186/1471-2458-8-91

Allen, D., Braithwaite, J., Sandall, J., & Waring, J. (2016). Towards a sociology of healthcare safety and quality. *Sociology of Health & Illness, 38*(2) 181–197.

American Nurses Association. (2001). *Code of ethics for nurses with interpretive statements*. Silver Spring.

Anderson, R.M. (1995). Patient empowerment and the traditional medical model: a case of irreconcilable differences? *Diabetes Care, 18*, 412–415.

Anderson, R. M., & Funnell, M. M. (2005). Patient empowerment: reflections on the challenge of fostering the adoption of a new paradigm. *Patient Education and Counseling, 57*, 153–157.

Austin, W., Goble, E., Leier, B., & Byrne, P. (2009). Compassion fatigue: the experience of nurses. *Ethics and Social Welfare, 3*(2), 195–214.

Austin, W., Lemermeyer, G., Goldberg, L., Bergum, V., & Johnson, M. S. (2005). Moral distress in healthcare practice: the situation of nurses. *Healthcare Ethics Committee Forum, 17*(1), 33–48.

Bachmann, R. (2003). Trust and power as means of coordinating the internal relations of the organization: a conceptual framework. In Nooteboom, B., & Six, F. (Eds.), *The trust process in organizations empirical studies of the determinants and the process of trust development* (pp. 58–74). Edward Elgar Publishing.

Barlow, N. A., Hargreaves, J., & Gillibrand, W. P. (2018). Nurses' contributions to the resolution of ethical dilemmas in practice. *Nursing Ethics, 25*(2), 230–242. https://doi.org/10.1177%2F0969733017703700

Barr, V. J., Robinson, S., Marin-Link, B., Underhill, L., Dotts, A., Ravensdale, D., & Salivaras, S. (2003). The expanded chronic care model: An integration health promotion and the chronic care model. *Hospital Quarterly, 7*(1), 73–82.

Baxter, P., & Jack, S. (2008). Qualitative case study methodology: Study design and implementation for novice researchers. *The Qualitative Report, 13*(4), 544–559. https://doi.org/10.1186/1471-2288-11-100

Benner, P. (2001). The phenomenon of care. In S. K. Toombs (Ed.), *Handbook of phenomenology and medicine* (pp. 351–369). Kluwer Academic.

Bodenheimer, T., Wagner, E. H., & Grumbach, K. (2002). Improving primary care for patients with chronic illness. The chronic care model. *JAMA, 288,* 1909–1914.

Boldt, J. (2018). The interdependence of care and autonomy. In Krause, F., & Boldt, J. (Eds.), *Care in healthcare. Reflections on theory and practice* (pp 65–86). Palgrave Macmillan.

Bostan, S., Acuner, T., & Yilmaz, G. (2007). Patient (customer) expectations in hospitals. *Health Policy, 82*(1), 62–70.

Broer, T., Nieboer, A. P., & Bal, R. (2012). Mutual powerlessness in client participation practices in mental health care. *Health Expectations, 17,* 208–219.

Bury, M. (1982). Chronic illness as biographical disruption. *Sociology of Health & Illness, 4*(2), 167–182.

Bury, M. (2001). Illness narratives: fact or fiction? *Sociology of Health and Illness, 23*(3), 263–285.

Busse, R. (2004). Disease management programs in Germany's statutory health insurance system. *Health Affairs, 23*(3), 56–67.

Busse, R., & Blümel, M. (2014). Germany: Health system review. *Health Systems in Transition, 16*(2), 1–296. https://www.researchgate.net/publication/264797649_Germany_Health_system_review

Busse, R., & Reisberg, A. (2000). *Health care systems in transition: Germany.* European Observatory on Health Systems and Policies.

Butts, J. B. (2015). Ethics in professional nursing practice. In Butts, J. B., & Rich, K. L. (Eds.), *Nursing Ethics: Across the Curriculum and into Practice* (pp. 71–121). Jones and Bartlett Publishers.

Butts, J. B., & Rich, K. L. (2008). *Nursing Ethics: across the curriculum and into practice* (2nd ed.). Jones and Bartlett Publishers.

Callaghan, D., & Williams, A. (1994). Living with diabetes: issues for nursing practice. *Journal of Advanced Nursing, 20*(1), 132–139.

Calnan, M., & Rowe, R. (2006). Researching trust relations in health care: Conceptual and methodological challenges. An introduction. *Journal of Health Organization and Management, 20,* 349–358.

Carey, N., Stenner K., & Courtenay M. (2009). *How nurse prescribing is being utilized in diabetes services: Views of nurses and team members.* (Poster abstract). FEND 14th Annual Conference, Vienna.

Carry, M. R., Gerlof, D. V., Lonneke, V. F., Franc, G. S., Jacques, T. M., & Gerrit, W. (2001). Long-term effectiveness of a quality improvement program for patients with type 2 diabetes in general practice. *Diabetes Care, 24*(8), 1365–1370.

Charmaz, K. (1983). Loss of self: a fundamental form of suffering in the chronically ill. *Sociology of Health and Illness*, 5(2), 168–195.

Chase, S. K. (2004). *Clinical judgment and communication in nurse practitioner practice*. F. A. Davis Company.

Christmals, C. & Gross, J. (2017). An integrative literature review framework for postgraduate nursing research reviews. *European Journal of Research in Medical Sciences*, 5(1). ISSN. 2056–600X:

Clark, M. (2005). Healthcare professionals' versus patients' perspectives on diabetes. *Journal of Diabetes Nursing*, 9(3), 87–91.

Clark, M., & Hampson, S.E. (2003). Comparison of patients' and healthcare professionals' beliefs about and attitudes towards Type 2 diabetes. *Diabetic Medicine*, 20(2), 152–4.

Cole, C., Wellard, S., & Mummery, J. (2014). Problematizing autonomy and advocacy in nursing. *Nursing Ethics*, 21(5), 576–582.

Conradi, E. (2003). Vom Besonderen zum Allgemeinen Zuwendung in der Pflege als Ausgangspunkt einer Ethik. In Behrendt, H., Erichson, N., & Wisemann, C. (Eds.), *Pflege und Ethik. Leitfaden für Wissenschaft und Praxis* (pp. 30–46). Kohlhammer.

Corbin, J. M., & Strauss, A. (1988). *Unending work and care: Managing chronic illness at home*. Jossey-Bass.

Corbin J., & Strauss, A. (1993). *Weiterleben lernen. Chronisch kranke in der familie*. Piper.

Corbin J., & Strauss, A. (1991). A nursing model for chronic illness management based upon the trajectory framework. *Scholarly Inquiry for Nursing Practice*, 5, 155–174.

Corbin, J. M., & Strauss, A. L. (1998). *Basics of qualitative research: Techniques and procedures for developing grounded theory*. Sage Publications.

Corley, M. C., Elswick, R. K., & Corman, M. (2001). Development and evaluation of a Moral Distress Scale. *Journal of Advanced Nursing*, 33(2), 250–6.

Cramm, J. M., Strating, M. M. H., Tsiachristas, A., & Nieboer, A. P. (2011). Development and validation of a short version of the Assessment of Chronic Illness Care (ACIC) in Dutch disease management programs. *Health and Quality of Life Outcomes*, 9(49). https://doi.org/10.1186/1477-7525-9-49

Creswell, J. W. (2007). *Qualitative inquiry and research design: Choosing among five approaches*. Sage.

Curtis, K. (2014) Learning the requirements for compassionate practice: Student vulnerability and courage. *Nursing Ethics*, 21(2), 210–223.

Daiski, I. (2004). Changing nurses' dis-empowering relationship patterns. *Journal of Advanced Nursing*, 48(1), 43–50.

Davies, C., Savage, J., & Smith, R. (1999). Doctors and nurses: changing family values? *British Medical Journal*, 319(7208), 463–64.

Davoodvand, S., Abbaszadeh, A., & Ahmadi, F. (2016). Patient advocacy from the clinical nurses' viewpoint: a qualitative study. *Journal of Medical Ethics and History of Medicine, 9*(5). Article PMCID: PMC4958925

Deber, R. B., Kraetschmer, N., Urowitz, S., & Sharpe, N. (2005). Patient, consumer, client, or customer: what do people want to be called? *Health Expectations, 8*, 345–351.

DeBusk, R.F., West, J.A., Miller, N.H., & Taylor, C. B. (1999). Chronic disease management: treating the patient with disease(s) vs treating disease(s) in the patient. *Archi Intern Med, 159*(22), 2739–2742.

de Casterle, B. D., Izumi S., Godfrey, N. S., & Denhaerynck, K. (2008). Nurses' responses to ethical dilemmas in nursing practice: meta-analysis. *Journal of Advanced Nursing, 63*(6), 540–549.

De Raeve, L. (2002a). The modification of emotional responses: A problem for trust in nurse-patient relationships? *Nursing Ethics, 9*, 465–471. https://doi.org/10.1191%2F0969733002ne536oa

De Raeve, L. (2002b). Trust and trustworthiness in nurse-patient relationships. *Nursing Philosophy, 3*(2), 152–162.

Deutsche Diabetes Gesellschaft Group. (2017). *Deutscher Gesundheitsbericht: Diabetes 2017*. Deutsche Diabetes-Hilfe und Deutsche Diabetes Gesellschaft (DDG). https://www.diabetesde.org/system/files/documents/gesundheitsbericht2017.pdf

Deutsche Diabetes Gesellschaft Group. (2020). *Deutscher Gesundheitsbericht: Diabetes 2020*. Deutsche Diabetes-Hilfe und Deutsche Diabetes Gesellschaft (DDG). https://www.diabetesde.org/system/files/documents/gesundheitsbericht2020.pdf

Dinc, L., & Gastmans, C. (2013). Trust in nurse-patient relationships: A literature review. *Nursing Ethics, 20*(5) 501–516.

Donchin, A. (1995). Reworking autonomy: toward a feminist Perspective. *Cambridge Quarterly of Healthcare Ethics, 4*, 44–55.

Dryzek, J. S., Hunold, C., Schlosberg, D., Downes, D., & Hernes, H. K. (2002) Environmental transformation of the state: the USA, Norway, Germany, and the UK. *Political Studies, 50*(4), 659–682.

Duttweiler, S. (2007). Vom patienten zum kunden? Ambivalenzen einer aktuellen entwicklung. *Psychotherapeut, 52*(2), 121–126.

Dwarswaard, J., Bakker, E. J. M., van Staa, A., & Boeije, H. R. (2016). Self-management support from the perspective of patients with a chronic condition: a thematic synthesis of qualitative studies. *Health Expectations, 19*(2), 194–208.

Dwarswaard, J., & Van de Bovenkamp, H. (2015). Self-management support: A qualitative study of ethical dilemmas experienced by nurses. *Patient Education and Counseling, 98*(9), 1131–1136.

Edwards, S. D. (2009). Three versions of the ethics of care. *Nursing Philosophy, 10*(4), 231–240.

Elissen, A., Nolte, E., Knai, C., Brunn, M., Chevreul, K., Conklin, A., Durand-Zaleski, I., Erler, A., Flamm, M., Frølich, A., Fullerton, B., Jacobsen, R., Saz-Parkinson, Z., Sarria-Santamera, A., Sönnichsen, A., & Vrijhoef, H. (2013). Is Europe putting theory into practice? A qualitative study of the level of self-management support in chronic care management approaches. *BMC Health Services Research*, 13(117). https://doi.org/10.1186/1472-6963-13-117

Ells, C. (2001). Shifting the autonomy debate to theory as ideology. *Journal of Medicine and Philosophy*, 26(4), 417–430.

Entwistle, V. A., Carter, S. M., Cribb, A., & McCaffery, K. (2010). Supporting patient autonomy: The importance of clinician-patient relationships. *Journal of General Internal Medicine*, 25(7), 741–745.

Fourie, C. (2015). Moral distress and moral conflict in clinical ethics. *Bioethics*, 29(2), 91–97.

Freidson, E. (2001). *Professionalism, the third logic. On the practice of knowledge.* University of Chicago Press.

Freitas, R. (2008). Undertaking a literature review: A step-by-step approach. *British Journal of Nursing*, 17(1), 38–43.

Fox, S., & Chesla, C. A. (2008). Living with chronic illness: A phenomenological study of the health effects of the patient-provider relationship. *Journal of the American Academy of Nurse Practitioners*, 20(3), 109–117.

Funnell, M.M., Anderson, R.M., Arnold, M.S., Barr, P.A., Donnelly, M., Johnson, P.D., Taylor-Moon, D., & White, N. H. (1991). Empowerment: An idea whose time has come in diabetes education. *Diabetes Education*, 17(1), 37–41.

Gastmans, C. (2002). A fundamental ethical approach to nursing: some proposals for ethics education. *Nursing Ethics*, 9(5), 494–507.

Gastmans, C. (2006). The care perspective in healthcare ethics. In Davis, A. J., Tschudin, V. L., & de Raeve, (Eds.), *Essentials of teaching and learning in nursing ethics* (pp. 135–148). Livingstone.

Gastmans, C. (2013). Dignity-enhancing nursing care: A foundational ethical framework. *Nursing Ethics*, 20(2), 142–149.

Gastmans, C., de Casterle, D. B., & Schotsmans, P. (1998). Nursing considered as moral practice: a philosophical-ethical interpretation of nursing. *Kennedy Institute of Ethics Journal*, 8, 43–69.

Gensichen, J., Muth, C., Butzlaff, M., Rosemann, T., Raspe, H., Müller de Cornejo, G., Beyer, M., Härter, M., Müller, U. A., Angermann, C. E., Gerlach, F. M., & Wagner, E. (2006). Die Zukunft ist chronisch: das Chronic Care-Modell in der deutschen. Primärversorgung: Übergreifende Behandlungsprinzipien einer proaktiven Versorgung für chronische Kranke. *Zeitschrift für ärztliche Fortbildung und Qualität im Gesundheitswesen*, 100(5), 365–374.

Gergen, K. J. (1995). Relational theory and the discourses of power. In Hosking, D., Dachler, H. P., & Gergen, K. J. (Eds.), *Management and organization: Relational alternatives to individualism* (pp. 29–49). Avebury.

Gilligan, C. (1982). *In a different voice: Psychological theory and women's development*. Cambridge, MS: Harvard University Press.

Gilson, L. (2003). Trust and the development of health care as a social institute. *Social Science & Medicine*, 56(7), 1453–1468.

Gimlin, D. (2007). What is 'body work'? A review of the literature. *Sociology Compass*, 1(1), 353–370.

Gittell, J. H. (2006). Relational coordination: Coordinating work through relationships of shared goals, shared knowledge, and mutual respect. In Kyriakidou O., & Ozbilgin M. (Eds.), *Relational perspectives in organizational studies: A research companion* (pp. 74–94). Edward Elgar Publishers.

Gittell, J. H. (2009). *High-performance healthcare. Using the power of relationships to achieve quality, efficiency, and resilience*. The McGrow-Hill Companies.

Gittell, J. H. (2011). New directions for relational coordination theory. In Spreitzer G. M., & Cameron, K. S. (Eds.), *The Oxford handbook of positive organizational scholarship* (pp. 400–410). Oxford University Press.

Gittell, J. H., Godfrey, M., & Thistlethwaite J. (2013). Interprofessional collaborative practice and relational coordination: Improving healthcare through relationships. *Journal of Interprofessional Care*, 27, 210–213.

Gittell, J. H., Seidner, R., & Wimbush, J. (2009). A relational model of how high-performance work systems work. *Organization Science, Articles in Advance*, pp. 1–17.

Gjengedal, E., Ekra, E. M., Hol, H., Kjelsvik, M., Lykkeslet, E., Michaelsen, R., Orøy, A., Skrondal, T., Sundal, H., Vatne, S., & Wogn-Henriksen, K. (2013). Vulnerability in health care – reflections on encounters in everyday practice. *Nursing Philosophy*, 14(2), 127–138.

Greener, I. (2003). Patient choice in the NHS: The view from economic sociology. *Social Theory & Health*, 1(1), 72–89.

Gröne, O., & Garcia-Barbero, M. (2001). Integrated care: a position paper of the WHO European Office for Integrated Health Care Services. *International Journal of Integrated Care*, 1, e21.

Gunnarsdóttir, S., & Rafferty, A. M. (2006). Enhancing working conditions. In Dubois, C. A., McKee, M. and Nolte, E. (Eds.), *Human resources for health in Europe* (pp. 155–172). Open University Press.

Gutierrez, K.M. (2005). Critical care nurses' perceptions of and responses to moral distress. *Dimensions of Critical Care Nursing*, 24, 229–241.

Hakesley-Brown, R., & Malone, B. (2007). Patients and nurses: A powerful force. *The Online Journal of Issues in Nursing*, 12(1). Article DOI: 10.3912/OJIN.Vol12No01Man04

Hardy, C., & Phillips, N. (1998). Strategies of engagement: lessons from the critical examination of collaboration and conflict in an inter-organizational domain. *Organization Science*, 9(2), 217–230.

Hardy, C., Phillips, N., & Lawrence, T. (2000). Distinguishing trust and power in inter-organizational relations: Forms and façades of trust. In Lane, C., & Bachman, R. (Eds.), *Trust within and between organization* (pp. 64–87). Oxford University Press

Hasseler, M. K., von der Heide, M., & Indefrey, S. (2010). Resources and barriers of an effective diabetes care management – experiences and perspectives of people with type 2 diabetes. *Journal of Public Health*, 19(1), 65–71.

Havens, D. S., Vasey, J., Gittell, J. H., & Lin, W. T. (2010). Relational coordination among nurses and other providers: Impact on the quality of patient care. *Journal of Nursing Management*, 18(8), 926–937.

Hedman, M., Pöder, U., Mamhidir, A., Nilsson, A. Kristofferzon, M., & Häggström, E. (2015). Life memories and the ability to act: the meaning of autonomy and participation for older people when living with chronic illness. *Scandinavian Journal of Caring Sciences*, 29(4), 824–833.

Heisler, M., Vijan, S., Anderson, R., Ubel, P., Bernstein, S. J., & Hofer, T. P. (2003). When do patients and their physicians agree on diabetes treatment goals and strategies, and what difference does it make? *Journal of General Internal*, 18(11), 893–902.

Hemberg, J., Nyman, H., & Hemberg, H. (2017). A vision of ethics in efficient occupational healthcare. *Nursing Ethics*, 1. https://doi.org/10.1177/0969733016689817.

Hibbard, J. H., & Greene, J. (2013). What the evidence shows about patient activation: Better health outcomes and care experiences; fewer data on costs. *Health Affairs*, 32(2), 207–214.

Hickman, M., Drummond, N., & Grimshaw, J. (1994). A taxonomy of shared care for chronic disease. *Journal of Public Health Medicine*, 16(4), 447–454.

Hinder, S., & Greenhalgh, T. (2012). "This does my head in". An ethnographic study of self-management by people with diabetes. *BMC Health Services Research*, 12, 83. https://doi.org/10.1186/1472-6963-12-83

Hoeve, Y., Jansen, G., & Roodbol, P. (2014). The nursing profession: public image, self-concept, and professional identity. A discussion paper. *Journal of Advanced Nursing*, 70(2), 295–309.

Holm, A. L., & Severinsson, E. (2014). Reflections on the ethical dilemmas involved in promoting self-management. *Nursing Ethics*, 21(4), 402–413.

Holman, H., & Lorig, K. (2000). Patients as partners in managing chronic disease: Partnership is a prerequisite for effective and efficient health care. *British Medical Journal*, 320(7234), 526–527.

Hörnsten, A., Sandström, H., & Lundman, B. (2004). Personal understanding of illness among people with type 2 diabetes. *Journal of Advanced Nursing*, 47(2), 174–182.

Hroscikoski, M. C., Solberg, L. I., Sperl-Hillen, J. M., Harper, P. G., McGrail, M. P., & Crabtree, B. F. (2006). Challenges of change: A qualitative study of chronic care model implementation. *Annals of Family Medicine*, 4(4), 317–326.

Hunt, L.M., Pugh, J., & Valenzuela, M. (1998). How patients adapt diabetes self-care recommendations in everyday life. *The Journal of Family Practice*, 46(3), 207–215.

International Diabetes Federation. (2019). *IDF Diabetes Atlas* (9th Ed.). Belgium. https://diabetesatlas.org/en/

International Diabetes Federation (2020). *IDF Diabetes Atlas*. Brussels: Belgium. https://diabetesatlas.org/en/

Jacobsen, R., Vadstrup, E., Roder, M., & Frolich, A. (2012). Predictors of effects of Lifestyle Intervention on diabetes mellitus type 2 patients. *The Scientific World Journal*, Article ID 962951. https://doi.org/10.1100/2012/962951

Jameton, A. (1984). *Nursing practice: The ethical issues*. Prentice Hall.

Jasmine, T. (2009). Art, science, or both? Keeping the care in nursing. *Nursing Clinic of North America*, 44(4), 415–21.

Jaworska, A. (2009). Caring, minimal autonomy, and the limits of liberalism. In Lindemann, H., Verkerk, M. & Walker, M. U. (Eds.), *Naturalized bioethics. Towards responsible knowing and practice* (pp. 80–105). Cambridge University Press.

Jormsri, P., Kunaviktikul, W., Ketefian, S., & Chaowalit, A. (2005). Moral competence in nursing practice. *Nursing Ethics*, 12(6), 582–594.

Joseph-Williams, N., Elwyn, G., & Edwards, A. (2014). Knowledge is not power for patients: a systematic review and thematic synthesis of patient-reported barriers and facilitators to shared decision making. *Patient Education and Counseling*, 94(3), 291–309.

Kälvemark, S., Höglund, A. T., Hansson, M. G., Westerholm, P., & Arnetz, B. (2004). Living with conflicts-Ethical dilemmas and moral distress in the health care system. *Social Science & Medicine*, 58(6), 1075–1084.

Kangasniemi, M., Stievano, A. & Pietilä, A. M. (2013). Nurses' perceptions of their professional rights. *Nursing Ethics*, 20(4), 459–469.

Kangasniemi, M, Pakkanen, P., & Korhonen A. (2015). Professional ethics in nursing: an integrative review. *Journal of Advanced Nursing*, 71(8), 1744–1757.

Kendall, E., Ehrlich, C., Sunderland, N., Muenchberger, H., & Rushton, C. (2011). Self-managing versus self-management: reinvigorating the socio-political dimensions of self-management. *Chronic Illness*, 7, 87–98.

Kleinman, S. (2004). What is the nature of nurse practitioners' lived experiences interacting with patients? *Journal of the American Academy of Nurse Practitioners*, 16(6), 263–269.

Kleppe, L. C., Heggen, K., & Engebretsen, E. (2016). Nursing textbooks' conceptualization of nurses' responsibilities related to the ideal of a holistic view of the patient: A critical analysis. *Journal of Nursing Education and Practice, 6*(3), 106–115.

Kitson, A. (1996). Does nursing have a future? *British Medical Journal, 13*, 1647–1651.

Koch, T., Jenkin, P., & Kralik, D. (2004). Chronic illness self-management: locating the 'self'. *Journal of Advanced Nursing, 48*(5), 484–92.

Kodner, D. K., & Spreeuwenberg, C. (2002). Integrated care: meaning, logic, applications, and implications: a discussion paper. *International Journal of Integrated Care, 2*(14). http://doi.org/10.5334/ijic.67

Kohlen, H. (2009). *Conflicts of care. Hospital ethics committees in the USA and Germany.* Campus Verlag.

Kohlen, H. (2019). Ethische Fragen der Pflegepraxis im Krankenhaus und Möglichkeiten der Thematisierung. *Ethik in der Medizin, 31*, 325–343.

Kohlen, H., & Kumbruck, C. (2008). *Care-(Ethik) und das Ethos fürsorglicher Praxis.* Bremen: Universität Bremen. http://nbn-resolving.de/urn:nbn:de:0168-ssoar-219593

Kramer, M., & Schmalenberg, C. (2003). Securing "good" nurse/physician relationships. *Nursing Management, 34*(7), 34–38.

Kukla, R. (2005). Conscientious Autonomy: Displacing decisions in healthcare. *Hastings Center Report, 35*(2), 34–44.

Kunyk, D., & Austin, W. (2011). Nursing under the influence: A relational ethics perspective. *Nursing Ethics, 19*(3) 380–389.

Lachman, V. D. (2007). Moral courage: A virtue in need of development? *MedSurg Nursing, 16*(2), 131–133.

Lachman, V. D. (2012). Applying the ethics of care to your nursing practice. *Medsurg Nursing, 21*(2), 112–116.

LaSala, C.A., & Bjarnason, D. (2010). Creating workplace environments that support moral courage. *The Online Journal of Issues in Nursing, 15*(3), Manuscript 4. Article DOI: 10.3912/OJIN.Vol15No03Man04

Laugharne, R., Priebe, S., McCabe, R., Garland, N., & Clifford, D. (2011). Trust, choice, and power in mental health care: Experiences of patients with psychosis. *International Journal of Social Psychiatry, 58*(5), 496–504.

Lawton, J. (2003). Lay experiences of health and illness: past research and future agendas. *Sociology of Health and Illness, 25*(3), 23–40.

Lemay, C. A., Beagan, B. M., Ferguson, W. J., & Hargraves, J. L. (2010). Lessons learned from a collaborative to improve care for patients with diabetes in 17 community health centers, Massachusetts, 2006. *Preventing Chronic Disease, 7*(4). http://www.cdc.gov/pcd/issues/2010/jul/09_0121.htm.

Lenzen, S. A., van Dongen, J. J., Daniëls, R., van Bokhoven, M. A., van der Weijden, T., & Beurskens, A. (2016). What does it take to set goals for self-management in primary care? A qualitative study. *Family Practice, 33*(6), 698–703.

Leykum, L. K., Palmer, R. F., Lanham, H. J., Jordan, M. E., Noel, P. H., & Parchman, M. L. (2011). Reciprocal learning and chronic care model implementation: Results from a new scale of learning in primary care settings. *BMC Health Services Research, 11*, 44. https://doi.org/10.1186/1472-6963-11-44

Liaschenko, J. (2001). Thoughts on nursing work. *Bioethics Examiner, 5*(2), 2–6.

Lindh, I. B., Severinsson, E., & Berg, A. (2007). Moral responsibility: A relational way of being. *Nursing Ethics, 14*(2), 129–140.

Lindh, I. B., Severinsson E., & Berg, A. (2009). Nurses' moral strength: a hermeneutic inquiry in nursing practice. *Journal of Advanced Nursing, 65*(11), 1882–1890.

Lisac, M., Reimers, L., Henke, K.D., & Schlette, S. (2010). Access and choice-competition under the roof of solidarity in German health care: an analysis of health policy reforms since 2004. *Health Economics, Policy and Law, 5*(1), 31–52.

Little, M. O. (1998). Care: From theory to orientation and back. *Journal of Medicine and Philosophy, 23*(2), 190–209.

Liu, P. Y., & Kohlen, H. (2018). Tensions in diabetes care practice: Ethical challenges with a focus on nurses in a home-based care team. In Krause, F. & Boldt, J. (Eds.), *Care in healthcare. Reflections on theory and practice* (pp. 211–235). Palgrave Macmillan.

Magnezi, R., Kaufman, G., Ziv, A., Kalter-Leibovici, O., & Reuveni, H. (2013). Disease management programs: Barriers and benefits. *American Journal of Managed Care, 19*(4), 140–147.

Maio, G. (2009). Dienst am Menschen oder Kunden-Dienst? Ethische Grundreflexionen zur sich wandelnden ärztlichen Identität. In C. Katzenmeier, & K. Bergoldt (Eds.), *Das Bild des Arztes im 21. Jahrhundert* (pp. 21–35). Springer.

Maio, G. (2018). Fundamentals of an ethics of care. In Krause, F. & Boldt, J. (Eds.), *Care in healthcare. Reflections on theory and practice* (pp. 51–63). Palgrave Macmillan.

Malloy, D. C., Hadjistavropoulos, T., McCarthy, E. F., Evans, R. J., Zakus, D. H., Park, I., Lee, Y., & Williams, J. (2009). Culture and organizational climate: Nurses' insights into their relationship with physicians. *Nursing Ethics, 16*(6), 719–733.

Manojilovich, M. (2007). Power and empowerment in nursing: Looking backward to inform the future. *Online Journal of Issues in Nursing, 12*(1), Manuscript 1. Article PMID: 17330984

Manski-Nankervis, J. A., Furler, J., Blackberry, I., Young, D., O'Neal, D., & Patterson, E. (2014). Roles and relationships between health professionals involved in insulin initiation for people with type 2 diabetes in the general practice setting: a qualitative study drawing on relational coordination theory. *BMC Family Practice.* https://doi.org/10.1186/1471-2296-15-20

Margalit, R., Thompson, S., Visovsky, C., Geske, J., Collier, D., Birk, T., & Paulman P. (2009) From professional silos to interprofessional education: campuswide focus on the quality of care. *Quality Management in Health Care, 18*(3), p 165–173. http://dx.doi.org/10.1097/QMH.0b013e3181aea20d

Martin, S., & Landgraf, R. (2010). *Systematische Analyse der Versorgungssituation bei Diabetes mellitus in Deutschland. Arbeitspapier als Ergebnis des Workshop Versorgungsstruktur der Klausurtagung des Nationalen Aktionsforums Diabetes mellitus zur Umsetzung der Diabetes-Agenda 2010 in Deutschland.* Leibniz- Institut an der Heinrich-Heine-Universität Düsseldorf.

Martin-Rodriguez, L., Beaulieu, M., D'Amour, D., & Ferrada-Videla, M. (2005). The determinants of successful collaboration: A review of theoretical and empirical studies. *Journal of Interprofessional Care, 19*(2), S132–147.

Matthews, D. (2007). Why we need a new model for diabetes care. *British Journal of Diabetes & Vascular Disease, 7,* 130–131.

Matziou, V., Vlahioti, E., Perdikaris, P., Matziou, T., Megapanou, E., & Petsios, K. (2014). Physician and nursing perceptions concerning interprofessional communication and collaboration. *Journal of Interprofessional Care, 28*(6), 526–533.

Maynard, A. (2006). Incentives in health care: the shift in emphasis from the implicit to the explicit. Human resources for health in Europe. In Dubois, C. A., McKee, M., & Nolte, E. (Eds.), *Human resources for health in Europe* (pp. 140–154). Open University Press.

McCabe, C. (2004). Nurse-patient communication: an exploration of patients' experiences. *Journal of Clinical Nursing, 13*(1), 41–49.

MacDonald, C. (2002a). Nurse autonomy as relational. *Nursing Ethics, 9*(2), 194–201.

MacDonald, C. (2002b). Relational professional autonomy. *Cambridge Quarterly of Healthcare Ethics, 11,* 282–289

McDonald, C. (2006). *Challenging social work: The context of practice.* Palgrave Macmillan.

McDonald, J., Jayasuriya, R., & Harris, M. F. (2012). The influence of power dynamics and trust on multidisciplinary collaboration: A qualitative case study of type 2 diabetes mellitus. *BMC Health Service Research.* https://doi.org/10.1186/1472-6963-12-63

McKee, M., Dubois, C. A., & Sibbald, B. (2006). Changing professional boundaries. In Dubois, C. A., McKee, M., & Nolte, E. (Eds.), *Human resources for health in Europe* (pp. 63–78). Open University Press.

McLaughlin, H. (2009). What's in a name: 'Client', 'patient', 'customer', 'consumer', 'expert by experience', 'Service User'. What's next? *British Journal of Social Work, 39,* 1101–1117.

McLeod, C., & Sherwin, S. (2000). Relational autonomy, self-trust and health care for patients who are oppressed. In MacKenzie, C., & Stoljar. N. (Eds.), *Relational autonomy: Feminist perspectives on autonomy, agency and the social self* (pp. 259–279). Oxford University Press.

Meetoo, D., & Gopaul, H. (2005). Empowerment: giving power to people with diabetes. *Journal of Diabetes Nursing, 9*(1), 28–32.

Miers, M. (2003a). Health care teams in the community. In Wilkinson, G., & Miers, M. (Eds.), Power and Nursing Practice (pp. 83–96). Palgrave.

Miers, M. (2003b). Nurses in the labor market: exploring and explaining nurses' work. In Wilkinson, G., & Miers, M. (Eds.), *Power and nursing practice* (pp. 83–96). Palgrave.

Miles, M. B., Huberman, A. M., & Saldana, J. (2013). Within-case displays: Exploring and describing. In M. B. Miles, A. M. Huberman, & J. Saldana (Eds.), *Qualitative data analysis: An expanded sourcebook* (pp. 90–142). Sage.

Milliken, A. (2016). Nurse ethical sensitivity: An integrative review. *Nursing Ethics, 26*. https://doi.org/10.1177%2F0969733016646155

Mol, A. (2008). *The logic of care: Health and the problem of patient choice.* Routledge.

Mol, A. (2009). Living with diabetes: care beyond choice and control. *The Lancet, 373*(9677), p. 1756–1757. https://doi.org/10.1016/S0140-6736(09)60971-5.

Mol, A. (2010). Care and its values. Good food in the nursing home. In Mol, A., Moser, I., & Pols, J. (Eds.), *Care in practice. On tinkering in clinics, homes, and farms* (pp. 215–234). Transcript Publishing.

Mol, A., & Law, J. (2004). Embodied action, enacted bodies. The example of hypoglycemia. *Body & Society, 10*(2–3), 43–62.

Mol, A., Moser, I., & Pols, J. (2010). Care, putting practice into theory. In Mol, A., Moser, I., & Pols, J. (Eds.), *Care in practice. On tinkering in clinics, homes, and farms* (pp. 7–25). Transcript Publishing.

Möller, J., Küver, C., Beyer, M., & Gerlach, F. M. (2004). Patientenschulung in der Hausarztpraxis als Beitrag zum Disease Management. Qualitative Studie über Motive und Hindernisse bei der Durchführung von Schulungen für Typ-2-Diabetiker. *Zeitschrift für Allgemeinmedizin, 80*, 146–149.

Morse, J. (1991). Strategies for sampling. In Morse J. (Ed.), *Qualitative nursing research: A contemporary dialogue* (pp. 127–145). Sage.

Moser, A., van der Bruggen, H., & Widdershoven, G. (2006). Competency in shaping one's life: Autonomy of people with type 2 diabetes mellitus in a nurse-led, shared-care setting: A qualitative study. *International Journal of Nursing Study, 43*(4), 417–427.

Mulball, A. (2003). In the field: notes on observation in qualitative research. *Journal of Advanced Nursing, 41*(3), 306–313.

Murray, J. S. (2010). Moral courage in healthcare: Acting ethically even in the presence of risk. *The Online Journal of Issues in Nursing, 15*(3), Manuscript 2. Article DOI: 10.3912/OJIN.Vol15No03Man02

Nagel, H., Baehring, T., & Scherbaum, W. A. (2008). Disease management programs for diabetes in Germany. *Diabetes Voice, 53*(3), 17–19.

Nimmon, L., & Stenfors-Hayes, T. (2016). The "Handling" of power in the physician-patient encounter: perceptions from experienced physicians. *BMC Medical Education, 16*(114). https://doi.org/10.1186/s12909-016-0634-0

Nordhaug, M., & Nortvedt, P. (2011). Mature care in professional relationships and health care prioritizations. *Nursing Ethics, 18*(2), 209–216.

Nortvedt, P. (2001). Clinical sensitivity: the inseparability of ethical perceptiveness and clinical knowledge. *Scholarly Inquiry for Nursing Practice, 15*(1), 25–43.

Nortvedt, P. (2003). Subjectivity and vulnerability: reflections on the foundation of ethical sensibility. *Nursing Philosophy, 4*(3), 222–230.

Nortvedt, P. (2008). Sensibility and clinical understanding. *Medicine, Health Care, and Philosophy, 11*(2), 209–219.

Nortvedt, P. Hem, M. H., & Skirbekk, H. (2011). The ethics of care: Role obligations and moderate partiality in health care. *Nursing Ethics, 18*(2), 192–200.

Nortvedt, P., Pedersen, R., Grøthe, K. H., Nordhaug, M., Kirkevold, M., Slettebø, A., Brinchmann, B. S., & Andersen, B. (2008). Clinical prioritisations of healthcare for the aged professional roles. *Journal of Medical Ethics, 34*(5), 332–335.

Nugus, P., Greenfield, D., Travaglia, J., Westbrook, J., & Braithwaite, J. (2010). How and where clinicians exercise power: interprofessional relations in health care. *Social Science & Medicine, 71*(5), 898–909.

Numminen, O., Repo, H., & Leino-Kilpi, H. (2017). Moral courage in nursing: A concept analysis. *Nursing Ethics, 24*(8). https://doi.org/10.1177%2F0969733016634155

Nutting, P. A., Dickinson W. P., Dickinson L. M., Nelson C. C., King D. K., Crabtree B. F., & Glasgow R. E. (2007). Use of chronic care model elements is associated with higher-quality care for diabetes. *Annals of Family Medicine, 5*(1), 14–20.

Ogden, J., Branson, R., Bryett, A., Campbell, A., Febles, A., Ferguson, I., Lavender, H., Mizan, J., Simpson, R., & Tayler, M. (2003). What's in a name? Patient views of the impact and function of a diagnosis. *Family Practice, 20*, 248–253.

Ogden, J., & Parkes, K. (2013). 'A diabetic' versus 'a person with diabetes': the impact of language on beliefs about diabetes. *European Diabetes Nursing, 10*(3), 80–85.

Ohman, M., Söderberg, S., & Lundman, B. (2003). Hovering between suffering and enduring: the meaning of living with serious chronic illness. *Qualitative Health Research, 13*(4), 528–42. https://doi.org/10.1177%2F1049732302250720

Olshansky, E., Sacco, D., Fitzgerald, K., Zinkmund, S., Hess, R., Bryce, C., McTigue, K., & Fischer, G. (2008). Living with diabetes. Normalizing the process of managing diabetes. *The Diabetes Education, 34*(6), 1004–1012.

Ouwens, M., Wollersheim, H., Hermens, R., Hulscher, M., & Grol, R. (2005). Integrated care programs for chronically ill patients: a review of systematic reviews. *International Journal for Quality in Health Care, 17*(2), 141–146.

Palviainen, P., Hietala, M., Routasalo, P., Suominen, T., & Hupli, M. (2003). Do nurses exercise power in basic care situations? *Nursing Ethics, 10*(3), 269–280.

Papastavrou, E., Efstathiou, G., & Charalambous A. (2011). Nurses and patients' perceptions of caring behaviors: a quantitative systematic review of comparative studies. *Journal of Advanced Nursing, 67*(6), 1191–1205.

Parker, J. M. (1999). Patient or customer: Caring practices in nursing and the global supermarket of care. *Collegian*, 6(1), 16–23.

Paterson, B. (2001). Myth of empowerment in chronic illness. *Journal of Advanced Nursing*, 34(5), 574–581.

Paulsen, J. E. (2011). Ethics of caring and professional roles. *Nursing Ethics*, 18(2), 201–208.

Peel, E., Parry, O., Douglas, M., & Lawton, J. (2004). Blood glucose self-monitoring in non-insulin-treated type 2 diabetes: a qualitative study of patients' perspectives. *British Journal of General Practice*, 54(500), 183–188.

Peter, E., & Liaschenko, J. (2013). Moral distress reexamined: A feminist interpretation of nurses' identities, relationships, and responsibilities. *Journal of Bioethical Inquiry*, 10(3), 337–345.

Pettersen, T. (2011). The ethics of care: Normative structures and empirical implications. *Health Care Analysis*, 19(1), 51–64.

Peyrot, M., Rubin, R. R., & Siminerio, L. M. (2006). Physician and nurse use of psychosocial strategies in diabetes care: Results of the cross-national diabetes attitudes, wishes, and needs (DAWN) study. *Diabetes Care*, 29, 1256–1262.

Pill, R., Rees, M. E., & Rollnick, S. R. (1999). Can nurses learn to let go? Issues arising from an intervention designed to improve patients' involvement in their own care. *Journal of Advanced Nursing*, 29(6), 1492–1499.

Polit, D. F., & Beck, C. T. (2004). *Nursing research: principles and method* (7th edition). Lippincott, Williams, & Wilkins.

Pols, J. (2005). Enacting appreciations: Beyond the patient perspective. *Health Care Analysis*, 13(3), 203–221.

Ponte, P. R., Glazer, G., Dann, E., McCollum, K., Gross, A., Tyrrell, R., Branowicki, P., Noga, P., Winfrey, M., Cooley, M., Saint-Eloi, S., Hayes, C., Nicolas, P. K., & Washington, D. (2007). The power of professional nursing practice: an essential element of patient and family-centered care. *The Online Journal of Issues in Nursing*, 12(1). Article DOI: 10.3912/OJIN.Vol12No01Man03

Pope, B., Hough, M. C., & Chase, S. (2016). Ethics in community nursing. *Online Journal of Health Ethics*, 12(2). https://dx.doi.org/10.18785/ojhe.1202.03.

Pope, C., & Mays, N. (1995). Qualitative research: reaching the parts other methods cannot reach: an introduction to qualitative methods in health and health services research. *BMJ*, 311, 42–45. https://doi.org/10.1136/bmj.311.6996.42

Porter, S. (2003). Working with doctors. In Wilkinson, & G., Miers, M. (Eds.), *Power and Nursing Practice* (pp. 97–110). Palgrave.

Powers, P. (2003). Empowerment as treatment and the role of health professionals. *Advances in Nursing Science*, 26(3), 227–237.

Rahman, S., & Myers, R. (2019). *Courage in healthcare. A necessary virtue or warning sign?* SAGE.

Ramvi, E. (2015). I am only a nurse: a biographical narrative study of a nurse's self-understanding and its implication for practice. *BMC Nursing, 14*(23). https://doi.org/10.1186/s12912-015-0073-y

Raspe, H. (1999). Patienten – Klienten – Kunden – Verbraucher. Sozialmedizinische Anmerkungen zu Beziehungsformen zwischen Kranken und Therapeuten. In A. Dörries (Ed.), *Patienten oder Kunden?* (pp. 9–19). Rehburg-Loccum: Evangelische Akademie Loccum.

Reach, G. (2014). Patient autonomy in chronic care: solving a paradox. *Patient Preference and Adherence, 8*, 15–24.

Redman, B. K. (2005). The ethics of self-management preparation for chronic illness. *Nursing Ethics, 12*(4), 361–369.

Rees, J., King, K., & Schmitz, K. (2009). Nurses' perceptions of ethical issues in the care of older people. *Nursing Ethics, 16*(4), 436–452.

Renders, C. M., Valk, C. M., Griffin, S. J., Wagner, E. H., Eijk Van, J. T., & Assendelft, W. J. (2001). Interventions to improve the management of diabetes in primary care, outpatient, and community settings: a systematic review. *Diabetes Care, 24*(10), 1821–33.

Robb, N., & Greenhalgh, T. (2006). "You have to cover up the words of the doctor". The mediation of trust in interpreted consultations in primary care. *Journal of Health Organization and Management, 20*(5), 434–455.

Robert Koch Institute. (2019). *National Diabetes Surveillance Report 2019. Diabetes in Germany*. National Diabetes Surveillance. https://diabsurv.rki.de/SharedDocs/downloads/DE/DiabSurv/diabetes-report_2019_eng.pdf?__blob=publicationFile&v=12

Robin, J. H., Callister, L. C., Berry, J. A., & Dearing, K. A. (2008). Patient-centered care and adherence: Definitions and applications to improve outcomes. *Journal of American Academic Nurse Practice, 20*(12), 600–607.

Robinson, C. A. (2016). Trust, health care relationships, and chronic illness: a theoretical coalescence. *Global Qualitative Nursing Research, 3*. https://doi.org/10.1177%2F2333393616664823

Rogers, A., Kennedy, A., Nelson, E., & Robinson, A. (2005). Uncovering the limits of patient-centeredness: Implementing a self-management trial for chronic illness. *Qualitative Health Research, 15*(2), 224–239.

Rørtveit, K., Hansen, B. S., Leiknes, I., Joa, I., Testad, I., & Severinsson, E. (2015). Patients' experiences of trust in the patient-nurse relationship. A systematic review of qualitative studies. *Open Journal of Nursing, 5*, 195–209. https://dx.doi.org/10.4236/ojn.2015.53024

Rosemann, T., Joest, K., Körner, T., Schaefert, R., Heiderhoff, M., & Szecsenyi, J. (2006). How can the practice nurse be more involved in the care of the chronically ill? The perspectives of GPs, patients, and practice nurses. *BMC Family Practice, 7*(14). https://doi.org/10.1186/1471-2296-7-14

Rothman, A. A., & Wagner, E. H. (2003). Chronic illness management: What is the role of primary care? *Annals of International Medicine, 138*, 256–261.

Rowe, R. E., & Calnan, M.W. (2006). Trust relations in health care: developing a theoretical framework for the "new" NHS. *Journal of Health Organization and Management, 20*, 376– 396.

Ryl, L., & Horch, K. (2013). Informiert und zufrieden? Auf dem Weg zum mitbestimmenden Nutzer des Gesundheitswesens. *Umwelt und Menschen Informationsdienst, 2*, 111–117. http://edoc.rki.de/oa/articles/rel3ottiLPdA/PDF/26zIiui31EOuI.pdf

Salloch, S. (2016). Same but different: why we should care about the distinction between professionalism and ethics. *BMC Medical Ethics, 17*(44). https://doi.org/10.1186/s12910-016-0128-y

Sayah, F. A., Szafran, O., Robertson, S., Bell N. R., & Williams, B. (2014). Nursing perspectives on factors influencing interdisciplinary teamwork in the Canadian primary care setting. *Journal of Clinical Nursing, 23*, 2968–2979.

Schei, E. (2006). Doctoring as leadership: the power to heal. *Perspectives in Biology and Medicine, 49*(3), 393–406.

Schlette, S., Lisac, M., & Blum, K. (2009). Integrated primary care in Germany: the road ahead. *International Journal of Integrated Care, 9*(20), 1–11.

Scott, P.A., Matthews, A., Kirwan, M. (2014). What is nursing in the 21st century and what does the 21st-century health system require of nursing? *Nursing Philosophy, 15*(1), 23–34.

Selling, J. (1999). Is a personalist ethic necessarily anthropocentric? *Ethical Perspectives, 6*(1), 60–66.

Serrano, V., Rodriguez-Gutierrez, R., Hargraves, I., Gionfriddo, M. R., Tamhane, S., & Montori, V. M. (2016). Shared decision–making in the care of individuals with diabetes. Shared decision–making in the care of individuals with diabetes. *Diabetic Medicine, 33*(6), 742–751.

Shaw, C. (2006). Managing the performance of health professionals. In Dubois, C. A., McKee, M., & Nolte, E. (Eds.), *Human resources for health in Europe* (pp 98–115). Open University Press.

Shenton, A. K. (2004). Strategies for ensuring trustworthiness in qualitative research projects. *Education for Information, 22*(2), 63–75.

Shigaki, C., Kruse, R. L., Mehr, D., Sheldon, K. M., Bin, G., Moore, C., & Lemaster, J. (2010). Motivation and diabetes self-management. *Chronic Illness, 6*(3), 202–214.

Shirley, J. (2007). Limits of autonomy in nursing's moral discourse. *Advances in Nursing Science, 30*(1), 14–25.

Siminerio, L. M., Funnell, M. M, Peyrot, M. & Rubin, R. R. (2007). US nurses' perceptions of their role in diabetes care: Results of the cross-national diabetes attitudes wishes and needs (DAWN) study. *The Diabetes Educator, 33*(1), 152–162.

Slaughter, A. (2011). A new theory for the foreign-policy frontier: Collaborative power. *The Atlantic.* https://www.theatlantic.com/international/archive/2011/11/a-new-theory-for-the-foreign-policy-frontier-collaborative-power/249260/

Smith, D. E. (1995). *The conceptual practices of power. A feminist sociology of knowledge.* University of Toronto Press.

Smith, K. V., & Godfrey, N. S. (2002). Being a good nurse and doing the right thing: a qualitative study. *Nursing Ethics, 9*(3), 301–312.

Smith, S. A., Shah, N. D., Bryant, S. C., Christianson, T. J. H., Bjornsen, S. S., Giesler, P. D., Krause, K., Erwin, J. P., & Montori, V. M. (2008). Chronic care model and shared care in diabetes: Randomized trial of an electronic decision support system. *Mayo Clinic Proceedings, 83*(7), 747–757.

Snow, R., Humphrey, C., & Sandall, J. (2013). What happens when patients know more than their doctors? Experiences of health interactions after diabetes patient education: a qualitative patient-led study. *British Medical Journal Open, 3.* https://dx.doi.org/10.1136/bmjopen-2013-003583.

Spiers, J. (2003). *Patients, power, and responsibility. The first principles of consumer-driven reform.* Radcliffe Medical Press.

Stock, S., Drabik, A., Büscher, G., Graf, C., Ullrich, W., Gerber, A., Lauterbach, K. W., & Lüngen, M. (2010). German diabetes management programs improve the quality of care and curb costs. *Health Affairs, 29*(12), 2197–2205.

Stock, S., Pitcavage, J. M., Simic, D., Altin, S., Graf, C., Feng, W., & Graf, T. R. (2014). Chronic care model strategies in the United States and Germany deliver patient-centered, high-quality diabetes care. *Health Affairs, 33*(9), 1540–1548.

Szecsenyi, J., Rosemann, T., Joos, S., Peters-Klimm, F., & Miksch, A. (2008). German diabetes disease management programs are appropriate for restructuring care according to the chronic care model: an evaluation with the Patient Assessment of Chronic Illness Care instrument. *Diabetes Care, 31*(6), 1150–1154.

Tamhane, S., Rodriguez-Gutierrez, R., Hargraves, I., & Montori, V. M. (2015). Shared decision-making in diabetes care. *Current of Diabetes Report, 15,* 112.

Taylor, K. I., Oberle, K. M., Crutcher, R. A., & Norton, P. G. (2005). Promoting health in type 2 diabetes: Nurse-physician collaboration in primary care. *Biological Research for Nursing, 6*(3), 207–215.

Temmink, D., Francke A. L., Hutten J.B.F., van der Zee, J., & Abu-Saad, H. H. (2000). Innovations in the nursing care of the chronically ill: A literature review from an international perspective. *Journal of Advanced Nursing, 31*(6), 1449–58.

Thompson, I. E., Melia, K. M., Boyd, K. M., & Horsburgh, D. (2006). Power and responsibility in nursing practice and management. In I. E. Thompson (Ed.), *Nursing ethics* (pp. 77–100). Churchill Livingstone.

Thorup, C. B., Rundqvist, E., Roberts, C., & Delmar, C. (2012). Care as a matter of courage: vulnerability, suffering and ethical formation in nursing care. *Scandinavian Journal of Caring Sciences, 26*(3), 427–435.

Tol, A., Alhani, F., Shojaeazadeh, D., Sharifirad, G., & Moazam, N. (2015). An empowering approach to promote the quality of life and self-management among type 2 diabetic patients. *Journal of Education and Health Promotion*, 4(13). https://www.jehp.net/text.asp?2015/4/1/13/154022

Torpie, K. (2014). Customer service vs. patient care. *Patient Experience Journal*, 1(2), 6–8.

Trapani, J., & Cassar, M. (2016). Dual agency in critical care nursing: Balancing responsibilities towards colleagues and patients. *Journal of Advanced Nursing*, 72(10), 2468–2481.

Tronto, J. C. (1993). *Moral boundaries: A political argument for an ethic of care*. New York: Routledge.

Tronto, J. C. (2009). Consent as a grant of authority. In Lindemann, H., Verkerk, M. & Walker, M. U. (Eds.), *Naturalized Bioethics. Towards Responsible Knowing and Practice* (pp. 181–198). UK: Cambridge University Press.

Tronto, J. C. (2010). Creating caring institutions: Politics, plurality, and purpose. *Ethic and Social Welfare*, 4(2), 158–171.

Tronto, J. C. (2013). *Caring democracy: Markets, equality, and justice*. New York University Press.

Tscheulin, D. K., & Dietrich, M. (2010). Das Management von Kundenbeziehungen im Gesundheitswesen. In D. Georgi & K. Hadwich (Eds.), *Das Management von Kundenbeziehungen im Gesundheitswesen. Perspektiven-Analysen-Strategien-Instrumente* (pp. 253–276). Berlin: Springer.

Twigg, J., Wolkowitz, C., Cohen, R. L., & Nettleton, S. (2011). Conceptualizing body work in health and social care. *Sociology of Health & Illness*, 33(2), 171–188.

Udlis, K. A. (2011). Self-management in chronic illness: concept and dimensional analysis. *Nursing and Healthcare of Chronic Illness*, 3(2), 130–139.

Ulrich, C. M., Taylor, C., Soeken, K., O'Donnell, P., Farrar, A., Danis, M., & Grady. C. (2010). Everyday ethics: Ethical issues and stress in nursing practice. *Journal of Advanced Nursing*, 66(11), 2510–2519.

Ulrike, R., Gabriele, M., Peter, E. H. S., Martin, S., Hildebrand, K., Rainer, K., Sybille, B., Ulrich, J., Stefan, R. B., Markolf, H., & Jan, S. (2008). Evaluation of a diabetes management system based on practice guidelines, integrated care, and continuous quality management in a Federal State of Germany. *Diabetes Care*, 31(5), 863–868.

Van den Berg, N., Meinke, C., Heymann, R., Fiß, T., Suckert, E., Pöller, C., Dreier, A., Rogalski, H., Karopka, T., Oppermann, R., & Hoffmann, W. (2009). AGnES: Supporting general practitioners with qualified medical practice personnel. *Deutsches Ärzteblatt International*, 106(1), 3–9.

Van den Hooff, S., & Buijsen, M. (2014). Healthcare professionals' dilemmas: judging patient's decision-making competence in the day-to-day care of patients suffering from Korsakoff's syndrome. *Medicine, Health Care and Philosophy, 17*(4), 633–640.

Van den Hooff, S., & Goossensen, A. (2014). How to increase the quality of care during coercive admission? A review of literature. *Scandinavian Journal of Caring Sciences, 28*(3), 425–434.

Van Heijst, A. (2011). Professionals as fellow human beings. In van Heijst (Eds.), *Professional loving care. An ethical view of the healthcare sector* (pp. 127–152). Klement Publishers.

Vanlaere, L., & Gastmans, C. (2011). A personalist approach to care ethics. *Nursing Ethics, 18,* 161. https://doi.org/10.1177/0969733010388924

Van Manen, M. (1990). *Research lived experience, human science for an action-sensitive pedagogy.* State University of New York Press.

Van Wynsberghe, R. (2007). Redefining case study. *International Journal of Qualitative Methods, 6*(2), 80–94.

Varcoe, C., Doane, G., Pauly, B., Rodney, P., Storch, J. L., Mahoney, K., McPherson, G., Brown, H., & Starzomski, R. (2004). Ethical practice in nursing: working the in-betweens. *Journal of Advanced Nursing, 45*(3), 316–325.

Varcoe, C., Pauly, B., Storch, J. L., Newton, L., & Mahoney, K. (2012). Nurses' perceptions of and responses to morally distressing situations. *Nursing Ethics, 19*(4), 488–500.

Varelius, J. (2006). The value of autonomy in medical ethics. *Medicine, Health Care and Philosophy, 9*(3), 377–388.

Verkerk, M. A. (2001). The care perspective and autonomy. *Medicine, Health Care and Philosophy, 4*(3), 289–294.

Ville, I., Ravaud, J. F., Diard, C., & Paicheler, H. (1994). Self-representations and physical impairment: a social constructionist approach. *Sociology of Health and Illness, 16*(3), 301–21.

Wagner, D., & Bear, M. (2009). Patient satisfaction with nursing care: A concept analysis within a nursing framework. *Journal of Advanced Nursing, 65*(3), 692–701.

Wagner, E. H. (1998). Chronic disease management: what will it take to improve care for chronic illness? *Effective Clinical Practice, 1*(1), 2–4.

Wagner, E. H. (2000). The role of patient care teams in chronic disease management. *British Medical Journal, 320*(7234), 569–572. https://doi.org/10.1136/bmj.320.7234.569

Wagner, E. H., Austin, B. T., Davis, C., Hindmarsh, M., Schaefer, J., & Bonomi, A. (2001). Improving chronic illness care: translating evidence into action. *Health Affairs, 20*(6), 64–78. https://doi.org/10.1377/hlthaff.20.6.64

Wagner, E. H., Grothaus, L. C., Sandhu, N., Galvin, M. S., McGregor, M., Artz, K., & Coleman, E. A. (2001). Chronic care clinics for diabetes in primary care: a system-wide randomized trial. *Diabetes Care, 24*(4), 695–700.

Walker, M. (2001). Seeing power in morality: A proposal for feminist naturalism in ethics. In: Des Autels, P., & Waugh, J. (Eds.), *Feminists doing ethics* (pp 3–14). Rowman & Littlefield Publishers.

Walker, M. (2003). *Moral contexts*. Rowman & Littlefield Publishers.

Watson, J. (1985). *Nursing: The philosophy and science of caring*. U.S.A: The University of Colorado.

Way, D., Jones, L., & Busing, N. (2000). *Implementation strategies: Collaboration in primary care – Family doctors & nurse practitioners delivering shared care* (Discussion paper), The Ontario College of Family Physicians.

Weaver, K. (2007). Ethical sensitivity: state of knowledge and needs for further research. *Nursing Ethics*, 14(2), 141–155.

Weaver, K, Morse, J, & Mitcham, C. (2008). Ethical sensitivity in professional practice: a concept analysis. *Journal of Advanced Nursing*, 62(5), 607–618.

White, W., Boyle, M. & Loveland, D. (2002). Addiction as a chronic disease: From rhetoric to clinical application. *Alcoholism Treatment Quarterly*, 3/4, 107–130.

Whittemore, R., & Knafl, K. (2005). The integrative review: updated methodology. *Journal of Advanced Nursing*, 52(2), 546–553.

Wikblad, K. F. (1991). Patient perspectives of diabetes care and education. *Journal of Advanced Nursing*, 16(7), 837–844.

Wilde, M. H., & Garvin, S. (2007). A concept analysis of self-monitoring. *Journal of Advanced Nursing*, 57(3), 339–350.

Wilkinson, G., & Miers, M. (2003). Power and professionals. In Wilkinson, G., & Miers, M. (Eds.): *Power and nursing practice* (pp. 24–36). Palgrave.

Wing, P. C. (1997). Patient or client? If in doubt, ask. *Canadian Medical Association Journal*, 157, 287–289.

Wolkowitz, C. (2002). The social relations of body work. *Work, Employment and Society*, 16(3), 497–510.

Yin, R. K. (2009). *Case study research: Design and methods* (4th ed.). Thousand Oaks, CA: Sage.

Young, J. (2016). A nurse-led model of chronic disease management in general practice: Patients' perspectives. *The Royal Australian College of General Practitioners*, 45(12), 912–916.

Zoffmann, V., & Kirkevold, M. (2005). Life versus disease in difficult diabetes care: Conflicting perspectives disempower patients and professionals in problem-solving. *Qualitative Health Research*, 15(6), 750–765.